# THE SOUTH REJECTS A PROPHET

David McKendree Key

David M. Abshire

# The South Rejects a Prophet

---

*The Life of Senator D. M. Key, 1824–1900*

FOREWORD BY RALPH McGILL

FREDERICK A. PRAEGER, *Publishers*

New York • Washington • London

FREDERICK A. PRAEGER, PUBLISHERS
111 Fourth Avenue, New York, N.Y. 10003, U.S.A.
77–79 Charlotte Street, London W.1, England

Published in the United States of America in 1967
by Frederick A. Praeger, Inc., Publishers

© 1967 by Frederick A. Praeger, Inc.

Library of Congress Catalog Card Number: 67-24671
Printed in the United States of America

*To*
James Ernest Abshire

# Acknowledgments

The inside story of D. M. Key's historic role is fully revealed only in the Key and Key-Patten Papers—the numerous letters, speeches, and clippings from newspapers no longer available elsewhere. This virgin source material has been either unknown to or unused by historians of the Reconstruction. It sheds new light on such events as the compromise leading to the Hayes election, the crisis of 1878, which was ended by Key's open letter to the South, the attempt to align permanently the Southern conservative Democrats and the liberal Northern Republicans, with the aim of cracking the solid South, and the involved charges of conspiracy and scandal in the Star Routes of the mail service. Above all, these sources give a new perspective on the hardening of racial lines in the South. The preserver of these papers was Mrs. Sarah Key Patten, ninety-three years old at the time of her death in 1958, and still the possessor of a sharp memory, keen wit, and sense of history—all of which aided this book.

Extraordinary gratitude is due to Professor of American History Joseph T. Durkin, S.J., of Georgetown University, under whom I wrote a doctoral dissertation on this same subject. The present book represents considerable additional effort and attempts to capture the spirit and drama of some critical days in American history. Toward this end, particularly helpful suggestions were made by Robert Selph Henry and my late father, from whom originated my interest in history and to whom this book is affectionately dedicated. Watt P. Marchman, the able Director of the Hayes Memorial Library at

Fremont, Ohio, did all possible to make my days at Fremont during and after a snowstorm both productive and comfortable. Through the thousands of sources in the Hayes collection, he expedited my progress.

Dean James Livingood and Librarian Gilbert Govan, both of the University of Chattanooga, have extended their interest over the years. Since 1957, interested people at one time or another have been helpful in this effort: Penelope Allen, William Baroody, Charles Bartlett, Richard Cushman, Professor Joseph Huthmacher, Hon. David Key II, Hilda Lawrence, Frances McGavin, Alfred Mynders, Martin Ochs, Mrs. Milton Ochs, Mr. and Mrs. Cartter Patten, the late Representative Carroll Reece, William C. Sullivan, Professor Richard Walsh, and finally Morton Puner and Edith Tarcov of Frederick A. Praeger, Inc., who bore the difficult task of final editing. Morris Leibman thoughtfully brought me together with Ralph McGill. My wife Carolyn, companion in this as in every endeavor, was ever present in the minute human-interest research necessary to reconstruct accurately the scenes in this book.

DAVID M. ABSHIRE

# Foreword

In my early boyhood, on a farm some twenty miles north of Chattanooga, and later, as I grew into my teens in Chattanooga itself, I heard stories of David M. Key, of William G. (Parson) Brownlow, and of the bitter and violent division between Unionists and those who sided with Jefferson Davis and the Confederacy.

Mr. Abshire's book is much more than an able biography of David M. Key. His book makes a valuable contribution to understanding the complex machinations, of both South and North, that were involved in the "steal" of the 1876 Presidential election, in which conservative Southern leaders, including a number of newspaper editors and former Confederate generals, joined to make Rutherford B. Hayes President of the United States. This was one of the great pivotal points in American history. The conservative Southerners wanted railroads and new industries to be developed in the South. They also wanted an end to Reconstruction. In going with Hayes, they obtained both.

The costs of this decision to the nation were evident early and are now coming due in full measure. In ending Reconstruction with the Hayes election, the Republican Party and the victorious North abandoned the newly freed Negro and returned him wholly to the control of the states under "states rights." There were then no segregation laws. The ballot was open to the Negro. But both parties had been guilty of manipulating and corrupting the Negro vote. Once "states rights" were again in the saddle, the various black codes, segregation, and the several devices that would effectively bar the Negro from a voice in choosing his representatives and that would separate him from the processes of democratic citizenship began to multiply. The consequences of this folly and injustice are being felt now, because millions of persons have migrated to the nation's industrial and urban centers, coming from a South where a segregated system debased education for both white and Negro citizens and denied millions of them the opportunity to acquire literacy and vocational and professional skills.

David M. Key, an emotional and yet a thinking man, saw far beyond his time. Originally deeply committed to the Confederacy, he lost patience in the postwar years with those who sought to return to the past. Many of these Southern leaders preached a new attempt at secession and war. It was a turbulent time, and none participated in it more fully than Key

Mr. Abshire's book is an excellent portrayal of this important period in history and of the efforts of one man to contend with the violent forces then loose in the land.

RALPH MCGILL

*Atlanta, Georgia*
*November, 1967*

# Contents

## CONTENTS

*A section of illustrations follows page 146.*

# THE SOUTH REJECTS A PROPHET

# 1

## The Angry Scowl

It was an evening of contrasts in Washington, that March 4, 1877. There was much jubilation and celebrating, much anger and discontent. The dark clouds that had been hovering over the capital for days seemed to some Southern dignitaries like an angry scowl in the sky—a scowl much like their own. Dusk was falling, and a lamplighter was riding into Lafayette Square, putting his blowtorch to the gas jets of the street lamps. Across the square, the White House loomed, a ghostly outline at this hour, and beyond it the unfinished Washington Monument, resembling a sheared tombstone.[1]

The dark sky and the fog had not dampened the jubilation and festivities. This evening a procession of boisterous people tramped up Pennsylvania Avenue, cheering and singing, carrying blazing torches and brightly painted signs that acclaimed the new President of the United States, Rutherford B. Hayes. Other Hayes partisans, at the foot of the Washington Monument, were about to set off a burst of fireworks.[2]

But there were other people, full of anger and frustration, and their scowls the night could not hide. These were disappointed and cantankerous visitors—most of them Southern politicians. They had traveled to Washington hoping to attend the inauguration of

Democrat Samuel Tilden. But now Republican Hayes had been inaugurated. For a while, one group of these grumbling dissenters had been posted near the White House gate; then, working off their anger, they had stalked restlessly across the brown lawns of the square, past the icy fountains, and onto the steps of white-columned St. John's Church. There they huddled together defiantly, scowling and grumbling and pointing occasionally across the square toward the lighted windows of the White House, where Hayes was celebrating his victory. They talked accusingly of a stolen election, murmured of retribution by rebellion, and threatened a second civil war. One of the group, wild-eyed and evidently under the influence of alcohol, yawped about an article by newspaperman Don Piatt that practically invited Hayes's assassination.[3] The scales of justice, it seemed to these Southern patriots, had been sorely tilted by political scoundrels and could be balanced only by the spilling of Northern blood.

The shame of it all, they said, was that the theft of the election had been made possible by one of their own kind—a former Confederate colonel and original secessionist, not long ago a rabid Solid South Democrat, who had taken the stump for Tilden only last fall. The scoundrel was Senator David Key from Chattanooga, Tennessee.

They all well remembered how Key's intrigue had begun last December, when the disputed Presidential election had been thrown into Congress. The Republicans were about to steal it, but the South was not caught napping. The Southern militia was alerted, ready to fight. In this near civil war, unlike the past one, Northern Democrats, particularly in New York City, said they would fight *with* the South. For the first time in decades, the balance of power favored Dixie.

Then Key had struck. He did it, first, by taking the floor in the Senate to call for peace and appeasement. Then he had proceeded to convince a group of Southerners to defect with him. No doubt he was secretly in league with Northern Republicans and greedy railroad lobbyists; thus he had enabled them to steal the election for

Hayes. Now Democrat Key, who had campaigned for Tilden only a few months before, was on his way to Washington to receive a cabinet appointment in the fraudulent administration.[4]

The Southern visitors had heard a rumor that Key planned to use this cabinet post to sabotage the Solid South and its cause of white supremacy. Still wearing the disguise of a Democrat, he might well subvert the whole Southern political machine. Key must be destroyed, or he would destroy the Southern way of life. Thus debated Southern politicians that evening in Lafayette Square.

At this moment, a horse-drawn cab had been hired at the railroad station, and the Negro driver, perched on his seat between two brass lanterns, peered uneasily into the foggy night ahead. He turned his horse to round the corner of Pennsylvania Avenue and Fifteenth Street, reassured himself by cracking the whip, and passed a horse-drawn streetcar.

In the back of the cab sat the hulky, middle-aged Tennessean David McKendree Key. He shivered in the damp Washington air and turned the lapels of his frock coat up around his stout neck and massive jowls, which were partly covered by a silvery spade-shaped beard. In the faint light, he strained his gray eyes under the bushy eyebrows to catch a glimpse of the city. He was tense, and his large hands were twisting his battered beaver hat.[5] The wooden carriage wheels clattered on the new slick asphalt of the wide avenue, and Key looked out at the colonnaded outline of the Treasury Building and the store fronts still covered with fluttering red, white, and blue bunting from yesterday's inauguration.[6]

This was one of Key's moments of doubt, when it seemed difficult to justify his controversial course. Soon he would have the dubious honor of being the first Southerner in the cabinet since the war. He would be Hayes's postmaster general, a job often called that of the "cabinet politician," because of the great patronage powers it entailed. In the history of the Republic, there was no precedent for a man from one party serving in the cabinet of the other. Key's appointment was particularly puzzling, for only last fall he had campaigned for Tilden, making speech after speech against Hayes.

How could he ever justify himself? In the South, they now called him a traitor, a combination Judas and Benedict Arnold, about to accept the biggest pay-off in American history. And they accused him of hiding behind his jolly-good exterior a slippery, self-serving nature as bad as Uriah Heep's. Key knew how Southern politicians spoke of him.[7]

Key's justification? He believed that small-minded, selfish Southern politicians were about to create and perpetuate a Solid South, perverse and unnatural, cemented by a one-party political machine, founded on the exclusive issue of color line. During the past few months, Key had feared that this political group might stir up a second civil war, which the country could not survive. Southern progress would certainly be stifled by a Solid South that would deprive the voter of real choice. Yes, Key thought, it would make the Southerner the dupe of New York's Tammany Hall, for Tammany controlled the Democratic Party. A Solid South would mean a solidly backward South, putting industrialization and economic progress last and racism first.

Before the Civil War, there had indeed been slavery, but there had also been some free Negroes. They had operated and still ran many small businesses in the South—all the barber and blacksmith shops and many little stores in larger Southern cities. Often, there had been camaraderie and political alliance between white conservatives and the elite free Negroes. The recent talk about passing segregation laws restricting Negroes to special cars on trains, setting afire the issue of white supremacy, was an effort by cheap politicians to strengthen their machine. New segregation laws would degrade the Negroes, isolate them, and stunt their educational and economic progress. All this was to ask for retribution and extremism in turn. Key felt an agonizing need for reappraisal amid such stupid radicalism on both sides.[8] He wanted the people of the South to look clearheadedly at the situation and chart the best possible course into the future.

And how would Southern politicians treat the man with this message? He wondered, as he shifted his bulky body, his large hands still fingering the battered beaver hat.[9] He looked out toward Lafayette Square, just now in sight. There in the night were those who hated Key; they little suspected that he was nearby. A burst of fireworks suddenly silhouetted the great elms and oaks lining the square. Their bare, crooked branches seemed to Key like cobweb-fingered ghosts haunting the martial statue in the center of the square. How often had Key, on his walks through the capital, looked at that statue of fellow Tennessean Andrew Jackson, defender of the Union against rebellious Southerners. Jackson reared high on his prancing horse, his cocked hat raised as if he were admonishing those who plotted civil war. His angry warning was etched on the base of the statue: "Our Federal Union. It must be preserved."

Key had spoken similar words three months ago in the Senate. Ironically, small-minded Southern politicians who now called Jackson a hero called Key a coward.

The coach jogged Key out of his thoughts as it turned past the watchman's house and through the big iron gate of the White House. The coachman reined his horse under the bright gaslight before the portico, and Key climbed out into the cold air and gave his name to the doorman. Stiff from the cold, he followed a butler into the main hall. A seedy bunch of office seekers suspiciously eyed the burly newcomer. Was he another office seeker, out to see what he could get?

Key followed the butler through the dimly lit Red Room and glanced in passing at the new Grant-family portrait over the fireplace. On the mantel, an ornate clock ticked the time that played such strange tricks.[10] Hayes had been one of Grant's generals, and now Key was about to embrace the men and the party against whom he had fought for four long, bitter years. No fire was laid in the hearth, and the room was cold and damp. The porous freestone kept the White House perpetually damp, and the air chilled the visitor to the bone. The butler led him through the Blue Room, swung open the heavy door to the Green Room, and announced the visitor.

There, by a grate fire, several men puffed on their cigars; the tallest among them was Rutherford B. Hayes. Key had not met the new President and knew him only from his photographs. Key's old campaign manager, Colonel Andrew Kellar of Memphis, and General Van Ness Boynton, an expert railroad lobbyist, rushed forward to greet him and introduce him to the President. Key approached uneasily between his two companions, conscious of the ambiguous aspect of his position and self-appointed mission.[11] The old butler left the room and closed the door.

What of this man he had just escorted? Was he a traitor or a new Moses who would lead the South in an exodus, out of the bondage of hate and backwardness? History would tell. Yet how Key fought to bring about such an exodus would long be withheld from history. Both Southern and Northern extremists would try to smear Key and later to bury his true message, the story of the daring course he undertook, and the relevant details of his controversial life. Paradoxically, these vocal and powerful extremists, who controlled the political machines, were merely a tyrannical minority; the majority of Southerners would gladly have followed Key's way.

Now that formerly hidden sources have come to light, Key's story can be told. Key's own papers and letters, newspaper clippings, diaries, and mementos tell of his pleading for the South, of the desire of the majority to follow his advice, and of the thwarting of this course with the passage of the Jim Crow laws that rang down the iron curtain of racial isolationism. Key's story not only reveals how a man's course was mired in the crisis of his time, but also mirrors the agony of the Southern conscience. It tells how a band of Southern politicians fanned hate and extremism to stay in power and cheated the South of economic development and progress.

# 2

---

# Secession Fever

To understand the sudden change in attitude and direction that made Key defy the Southern political leaders in 1877, one must begin some sixteen years earlier.[1] Key was then a stocky, thirty-six-year-old Chattanooga lawyer, with curly black hair and whiskers, noted throughout the eastern Tennessee hills for his ability to beguile a jury. He knew these hills. His father, a gospel-preaching Methodist circuit rider, had taken young Dave, toting Bible and gun, through every hill, dale, and hamlet, from the rich plantations near Knoxville to the unproductive, steep, rocky farm tracts in the foothills of the Smokies. Parson Key had been both preacher and farmer, and, near a tiny eastern Tennessee town, his boy had sweated between the plow handles, as he was later to put it, from the time he was a chunk of a lad until he was twenty-one.

The hillbilly people, the country drawl, and the rocky soil got into Dave Key's blood; but he left this rustic life. He worked his way through law school at a newly established college and later was tutored by an influential Democratic politician, not only for the bar, but also in expounding from atop a cracker barrel the fiery spirit of the Southern Democratic Party that taught suspicion toward every Yankee. Key perfected a ring in his voice, a sharp wit, and the skill to spin a yarn that made a listening mountaineer snap his suspenders in appreciation. In those days, young Key supplemented his salary by being about the best poker player around.[2]

On a chilly January day in 1861, the blue sky over the little town of Chattanooga afforded a clear view of the brown mountains and ridges making a natural bowl into which rushed the Tennessee River. Seeking an escape after being rebutted by the southwest palisades of Lookout Mountain, the river coiled into what looked like an Indian moccasin, then swept out of the valley through a series of canyons.

On this wintry afternoon, Key stood in the master bedroom of his red-brick house in Chattanooga, dressing to go out for the evening. His head swam with the news of secession. The governor of Mississippi had ordered cannon placed at Vicksburg. Georgia had passed an ordinance of secession; South Carolina had seceded the previous December, after Abraham Lincoln's election to the Presidency. In Tennessee, a bill calling for a convention to consider secession had passed the state legislature. And Jefferson Davis, who had resigned from his Senate seat and was en route to his home in Mississippi, would pass this night in Chattanooga.[3]

Secessionists fervently hoped that Davis would make a dramatic, perhaps decisive, speech this evening. They had selected their most inspired young apostle of secession, Dave Key, to escort Davis and to persuade him to speak.

Key picked up his tie from the white marble dresser top and slipped it around his collar. Davis indeed might sway Chatta-noogans toward secession. The town was bitterly divided. One Chattanooga newspaper, the *Gazette,* warned, on January 24, against politicians who would plunge the nation into rash action and proclaimed that if Tennessee entered a Southern confederacy, the state would live under military rule and the people would have to "submit like slaves."

The other newspaper, the *Advertiser,* the same day quipped that the Union was no more, that "the man [who] would so act, or vote, as to tie Tennessee on to the North deserves the fate which awaits him . . . being placed on the broad platform of social and political equality with the kinky head." If Tennessee did not stand with the South, continued the *Advertiser*, "we sound the death knell of our liberties. . . . Let the patriotic outbursts of every true Southerner be 'Resistance to tyrants is obedience to God.'"

Resistance to tyrants meant resistance to Lincoln and his gang, Key reasoned. They were trying to foist tyranny upon the South— a South that wanted only to leave the Union peacefully.

Key asked Lizzie, his comely brown-eyed wife, to hurry; she was instructing the house girl how to care for the two babies that evening. He went outside, hitched the horse to the family carriage, and watched the setting sun play across mountaintops and ridges and rest on Lookout Mountain's giant boulders. Key helped Lizzie onto the seat, waited till she had arranged her bustling skirts, and climbed up himself. He turned the horse, and they started down the hill.

There, sprawled before them, was what looked more like a grubby, mushroomed mining settlement of the Far West than a town of the old South. In the business section, most of the buildings were wooden, crude, and dingy. This was Key's town; less than a quarter of a century ago, it had been Indian territory. At the bottom of the hill, they turned into slushy Market Street, the town's main thoroughfare. Before city hall, several unattended squealing pigs and cows crossed the street just in front of them, and Lizzie commented that the town should have passed laws long ago against animals roaming through the business section. In the heat of summer, this made for an inelegant stench, not at all suitable for the center of a city.

Lizzie waved to a group of children across the street. Unaware of the crisis, they congregated as usual in front of DeGeorges' and D. Devote's Confectionery, Ice Cream Parlor, and Oyster Saloon. The sweets attracted more children than any other place in town except big Bill Lewis' blacksmith shop, where one would often find a wide-eyed child watching strong Bill Lewis send wild sparks flying from his forge. Lewis, a mulatto, had been his own white father's slave. Strangers to the South had to think a bit about that, and the children did not understand. "He hammered his way out of this unholy relationship," some townsmen said. "William Lewis bought his freedom with his labor, married a Chattanooga slave girl, and purchased her freedom and then the freedom of other relatives with more labor."

Lewis' industrious, capable brown hands had forged the bell for the white folks' First Baptist Church. Every Sunday, Bill Lewis and his wife, who were members of the Old Plank Methodist Church, sat in the back of the church for services, singing, and praying. The whites sat all around them. Bill Lewis, solid and respectable, paid no mind to the Yankee abolitionists' ideas. In politics he was a strong Democrat. By the sweat of his brow he had earned his place in the sun, and the rest of his race could do likewise as far as he was concerned. They needed no help from Northern abolitionists, nor from that politician from Illinois.[4]

A shrill train whistle sounding in the distance made Key pull at the reins to hasten the horse's pace. They stopped before Crutchfield House, the town's handsome three-storied hotel. After escorting Lizzie up to the long wooden porch, Key walked quickly across the street to the railroad station to await the 6:55. John Hopkins, a secessionist neighbor, greeted Key and pointed out a puff of smoke that marked the train's path through the cut in the eastern part of the valley's mountain wall, known as Missionary Ridge.

Hopkins and Key admired the big black engine with its bright-red bumper and red caboose, pulling the yellow railroad cars and racing through the valley. The whistle screamed, the wheels ground against the rails, and the train chugged to a halt. Onto the platform stepped Varina Davis, helping her two children down from the car. She smiled, greeting the two men, and straightened her bonnet above the center part of her black hair. Now tall, thin, wiry Jefferson Davis greeted Key and Hopkins. Davis was a gaunt-faced man with deep-set eyes, sharp features, and a meticulously trimmed goatee; his bearing reflected a man of determination and vigor.

Key smiled broadly, extending a cordial greeting. Davis replied, his voice hoarse from making too many speeches at whistle stops.[5]

The group went across the street, up to the wooden porch of the Crutchfield House, and entered the partially finished lobby, furnished with pieces varying from heavy mahogany couches to cracker boxes. The logs were blazing red in the two huge fireplaces, warming the large room pleasantly. Short, round-faced Tom Crutchfield, the proprietor, gripped Davis' hand and offered warm hospitality to him and his family. Other secessionists poured in, eager to greet Davis.

In the doorway to the saloon, Key saw Tom Crutchfield's brother, Bill, who shared none of his brother's hospitable feelings toward Davis. Bill was a tall man with curly red hair and beard and persuasive, gesticulating hands. The townspeople said that Bill Crutchfield was as "rough as pig iron, eccentric . . . peculiar," and absolutely fearless. Bill had a mountaineer mind, unyielding when made up. It was indeed made up now—in favor of Unionism.[6]

Lately, Bill had been unusually excitable, perhaps because his beautiful wife, Nancy Jane, a cultured belle from the Deep South, had argued so violently for secession that the town gossips said their marriage would not last. Tonight, Bill might well be a threat to Key's plans. And at any moment, other aggressive Unionists would arrive, men like Colonel Clift, who commanded a regiment of Tennessee militia. Key had to convince Davis to speak quickly— before Bill Crutchfield's gang could start trouble. Meanwhile, the hospitable Mrs. Thomas Crutchfield, as stout, round, and good-natured as her husband, was showing the Davis family upstairs.[7] As the guests began to arrive and the tempting smell of supper preparations filled the room, Key and Hopkins took Davis aside to a little table lit by a low-burning whale-oil lamp to talk business.

Key pressed the tired, hoarse Davis. He need not make an irate or passionate speech, he explained. He merely needed to say a few calm, common-sense words urging secession. But Davis refused. He was a Mississippian, he said, not a Tennessean. Besides, he had almost lost his voice, as they well knew. He was tired. Key con-

tinued to press, insisting that his speech might tip the scales for
secession. Davis gave in.

The crowd, realizing that Jeff Davis was about to speak, chat-
tered louder; there were a few cheers and hillbilly hoots. Bill
Crutchfield stood under a big cream-glass chandelier, his face blazing red. He elbowed his way into the lobby, and his gang followed.
Bill Crutchfield's hands waved carelessly, his voice became louder
as he turned from side to side, pointing to Davis, telling all within
earshot that he would take it personally if that Mississippi meddler
spoke here for secession.

Davis climbed onto a chair. Spirits churned, and voices were
raised so high that three floors up, Varina Davis could hear the
commotion and rushed downstairs. Near the door to the big lobby, a
rough-looking mountain man, sitting on a barrel, turned to a
Negro nearby and said unsteadily, "Tell that lady she need not be
uneasy. Jeff Davis ain't afraid. He will make his speech."[8]

Jefferson Davis' gaunt cheekbones seemed to reflect the glow of
the crackling fire. He strained to raise his hoarse voice, lifted his
hand to silence the crowd, then took up an even, guttural tone. He
calmly discussed the present crisis; he neither denounced the federal
government nor reviled Lincoln. The South did not want war, he
said; it merely wanted to leave the Union, go its own way in peace.

He ended his speech lauding states' rights and secession. Now
he revived, recovered the force of his voice, and exhibited true en-
thusiasm. His voice grew louder. He wanted everyone present to
understand that he was a secessionist and believed that every state
in the Union had the constitutional right to secede.[9]

Secessionists applauded and cheered. Key, jubilant, was among
those who ushered the hero into the bar for brandy to soothe the
hoarse throat.

Suddenly, there were excited shouts and female screams in the
big lobby, and Key and Davis rushed back to the door. There was
Bill Crutchfield on top of the clerk's counter, speaking against
secession and reviling Jefferson Davis. Several of Davis' supporters
were drawing their pistols, each cock producing a new female

scream. There must have been a dozen pistols pointed at Bill Crutchfield, a dozen fingers each on a trigger that could bring him down in cold blood. Bill Crutchfield alone seemed oblivious to the danger as he shouted that Davis and his ilk had deserted Congress in the decisive hour of the Republic. And these deserters claimed to protect the South! Who had been in the majority in that Congress? The Democrats. They could have protected the South. How? By merely remaining in Congress, shouted Crutchfield passionately. But traitors like Davis had walked out.

Defying the cock of another pistol, Crutchfield yelled that Davis had deserted both the Union and the true interests of the South. And now he was here in Tennessee to meddle in Chattanooga affairs. Tennessee was none of his business. Mississippi was his state! And if Tennessee would foolishly walk out of the Union, it would walk into a military dictatorship.

"Behold," cried Crutchfield, pointing to Davis, who stood in the doorway, "your future military despot!"[10]

Jefferson Davis' gaunt face had turned red. The room grew quiet. Everyone was aware of Davis' burning rage. Meddle in Chattanooga affairs! It was Key's idea that he speak in the first place! He started through the crowd toward the counter, where Bill Crutchfield, undismayed, continued his speech. Shots rang out, shattering the glass chandelier. A scuffling started in the darkened room, now dimly lit by the glow of the two hearths. Thomas Crutchfield moved through the crowd with catlike alacrity. He beat Davis to the counter and grabbed his brother. By the time the oil lamps were lit, Tom had Bill halfway out of the main door.

Before parting, Bill Crutchfield hurled more insults at Davis. Davis jumped on the clerk's counter. His voice breaking with hoarseness, he announced that he would not fight the man who had attacked him while his back was turned. But he would seek satisfaction and duel with any gentleman in the crowd who was Crutchfield's friend, if Crutchfield had a friend who was a gentleman.

The last challenge petrified Tom Crutchfield. But Bill glowered, turned back to the dimly lit, crowded room, caught his breath, and shouted, "I am ready to meet you now or any time hereafter."[11]

Tom Crutchfield pushed his brother into the hall and out the front door. Now Bill's followers were ready to start a fight. But as the lamps were relit the secessionists' drawn pistols all around the room were visibly in the majority.

Key quickly moved to Davis' side and tried to calm him. Davis had lost his voice completely now. He was utterly exhausted, and his high cheekbones seemed to protrude more than ever in his gaunt face.

The ladies reappeared, and dinner was being served. Key and Hopkins led the group to the dining room and tried to make small talk. Now Key felt awkward, aware of his big hands and country manner. He knew he had mishandled the big moment. The evening had been miserably unsuccessful. The guest of honor had been in great danger, might even have been killed. Of that Davis seemed all too aware while he ate the tasty dinner at Crutchfield House and rested his husky voice. All the table companions looked forward to the next morning, when the 7:30 whistle would announce the departure of Davis' train for Mississippi.[12]

# 3

---

# Guerrilla War

For days afterward, Key often sat at his big mahogany desk, doing no work but recalling the events of that hectic evening at Crutchfield House. He had hoped that Davis would make a persuasive speech that would convert many, perhaps even Bill Crutchfield himself, and turn the tide in the southeastern part of the state for independence.

But Davis' speech and its sequel had merely set off a wave of rifts.[1] The secession issue now divided families like the Crutchfields and could no longer be debated dispassionately. It seemed to bring out the beast in people, as it had in Bill Crutchfield. The old friendship between Crutchfield and Key had given way now to suspicion and misunderstanding.

Key frequently looked up from his law briefs and out of the window to watch the crowd of mountaineers and small farmers milling about the Saturday market and drawing water from the large cistern. He knew those people and had defended many of them in court. The farmers and mountaineers distrusted wealthy planters like Jefferson Davis and stood against the secessionist cause. Many of them felt estranged from Key after hearing of the explosive evening that he had allegedly engineered. Most of the townsmen had also drawn back into their shells. It seemed that

Chattanooga, like all of eastern Tennessee, would prefer neutrality should rebellion break out.[2] Key and his secessionist allies were unable to change this neutralist temperament. Were they to try harder, they would only drive more people into the Northern camp. Only a dramatic affront on the part of the Northern states could move the townsmen to take sides against the North.

The weeks slipped by, and the spring rains began. Market Street seemed about to float away, and green shoots appeared on the slopes of Lookout Mountain. Early in April, news came over the telegraph of the much needed Northern provocation. It was reported that President Lincoln, disguising the attempt as a provisional expedition, had tried to send reinforcements to Fort Sumter. There had been a fight, and Southerners had fired at the fort. That message hit Chattanooga like a thunderclap.

At the courthouse, the tavern, Devote's Confectionery, the docks, and Lewis' blacksmith shop—everywhere—Key and his secessionist friends were telling the news of the firing on Fort Sumter and giving their interpretation of it. According to them, President Lincoln had maneuvered the South into firing the first shot, and loyal Southerners at Charleston had fired in defense of Southern honor and rights. They said that neutrality was no longer an alternative. The South had to stand together to defend the sister state and whip the Yankees if they really wanted to make war.

One secessionist gathered together the school children on top of Lookout Mountain. Barrels of coal tar were collected and set ablaze, and the black smoke could be seen throughout the valley. The youngsters danced around the bonfire and sang songs of Dixie Land, their new nation, which was born out of the Yankee challenge to their freedom.[3]

Events moved swiftly. It seemed that Lincoln really would fight secessionists; on April 15, he called into service 75,000 militiamen. This inspired Isham Harris, the rabid secessionist governor of Tennessee, a self-made, domineering young man who was determined to lead Tennessee out of the Union. He sent a sizzling wire to President Lincoln: "Tennessee will not furnish a single man for coercion, but fifty thousand, if necessary, for defense of our rights or those of our Southern brethren."[4]

Harris infuriated eastern Tennessee Unionists when he instructed the state commissioners to sign an agreement with the Davis government declaring that until Tennessee passed a referendum on joining the Confederacy, the state would be under the direction of the president of the Confederacy. To ensure that the referendum, set for June 8, would turn out as he wished, Harris dug into the state treasury for funds to pay for a canvass of the state for secession. After setting up his military government, he called in his chief lieutenants for consultation and to hear reports on the attitudes of different sections of the state. In Chattanooga, the city council met and voted D. M. Key powers to confer with Harris about supplying the area with arms and ammunition. Chattanooga community leaders were alarmed by the increasing strength and activity of the Unionists in southeastern Tennessee. Incensed by the governor's strong-arm methods, these Unionists were preparing to use all means to destroy the secessionist movement. The most prominent Unionist, Colonel Clift, set up a secret Unionist camp, well concealed in the thickets of the overgrown banks of the Tennessee River, and stocked it with rifles and supplies.[5]

Special policing and safety measures were instituted in Chattanooga; slaves were prohibited on the streets after 7:30 P.M., and a twelve-man vigilance committee was to judge persons "suspected of being dangerous to the community."[6] Key and the secessionists steadily gained the upper hand over the Unionists. But Bill Crutchfield, who had been disowned by his family, continued to speak out against secession, until he realized that further agitation would land him in jail, perhaps with Key as his jailor. Only late at night did he dare to go out into the streets, but soon even that became too dangerous. Eventually, he had to leave his beautiful wife behind and flee North—vowing he would fight with the Yankees.

Key continually received reports that in the mountains of eastern Tennessee the flames of Unionism were spreading as if caught in a March wind. Parson Brownlow, thinking he was God's own messenger, called Unionism God's will and damned secessionists from his Methodist pulpits. People in every town hall and village square knew the preacher with the wild eyes, homely nose, gaunt cheeks, and unkempt long hair. They all had heard his voice. Key knew the parson well, for Parson Brownlow and Parson Key had visited the same pulpits, preaching Isaiah and Moses to the same brethren.[7]

But there was another Unionist who was far dearer to Key than evangelist Brownlow. This was U.S. Senator Andrew Johnson. Johnson, like Congressman Nelson, had just returned to his native state from the session in Washington. On Key's cluttered desk lay a letter from one of Lizzie's cousins who lived near Knoxville:

> If Johnson and Nelson go around here speaking much more, they will make some of our backwoods yeomanry think that the Southern Confederacy is about to try to coerce them, take away all their liberties and elect a king to rule over them and grind them to powder, and that their only hope of deliverance is in the bosom of Abraham and under the sheltering wing of his Black Republican cohorts. Nelson tells them to die before they will go with the Southern Confederacy and some say they will die.[8]

Nelson had never been close to Key, but Andy Johnson, a self-made eastern Tennessean, who had once been a poor, orphaned young tailor's assistant, had been one of Key's early heroes and mentors, and he had worked diligently in Johnson's last campaign. When Dave Key was a young man, Johnson had developed a special liking for him, and he had often invited young Key to his fine home on Main Street in Greeneville. Dave had sat by the fire in Johnson's special overstuffed chair, adorned with silk-rope piping and velvet trim, which was usually reserved for Johnson himself. As the fire burned low, they would talk, Johnson explaining why his attitudes enraged the Southern planter class and why the working class should get a fair break in legislation. And Johnson would insist that no Northern provocation was worth breaking up this great Union.[9]

If David Key, on the eve of secession, had harbored some lingering hope that Johnson might change his attitude in the eleventh hour and support secession once the war had begun, such hope was shattered soon after the letter had come from Lizzie's kin. Union leaders held a tumultuous convention in Knoxville, where Brownlow, Nelson, Johnson, and others pledged to defy Governor Isham Harris, whom they called a devil and a tyrant.[10]

But Harris was undaunted. He sent provisional regiments and his most able orators for secession to the eastern part of the state to counteract the influence of Senator Johnson and his followers. One of the speakers Harris selected was D. M. Key. He quickly commissioned Key a major and assistant adjutant general and sent him into the very territory where Johnson was making his greatest progress. Who could oppose the Senator more effectively than his erstwhile protégé?

This assignment was unpleasant for Key. But he believed in the cause of secession and spoke out for it. With other orators for secession, he traveled back and forth on the East Tennessee Railroad, from Georgia to Virginia, stopping at every major town. He used a strong homespun approach, shaking fists on courthouse steps and crying that Johnson and Brownlow were wrong, that the Confederacy meant the birth of liberty, not its death. At his best, Key was artful, friendly, and jovial. His effectiveness was enhanced by the arrival of the first uniformed Confederate soldiers and the sound of the first fifes and drums. Then the pretty eastern Tennessee girls flocked to the Confederate cause and brought out the recruits in droves. All forces were pooled to work for Harris' victory and for Brownlow's and Johnson's defeat in the state-wide referendum.[11]

Tennesseans voted on the referendum on June 8, 1861. On that hot and sultry day, Major Key stationed himself just outside a dingy wooden building, the polling place of a small eastern Tennessee hamlet. He greeted the voters jovially on behalf of the glorious secessionist cause and kept a watchful eye open for any disorderly Unionist dissenters.

As the humidity rose and the stream of voters slackened off to a trickle, Key had time to remember that night at Crutchfield House, and he now felt that Bill, drunk and violent, had yet managed to bring forth a few strong, logical arguments. What if the Southerners had never walked out of Congress? Perhaps they really should not have done so. Yet, all the South had asked was peaceful secession, and was it not tyranny to prevent free people from such a choice? The South and the Confederacy were one and the same, so why should anyone question the methods of Governor Harris—granted they were highhanded—to bring Tennessee into the Confederacy where it belonged? Secession from the Union was a right, as indicated in the Virginia and Kentucky resolutions of 1798 and in Calhoun's speeches of the 1830's. Lincoln was indeed interfering with this right, as George III had interfered with the rights of the colonists.

Yet, Key was disturbed that all over eastern Tennessee, friends of the late Parson Key, now following Brownlow, were trooping to the polls to vote against what they called tyranny, and their tyrant was Governor Isham Harris. Some were proposing to hold a convention to pass a petition asking for the right of the pro-Union counties of eastern Tennessee to secede from the state if Tennessee seceded from the Union. Counties seceding from a state? Where did the right of secession end? These were disturbing questions for Key.

At the end of the day, Major Key headed back toward the dirty little railroad station to travel on to Knoxville. There he received the glorious news: Tennessee had voted for secession. Although many eastern Tennessee counties had remained Unionist, the efforts of Key and others had gained enough eastern Tennessee votes for the Confederacy to carry the state. Elatedly, Key wrote Lizzie: "We are in the South and long live the South, I say."[12]

But Tennessee's Unionists were not reconciled to defeat. They met in Greeneville and passed a petition to the state general assembly that pro-Unionist counties be allowed to secede from the state. The general assembly, however, rejected the petition and reasoned that states were sovereign and could secede from the Union whenever their conscience demanded it, but that counties did not have that right. This settled the issue, though Key would have hated to debate the logic of the argument with his old mentor Andy Johnson. He knew Johnson would argue that this decision proved the hypocrisy of the Confederate cause, both on the issue of freedom for slaves and on that of freedom for eastern Tennessee Unionists.

Key spent much of the following summer in the new army camp, staked out on the former fairground near Knoxville, mustering in regiment after regiment of recruits, advising them to take military life seriously and to prepare for battle. He hoped that this task would be temporary and that he too would soon see battle.

The sprawling provisional campsite still looked to Key like one of the county fairs he used to visit on these grounds in his youth. Rows of shelter tents, gray tepee tents, and brush lean-tos stood along the company streets and log corduroy walkways. Covered wagons arrived, bulging with supplies. And sun-tanned recruits were always about, washing their odd assortments of clothing in the nearby creek, polishing their brass, or working with their haversacks. Some of the soldiers were not yet in Confederate gray, and men still in suspenders and checkered trousers were playfully calling out the commands for each step in the drill of loading the rifle nine times.

Soon, the raising and organizing of a company became routine procedure for Key. At mass meetings in the various county seats, Major Key would drum up volunteers; community leaders who hoped to become officers would pass around a list at the meeting or later in town; after recruitment and farewells, the volunteers would set out for the camp near Knoxville. Some traveled in comfortable, decorated railroad coaches, others in plain boxcars. The recruits had to pass a most lenient physical examination and were mustered in. Then came the election of officers. After several weeks of basic training, the new soldiers boarded the train again to go off to their posts of duty.[13]

One late summer evening, after the sun had set and the gnats swarmed about the campsite, Major Key rested on a camp stool inside his faded tent. Across the tent, Colonel J. W. Gillespie lay sprawled on a cot, sleeping like a child. When Tennessee had officially joined the Confederacy, Governor Harris had appointed both Gillespie and Key to raise regiments in eastern Tennessee. Key enjoyed working with Gillespie, who had more style and reputation than any other Mexican War hero in the Chattanooga area. Gillespie had been merited for gallantry at Cerro Gordo and was a real hero to recruits. Although he had been a major general of the Tennessee Militia and a state legislator, he was at heart an easygoing aristocrat, and Vechee, his place in the hilly country outside Chattanooga, was among Tennessee's finest plantations.

Key was in a thoughtful mood, recalling the events of this fading summer. After the great elation over the victory of Bull Run, there had been no quick follow-up, no fall of Washington—only the bickering of Confederate commanders. Perhaps a long war was in store; perhaps Abe Lincoln and the Federals would not cry for peace.

The difficulties had often seemed insurmountable. Tennesseans had neither ammunition nor guns, except for sporting weapons and a few old flintlock relics of the Mexican War that, in fair weather, might kill a squirrel at short range. On other supply items, Key and Gillespie had made out slightly better.

Key's responsibilities went beyond supply, drill, and discipline in camp. He was also serving as a roving trouble shooter and spending much time raising recruits and inspecting troops on duty on strategic railroad bridges throughout eastern Tennessee. The flow of supplies to the Confederate armies in Kentucky and in western Virginia depended on these railroad lines, and the destruction or sabotage of one of them could cut off supplies for the forces in Virginia and on the Kentucky border and cripple the center of the Confederacy.[14]

Key had written to Lizzie that he enjoyed camp life, that it was "first rate." And he did enjoy life at Camp Cummings in good weather—but not riding a circuit in the rainy season or cooking, eating, and sleeping in the rain and red mud. Some of his duties he found bitter and detestable, such as policing Unionist prisoners and reasoning with packs of teen-age hoodlums who claimed they were patriots of the Confederacy but dodged enlistment. These youngsters traveled in droves, spied out every Union suspect, and harrassed the old, the defenseless, and those who tried to stay neutral. Their victims were often descendants of Tennessee pioneer families, and Key was much concerned with their difficult position and the problems of their protection. After all, they had not followed Colonel Clift or taken up arms against the Confederacy.

Key, accompanying a general, had come upon one such camp of a hoodlum band. There had been about 200 excited, noisy youths, none of them in the Confederate service but all eager to fight a group of unarmed Lincoln supporters who were seeking shelter in a nearby hollow. All the youngsters were armed—although there were not enough guns for half of Key's trainees at Camp Cummings.

While some loudmouths continued to talk back, Key told them sternly that their wanton attacks on civilians were hurting the cause, that they belonged in uniform anyway. The more Key talked about signing up, the weaker became their bold talk and the smaller became the group as more and more of the boys sneaked away.

Key frequently worried that the Tory opposition was often handled not with skill and diplomacy but with bitter, destructive antagonism. He feared that treating Tennessee Tories like Yankee enemies might breed one civil war within another. Key had learned a lesson that night at Crutchfield House upon which he still pondered. And if the Tennessee Tories began to act like Yankee enemies or like Colonel Clift, every strategic railroad bridge in eastern Tennessee would be in danger. Key had failed to pause and think that night at Crutchfield House, and he now warned many a Confederate officer to pause and consider. People who bitterly opposed secession could simply not be forced to support the Confederacy.

Key stripped off his jacket and boots and lay down on his bunk. He closed his eyes and listened to the doleful lament of an old

Guinea Negro whom one of the colonels had brought along to entertain the camp with his music until the arrival of the military band. But the old man would sing only one song: "My wife is sick, my wife is sick." Perhaps indeed he was worrying about his spouse. In the distant night, the guards called out, "Post number one all is well. . . . Post number two all is well." All might be well if only the Confederate leaders would learn to handle the Unionists with wisdom, thought Key as he dropped off to sleep.[15]

But all was far from well; a nightmare for Tennessee was being prepared in the purple mountains to the east.

For weeks, the strategic bridges along Key's route of inspection had been stealthily watched by William B. Carter, a loyal Unionist mountaineer. Carter was carefully planning a guerrilla attack on nine strategic bridges whose destruction would immobilize the Confederate defenses in northeastern Tennessee and Kentucky. Carter hoped that his offensive would enable the Union forces in Kentucky to attack through Cumberland Gap, overrun all of eastern Tennessee, and slice it off from the Confederacy. Using this mountain base, the Union forces were to push southward through Alabama and Georgia. It was a most ambitious plan.

Carter made his way through Confederate troop concentrations and arrived in Washington. There he presented his bold plan, first to influential eastern Tennessee refugees like Andrew Johnson, then to Generals McClellan and Thomas, and finally to President Lincoln himself. The plan was adopted and carefully mapped out. Then Carter returned to Tennessee. He chose nine guerrilla leaders and prepared them to help organize the raiding patrols. While the raids were taking place, other Union sympathizers were to assemble in secret coves, hollows, and barns, form new companies, and elect officers.

The surprise attacks took place on the dark night of November 8. Near the Holston River bridge at Strawberry Plains—not far from where Key had made his recent speech in the camp of the young hoodlums—a patrol crept toward the river and stealthily made their way downstream to the abutment under the bridge, creeping through bushes and reeds. They watched and listened for some time and concluded that there were few if any guards on the bridge. The patrol split up. While most of the men served as security guards, the leader and another man climbed up the abutment and onto the bridge. Still there were no signs of guards. The leader had prepared some flammable material. As he struck a match to ignite it, suddenly at the other end of the bridge, an unobserved Confederate guard came to life, spun around, and fired at the flame. Hit, the patrol leader moaned and fell. The guard rushed forward and pounced upon the wounded figure. As guard and patrol leader wrestled in the night, the other man rushed up, unsheathed a hunting knife, grabbed what he thought to be the Confederate guard's hand, and began to hack away at wrist and arm. Horrible screams told him of his monstrous error: the hand, almost amputated, was his patrol leader's.

By now the others in the Tory band had scurried up the abutment. They jumped into the fray, separated the fighters, shot the Confederate guard several times, and threw him down into the river. The Tory men huddled around their wounded leader, trying to help control his profuse bleeding. When they heard splashing movements in the water, they assumed that the Confederate soldier was swimming downstream to alert nearby Confederate units.

The rattled patrol then started a frenzied search in the leader's bloody clothing and peered around the railroad ties on the bridge for the matchbox to set the bridge on fire. They could not find a single match! Near panic, they carried their leader away, leaving the bridge intact—their mission unaccomplished.

But other raids were more successful. Shrill cries, flames, and dead Confederate bodies heralded the destruction of the bridges over the Hiwassee and Holston rivers and Lick and Chickamauga creeks.

News of the uprisings and bridge burnings swept through the Confederacy. The president of the East Tennessee and Virginia Railroad reported vast destruction and warned that the guerrillas would soon demolish the entire line from Bristol to Chattanooga. In his Richmond office, the adjutant general of the Confederacy paced nervously about as the alarming wires ticked in. 500 Tories threatening Strawberry Plains; 1,500 Tories assembling for action in Hamilton County at Colonel Clift's camp, somewhere on the Tennessee River; 500 Chattanooga Unionists headed for the bridge at Loudon.

Governor Harris wired Jefferson Davis, reporting that this was a "deep-seated rebellion." It had to be "crushed instantly, the leaders arrested, and summarily punished." A Chattanoogan notified high-ranking Confederate officers that Chattanooga was exposed to the ravages of Colonel Clift. In western Tennessee and Kentucky, General Albert Sidney Johnston was concerned about the security of his right rear guard and urged Harris "to put arms into the hands" of unarmed levies. Knoxville panicked at the thought of a major invasion by Union forces.

Large-scale reinforcements poured in, many to Chattanooga. Gillespie and Key led an attack on Clift's secret camp at Sale Creek, but they found the camp abandoned. Half of Clift's forces had taken to the mountains, the others had fled north to join the federal armies in Kentucky. All escape hatches in the Cumberland Mountain passes were now heavily guarded, and many Union sympathizers were captured, among them Andrew Johnson's son-in-law.[16]

But there still was no federal invasion. Unbeknown to Carter, as well as to the Confederates, General Sherman, taking command of the invasion forces, had canceled the daring plan. Sherman feared that such a thrust into eastern Tennessee would dangerously expose his forces' flanks. But it was too late to get word to Carter, who was somewhere in the eastern Tennessee mountains. Since there was no follow-up invasion, many high-ranking Confederate officers were now convinced that eastern Tennessee Unionists were conducting warfare on their own; this constituted treachery. During these trying weeks, Key abandoned his attitude of moderation. He now agreed with those who maintained that there could be no more appeasement of active Unionists.[17]

Colonel W. B. Wood notified the adjutant general that he had captured six of the Lick Creek assailants. He asked for vigorous measures to put down the rebellion and declared that "a mild or conciliatory policy will do no good; they must be punished. . . . The slow course of civil law in punishing such incendiaries" would not have the needed effect.

The authorities in Richmond complied with Colonel Wood's demand. The Secretary of War ordered that those engaged in the bridge burnings should be tried by court-martial; the guilty were to be hanged, if possible in sight of the burned bridges. All other Tories, even those not involved in the bridge burnings or other acts of aggression, were to be shipped off to a prison at Tuscaloosa, Alabama. Now Key's worst fear had come true; it was a reign of terror.[18]

Colonel Gillespie grudgingly obeyed orders to arrest Key's friend Levi Trewhett, an eighty-year-old attorney who lived about thirty miles from Chattanooga. Trewhett, like Andy Johnson, was dedicated to helping the common man; he let the poor farmers pay for his counsel with a load of hay or a pile of wood. Although Levi Trewhett denounced Isham Harris as a tyrant coercing defenseless eastern Tennesseans, he had never advocated that Tories take up arms against the Confederacy.

Some months later, Key made a hectic train trip to Richmond, by now the capital of the Confederacy. The train was packed, and all the way there he had to stand in the crowded aisle, but he was buoyed up by the hope that he would accomplish his mission. His official duty in the Confederate capital was to arrange for fresh supplies. He was indeed glad that this assignment gave him the opportunity to ask clemency for Levi Trewhett. Trewhett, with other such Unionists, had been herded into an overcrowded Knoxville jail. A high-ranking Confederate officer had decided to skip the slow court-martial process. He had shipped the prisoners off to Tuscaloosa in boxcars without a hearing.

Key had been stunned by this injustice, and it was much on his mind during this difficult journey to Richmond. Not long before, serving as spokesman for a group of Confederate officers, he had urged citizens of the county to write a petition protesting against Trewhett's unjust imprisonment. Key and other officers had endorsed the petition, and it was mailed to President Davis. But no answer had come from Richmond. Was this the justice of the new Confederacy?

If a man never proven guilty was imprisoned without trial, Key's speeches throughout eastern Tennessee, promising the freedom of the Confederacy, had become a farce. He had often spoken of Madison's and Jefferson's resolutions of 1798, which had condemned the Alien and Sedition laws and imprisonment without trial. It was one thing, he felt, to take William Carter to prison, to hang in sight of the burned Lick Creek bridge its would-be saboteurs; but it was another to take an old and ailing man who had not raised a finger in violence against the Confederacy and ship him off to prison.

When Key arrived in Richmond, he found the city a madhouse and his supply duties difficult. But worst of all, he did not obtain clemency for Trewhett. Dejected, he boarded another crowded train and started his journey back. Miles down the track, in western Virginia, the train screeched to a halt and the conductor announced a landslide ahead. That night, the passengers slept in their seats. The next morning, Key set out on foot to find a place to eat breakfast. When he reached an inn, he was offered stale food. At the sight of it, he felt ill. He put it to lack of sleep, bad nerves, and the poor food, and he walked back to the train.

Finally, the train started off, chugged down the track for five miles, and again broke down. Disheartened and nauseous, Key wondered whether the Confederacy could possibly win the war with the railroad system a shambles, justice in jeopardy, and men like Trewhett in prison.

Not long after this painful journey, he found he need no longer worry about his friend suffering in the Tuscaloosa prison. Trewhett was dead.

Colonel Key's romance with the Confederacy was sick. "I think, I hope," he wrote to Lizzie, "I shall be able to see you soon. I must do so even at the risk of a Court Martial. I want to see badly the babies, all of them, and more than all I want to see my dear Lizzie." But, like a good soldier, he regained his dedication and blamed it all on the enemy: "If the Yankees had not started the war, even old Levi would be living today." And he wrote to Lizzie: "What privations, miseries and wrongs these Yankees inflict upon us."[19]

# 4

## The Faltering General

At the railroad station across from Crutchfield House, on a balmy May afternoon in 1862, weary soldiers of the 43d Regiment left their trains to receive coffee and cookies from the town's ladies. One might have expected to see Lizzie among them, but she was not in town. She was now staying with the children at the Lenoir plantation of her father, in eastern Tennessee. The engine's bell-like smokestacks were still puffing. They had pulled into Chattanooga an array of passenger coaches and cattle and freight cars whose boards had been removed to give the traveling soldiers a view of the countryside.

In a group of townspeople stood Colonel Key, sipping coffee from a tin canteen cup and eating hard crackers, a long troop-roster roll clamped under his left arm; he was conversing with old friends. The station attendant joined the group and greeted the colonel. He told him that companies, battalions, and regiments were pouring into Chattanooga every day and that excitement filled the air like the winds of an oncoming storm.

Everywhere was the mark of war, even though no shell had yet touched Chattanooga. The long wooden porches of Crutchfield House were spilling over with the sick and the wounded. They had come from all over the South, civilians evacuated from cities like Nashville, soldiers from battlefields like Shiloh. Sometimes, in that hospital, so many pulses stopped beating at the same time that doctors and nurses could not attend to the dying, and it was often impossible to carry out the dead quickly enough to shield the living from the thought that their hospital resembled a morgue.[1]

Key had listened with grief to the station attendant's grim report. His friends now added that trains full of the wounded and the sick had rolled into Chattanooga after the loss of Fort Henry and Fort Donelson in northwestern Tennessee. That had been in February. After these defeats, Nashville had been in panic, for the northernmost border of the state was wide open to the enemy. When a cold spell hit the city, civilians, supplies, wounded, sick, nurses, and hospital facilities had been loaded onto trains bound for Chattanooga. Because of lack of passenger compartments, many of the sick had been piled into drafty cattle cars; for more than eighteen hours they had been exposed to freezing weather. When they arrived, it had been hard to tell the living from the dead.

Key learned that many of the women from Chattanooga and other towns were now volunteer nurses at the hospital. They were performing all sorts of duties, from tending the sick to sewing canvas on new cot frames. Many Negroes had volunteered and helped staff the hospitals there and elsewhere; not only free men like Bill Lewis but slaves who could have escaped and fled north chose this service instead. The Negroes in the Chattanooga area had instigated no insurrection, no rebellion, but had behaved with magnificent loyalty. This made a profound impression on Key, one he would never forget.[2]

Key was eager to hear more about the military situation in his hometown, for Chattanooga was now the biggest military base in Tennessee. Obviously, General Grant would want to take the town. How long could it be protected? Would Grant move now in this direction and on down the Mississippi toward Vicksburg? Obviously, Confederate strength was being built up in the area by the transfer of the 43d and other regiments. But more reinforcements would be needed, more troops than had been at Fort Henry and Fort Donelson and Island Number Ten in the Mississippi, all of which had fallen.

After the battle of Shiloh a few weeks before, some Union troops had pushed as far south as Huntsville, Alabama, southwest of Chattanooga. Then came a big scare. A bold group of Yankees, disguised as Confederates, had seized the "General," a Confederate engine, and had left a trail of destruction along the tracks between Atlanta and Chattanooga. Rumors grew, until Chattanoogans feared that a whole federal army was marching upon them. Ever since, the townsfolk were tense and aware that Federals could pop into this valley unexpectedly, like rats out of their winter holes. They were indeed glad to see their own boys of the invincible 43d back home to defend them.

Key knew that the 800 youngsters who made up the regiment were not quite so invincible. He recalled how low their morale had been last February, when the regiment, barely assembled and trained, had been broken up into small groups to be placed on bridge duty. The men wanted action, not bridge guarding. Key remembered that even Colonel Gillespie's interest had dropped to zero at this point. Instead of traveling to the various companies to cheer them up and restore morale by telling his stories of Cerro Gordo, he had left the regiment to Key and taken a trip to Vechee, his grand plantation. If Jefferson Davis wanted the 43d to fight in battle, Gillespie would be at the forefront. But if he wanted a bridge guard, the colonel would go off, back to the good life at Vechee, as in the happy days before the war.[3]

Gillespie set an example for the officers in the regiment. Soon, the ranking major decided he was sick and needed to go to the resort town Augusta, Georgia, to take his cure. And so it went. It seemed that the only officer on whom Key could count was his younger brother, Lieutenant Summerfield Key. When under pressure or under fire, the men of the regiment had behaved well. Several companies of the 43d, under Key's personal command, had recently passed through dangerous Laurel Valley. They had destroyed a bushwhacker camp and returned safely despite the sharp-shooters in the hills who had tried to turn the expedition into a disaster. Several of Key's men had been wounded, and one was killed; but the whine of Minié balls, the smell of action, and a commendation of General Kirby-Smith had uplifted the men's spirits.[4]

Yet Key felt that running the regiment was like running a boarding school for boys. Many of his men got off the train in Chattanooga still wearing their bright-checkered trousers, wide suspenders, and hillbilly hats. Confederate uniforms were still hard to come by.

Key was much relieved when Colonel Gillespie returned in time to aid in the defense of Chattanooga. He arrived nonchalantly, strode out of the station house, and examined the orders he had just received as to where the 43d would be stationed. The com-panies formed up and started, fife and drum, down Market Street —past the cistern, Key's old law office, Devote's Confectionery, and the courthouse. All along the way, the townspeople waved, shouting their welcome. For 800 young men, untested by battle but now quite confident, it was a proud moment. Now they knew what they were fighting for—this town, their friends, their families.

June 10, 1862, dawned, a hot, humid day. The sun beat down on the fields, near a red-brick mansion, where the 43d had pitched tents. The humidity climbed as the men hustled about their morn-ing duties, beads of perspiration already on their faces. A Union attack on the town was imminent. For several days, Yankees in force had appeared on the other side of the river, opposite the town. Federal artillery had been positioned in the hills, and shot and shell spun into the town. The day before, some shots had landed in Market Street, and one or two had hit Key's bivouac area and caused casualties.

The federal units across the river had been at Huntsville, Ala-bama; they were a battle-seasoned force. Chattanoogans were glad they had the Tennessee River, a sizable natural barrier against the enemy's crossing. Confederate artillery batteries had already been placed on steep Cameron Hill jutting out above the river bank. Shortly before 9:00 A.M., General Kirby-Smith ordered the 43d to strike camp and onto Cameron Hill, where the regiment could give support to the artillery fire, sniping and firing at the Yankees.

Soon the companies of the 43d Regiment were on their way across Market Street and up to Cameron. As Key marched, occasional shells whined overhead. Key, dripping with perspiration after leading a company up Cameron Hill, pulled out his watch. It was twelve minutes after nine. He scurried over the steep hillside making his final inspection. Suddenly, all the Yankee artillery opened fire on the town. Key crawled through some underbrush until he could see the town below—the rows of wooden houses, the public buildings, the station, Crutchfield House, and the cistern —and puffs of smoke marking the exploding shells. Frenzied animals and excited people were running through the streets. The Yankees had sent no notice or warning to the women and children or to the hospital—civilians had not thought that they were going to shell the town. Glancing back at his own batteries, Key heard artillerymen calling out to hold fire until a major crossing was attempted.

The sun reached its height over the town, as Key and Gillespie, well concealed in the bushes, continued to watch the shelling of Chattanooga. By noon it became evident that the Yankees were pulling out, and the Confederate cavalry was ordered to take up the pursuit. Apparently, this had been only a raid, even though the Federals numbered between 7,000–15,000 men. Union soldiers robbed and looted the little settlement across the river, north of Chattanooga, and took a few prisoners. But their force had been pulled back from Chattanooga. For the moment, the town was safe.

The men of the 43d remained on Cameron Hill through the night. They were in fine spirits, still relishing the smell of powder. They slept without tents and baggage that night on the steep hillside.

From his bedroll, Key looked out toward the dark, shimmering stretch that marked the Tennessee River, at the lights lining Market Street, and at the hill beyond, where he and Lizzie had spent happy years. Secession and war had taught him to value simple family life. He thought of his children, of Lizzie. A few days earlier, he had written to her at the Lenoir plantation, telling her it was his duty to ensure that she and the children would enjoy the blessings of liberty; beyond this, his aim was to live and die with his family, for which he now longed in the darkness of the night.[5]

The Yankees' early summer raid on Chattanooga had not been the prelude to a major move on the Chattanooga railroad center. In mid-June, news came to the troops in Chattanooga that Cumberland Gap had been occupied by Union forces. But General Grant's attention seemed focused on Vicksburg, not Chattanooga.

There also was much good news. In battles lasting seven days, Robert E. Lee had driven the massive Union armies from the doorsteps of Richmond and completely off the peninsula. And in Kentucky, John Hunt Morgan had undertaken a daring and successful raid. Early that August, the Confederate cause looked bright.

The morale of the 43d soared when it was announced that the forces of Generals Braxton Bragg and Kirby-Smith would mount an offensive into Kentucky. The regiment had already been assigned to Brigadier General Humphrey Marshall's brigade and ordered to move to Castlewood, Virginia, in the Shenandoah Valley. If Key and his men had craved activity, now they would get it. They arrived in the southeastern Virginia mountains, and after a brief respite in the little sleepy town of Castlewood, the entire brigade received orders for a forced march into Kentucky.

Meanwhile, General Kirby-Smith's divisions had swept into Kentucky and won a battle; they were now moving toward Cincinnati. Federal troops, retreating at Cumberland Gap, were fleeing north. The brigade to which Key was assigned, along with General John Hunt Morgan's cavalry, was ordered to intercept this force.

The march started. It was late in September and unseasonably hot. Gillespie and Key had to urge their men to move on, day after day shouting to their columns, "Close up, close up, close up." Soon their water supply ran low, and there was only corn bread left to eat, with a few hot cakes and biscuits to break the monotony. But despite their hunger and thirst, the men were cheerful as they pushed deeper into the bluegrass regions of Kentucky. They talked about an expected uprising of Confederate sympathizers and planned great victories, like Lee's at Seven Days and in the second battle at Bull Run.

But eventually it became apparent that the retreating Yankee forces had escaped the trap. The men's disappointment was great, but soon there was more marching to be done and more new country to be seen. At Mount Sterling, the 43d joined Bragg's main forces; the town's belles presented the troops with the regimental colors. Colonel Gillespie convinced the regiment's finest orator, a man with a beguiling voice, to speak to the ladies and the assembled townsfolk. It was a memorable occasion, and everyone was deeply stirred by Colonel Key's Tennessee eloquence.[6]

The 43d moved on toward Frankfort, where General Bragg was planning an elaborate ceremony for the inauguration of the provisional Confederate governor of Kentucky. For a few days, it seemed that the Yankee forces were entirely forgotten by General Braxton Bragg, who suddenly had become a political dilettante. On September 26, Bragg issued an elaborate proclamation telling all Kentuckians that they had been rescued from the "meddlesome, grasping and fanatical disposition of the East." Some soldiers carped that Bragg should march on the Federals before they recouped and struck back.

There was more delay, little drinking water, and no rain. Key's thirsty men would cheer as they approached a stream bed, only to find dry rocks and sand. And it was over just such a creek of flowing water that a fight began between federal units and some of Bragg's forces. The skirmish turned into the Battle of Perryville.

Kirby-Smith's troops and Humphrey Marshall's brigade, to which Key's regiment was attached, were miles away. After indecisive fighting, Bragg ordered a junction with Kirby-Smith's forces at

Harrisburg. At last the 43d would fight a major battle. On the night of October 11, two great armies finally were drawn up in battle order on the outskirts of town. The men of the 43d, together with their comrades of all the other Confederate regiments there that autumn night, sensed the importance of the coming contest. Defeat would be catastrophic; it would carry the war back to their homes in Tennessee and perhaps even further south. There could be no retreat. Tomorrow's sun must see the beginning of the long-sought victory. That night, many men slept soundly and dreamed of glory.

But General Bragg faltered. He did not speak to his officers of victory, did not make plans for combat. The next morning, when Gillespie received the general's orders, he handed them to Key, wordless: the retreat was to begin immediately.[7]

And retreat it was, inglorious and devastating. Caravans of refugees led the way, with stagecoaches and farm wagons loaded with family possessions and furniture. Then followed the troops, unit after unit, lifting sore feet and worn-out shoes. Few jokes were heard, but many a bad word for Bragg, mile after mile, on the dusty, rocky way back to Tennessee. After marching 1,000 miles, the 43d still had not met the Federals in a major battle.

At the end of the long road, in eastern Tennessee, the regiment was granted a furlough. Key went to join Lizzie at the Lenoir plantation, and the children learned to know their father again. But never had they known him so discouraged over the war.

# 5

## Vicksburg

Though faded and badly in need of paint, the doric columns of the red-brick Lenoir mansion looked lovely to Key during those fleeting, happy weeks in the late autumn of 1862. It was good to be with Lizzie at her girlhood home, and Dave and Lizzie roamed through the autumn fields and woods and helped with the farm work. They walked down the paths, shuffling through the brown, red, and yellow leaves, collected chestnuts, and sat by clear, splashing brooks. Sometimes they took Emmie and Albert along, the oldest of their children. They came to feel again that life had meaning and hope.

Most of the slaves had remained loyal to the Lenoirs. This was a great comfort now that all the Lenoir men, except Lizzie's father, aging and ailing Albert, had left for the army. Although the Yankee armies were in the state, there had been no violence and few runaways. Many slaves had joined the Confederate armies to help with supply. Those who worked around the house under the supervision of "Aunt" Clarsie and her husband, who spoke with aristocratic Charleston accents, still looked devotedly after the welfare of their aging master and his family. In a bitter moment, he had predicted that the war would make his wife a widow, his children paupers, and his plantation a heap of ashes. Aunt Clarsie scolded him for such lack of hope. She was determined to keep him alive. She and her husband were now a combined chief of staff for the plantation, and the visiting Colonel Key was overwhelmed by the thoughtfulness and competence of their stewardship. Yet, there was no adequate manpower to till the farms, to work the grist mill, to grow and harvest the vegetables, to tend the lathe in the furniture factory, or to make the cots needed at the fronts and in the hospitals. Albert Lenoir drove himself beyond his strength, as if in self-punishment because his health did not permit him to go to the front or do the job on the plantation. His father-in-law's condition was the sole note of sadness during Dave's autumn furlough.

At night, after the sumptuous dinners of turnips and sugar-cured ham, Key would sit in the living room before a crackling fire. He dreaded the inevitable moment of his departure and hoped to be able to remain long enough to celebrate Christmas with his family. Aunt Clarsie was already preparing for a huge feast. She was bitterly disappointed when Key received orders to assemble his companies at Lenoir Station and to depart by train for Vicksburg. Vicksburg—the name seemed to chill Lizzie strangely.[1]

Near the Tennessee border, General Grant was pushing forward toward the stronghold, while General Sherman moved down the western side of the Mississippi River; other federal units were inching their way up the river from New Orleans. Jefferson Davis feared that Vicksburg, the link between the eastern and western halves of the Confederacy, might fall. He ordered General Bragg to send Stevenson's division of 10,000 men to aid General Pemberton, who was in charge of the defense of Vicksburg. Since the 43d was now a part of Stevenson's division, it was this decision that had interrupted Key's bliss.

At Lenoir Station, Dave bade a fond farewell to his family and the Lenoir household. He hugged his mother-in-law, listened to Aunt Clarsie's warnings not to catch the fever, and joked with little Albert, Emmie, and Kate. Then Dave shook hands with his father-in-law. The aging Albert looked at him affectionately and sadly, and they both sensed that this was their last farewell. There were last dear words with Lizzie, tears, and final good-byes. But now Key had to look after his men. At the engineer's signal, the engine pulled away a long train of boxcars full of soldiers and puffed out of Lenoir Station. It was four days before Christmas, and Vicksburg was hundreds of war-torn miles away.

On New Years Day, 1863, the long train carrying the 43d Regiment rolled into that Confederate citadel. Dampness and fog hindered the men's view of the town's roofs and belfries, its plush homes, and its great cotton warehouses—all perched 250 feet high on the cliffs above the broad Mississippi River. From the city, the cliffs extended northeastward along the Yazoo River, which flowed into the Mississippi north of Vicksburg. It was this general area, at Chickasaw Bluffs, that General Sherman was attacking as the 43d arrived in Vicksburg. Soon the long columns of the regiment set out, marching off on the road leading north to the crest of the bluffs. Key's men looked forward to the battle; they were in good spirits.

Guides directed the various platoons into positions along the cliff line, while Key strained his eyes to see through the thick fog. Below, the Yankees had tried to make camp on the previous day. Key could faintly make out the Yazoo River and the outline of a mysterious, densely wooded island. Except for the distant whistle of the troop trains arriving at Vicksburg with reinforcements, all was quiet.

A heavy rain began to fall. Key's men stood around their rifle holes, watched them fill up with water, and listened to stories about Sherman's assault. With nightfall, the rain stopped. The sky became clear, and the moon gave an eerie light to the foggy landscape.

The next morning, the men of the 43d were alerted for an attack. They watched the fog pockets and the clear areas in the bayou below, hour upon hour. As the fog lifted, faint columns could be made out loading onto gunboats and transport steamboats on the Yazoo. Sherman had evacuated his troops.[2]

The men of the 43d were depressed and disgusted. They had missed another battle. Again, they were just a day too late, a habitual story by now. This was another low point in morale, and Key and Gillespie used every device—jokes, marches, and hard work— to divert the men's attention.

Morale was not helped by news about a big battle in central Tennessee. A Union general, Rosecrans, had attacked Bragg's forces at Murfreesboro, just south of Nashville. The 43d would have been in that battle had they not been dispatched to Vicksburg. The Confederates had suffered grave losses and were falling back in central Tennessee to seek a new defensive line from which to block a Yankee campaign to take Chattanooga. Again Bragg had failed.

When Grant despaired of taking Vicksburg by frontal assault and ordered Sherman to evacuate, General Pemberton had time to improve the fortifications. He ordered the 43d to assist in defensive preparations near the little river town of Warrenton, along the cliff line about ten miles south of Vicksburg. Throughout the winter, the regiment took to spade and shovel and to patrol duty along the Mississippi River.

From a range of bluffs more than 200 feet high, Confederate batteries had been able to wreak havoc in broad daylight upon river transport and General Sherman's troops across the river. Now Union troops were trying to dig a canal across the neck of the Mississippi River so that their transports would not have to pass the deadly Confederate batteries at Vicksburg.[3]

On the bright, clear morning of April 30, 1863, at about ten o'clock, as the waters of the Mississippi sparkled in the sun below Warrenton, Key paced restlessly along the levees in a dirty uniform that showed the effects of two solid days of picket duty. He watched a battalion of the 43d file in to replace one that was returning to the main camp for rest.

He gazed at a stack of cotton bales piled up not far from the levees. Cotton, the pride of the South, was the main product of this area. Because of overdependence on this one crop, food supplies always had to be shipped in from farther up or lower down the Mississippi. But Vicksburg faced blockade from both above and below. The local farmers and plantation owners did not know how to convert the cotton land quickly into vegetable or grain fields, and soon the citadel would be threatened by starvation. Key came to feel that perhaps something had been deeply wrong with the economy of the South for a long time and that the war had merely accentuated this wrong. The crisis at Vicksburg seemed more than a military or an economic crisis—it now seemed to Key the crisis of a way of life, an archaic way, devoid of diversity and flexibility.[4]

Although it was early in the day, Key was already plagued by mosquitoes. Mosquitoes were swarming around the river bed. During Key's past two days on levee duty, these tough and impartial enemies of all soldiers had bitten him mercilessly. He felt ill and chilly, and he remembered Aunt Clarsie's warning to beware of the fever.

Several officers climbed the levee, saluted and greeted Colonel Key, and reported the change-over completed. The colonel briefed the new company commanders and stressed the importance of this river post in the scheme of the Vicksburg defense. After the Union capture of New Orleans, General Banks had moved north to Baton Rouge with about 20,000 men, while Grant's main forces had started some mysterious operation down the Mississippi River. Strange gunboats, looking like funny, slanted cracker boxes, steamed up and down the river, passing tauntingly close to the Confederate fortifications and batteries at Warrenton and Vicksburg. One night, six gunboats and several tall-stack steamboats, protected by cotton bales, and barges, piled with coal and forage, passed the batteries at Vicksburg and headed toward Warrenton.[5]

Key told the officers that only the night before, the main fleet, carrying Union troops, had passed Vicksburg and Warrenton. It had moved farther south, firing away all day at Confederate positions at Grand Gulf, near the junction of the Big Black River and the Mississippi. Key, pointing to the smoke rising in the direction of Grand Gulf, told them that the Federals had withdrawn temporarily. At least one of their boats was badly damaged, and only one out of seven Confederate guns was dismantled. But all this activity along the river indicated a major shift of Union troops from the north to the south of Vicksburg.

The colonel's description was interrupted by a sudden cannonade in the direction of the Yazoo. It seemed that the Yankees were starting operations in earnest, from north, south, and east. And General Stevenson's division was spread out too thinly from Haynes and Chickasaw Bluffs, north of Vicksburg, to Grand Gulf in the south.

At midday, Colonel Key left the river post with the companies that had been relieved and returned to the base camp. He found his brother, Summerfield, seated amidst blooming magnolia trees and wild flowers. Nearby were several log huts with thatched roofs and chimneys crowned with a commissary barrel to step up the draft. Writing a letter to sister-in-law Lizzie, Summerfield put down his pen to tell Dave again about the two girls who had visited camp the day before, one a widow, fat and forty, the other a blooming girl of seventeen. They were not at all the usual camp followers, Summerfield insisted, despite his brother's teasing. That morning, the handsome young lieutenant had already received a bouquet, a cake, and a tobacco pouch from a less attractive man chaser with pitiful false teeth. The colonel asked his brother in vain for mail from Lizzie. Disappointed, he went off to join some of the officers at a game of poker. Dave Key had not lost his skill at the game and often piled up stacks of inflationary Confederate dollars. The more the future seemed a gamble, the more the colonel sought out the distraction of the cards.[6]

That night, he went to sleep listening to the increasing rumbling of the cannons to the south. His rest was brief. Shortly after midnight, he received orders from the division commander. Soon the long, ominous roll of drums in the night signaled the startled men to prepare for a march. By dawn, the companies were on the road to Port Gibson and Grand Gulf, where Grant had struck in full force.

The sun was high and the noise of gunfire from Port Gibson and Grand Gulf was swelling as they waded into the cold, slimy bottom of the Big Black River and labored to move along their wagons.

When they got across, Gillespie and Key received news that a fierce battle had raged all day; the Confederate position had been routed, and Grant had taken prisoners by the hundreds.[7]

Down the road they pushed. After passing a bend in the road, they encountered a group of exhausted, beaten Confederate troops, who told them that all of Grand Gulf was being evacuated; all troops were falling back across the Big Black River. About midnight, Key and Gillespie reversed their course. Once more their weary columns, with soaked and aching feet, recrossed the slimy river, to move into assigned positions by a ferry. There they slept and waited. They waited a day, then another day; they collected corn, rounded up cattle, cleaned their weapons, and worried about what Grant was up to now. Eventually, they received orders to make a forced march to Edwards Depot, a station on the railroad line running east of Vicksburg to Jackson, Mississippi. Rumor had it that General Joseph E. Johnston was moving west with a large force to reinforce Pemberton. Combined, they would crush Grant! Pemberton believed that Grant would not be able to replenish his supplies after crossing the Mississippi and soon would be compelled to move on Vicksburg.

Soldiers sometimes sense when the generals are wrong, and Pemberton was wrong. Grant had boldly decided to cut himself off from his supply line, live off the land, and maneuver between Pemberton and Johnston. While Pemberton dawdled, Grant raced eastward, drove Johnston's forces out of Jackson, and moved west in search of Pembertson's scattered army.

In a pouring rain, with mud-filled shoes and aching legs, Key's tired column reached Edwards Depot. Delay had followed delay; the troops had been held up first by a flooded creek, which had forced them to construct a bridge, then by the need for fresh supplies. Men grumbled and cursed. Finally, marching orders came. They moved southeast, marching in the rain along muddy, narrow country roads bordered by dense woods. About midnight, they bivouacked for the first time after two weeks of incessant marching. They were too wet, tired, unhappy, and unsure of their generals to enjoy this long-awaited rest.[8] Early in the morning, Pemberton's frantic order was relayed: the entire column was to reverse its course again and move north. Key was confused; he could not make out what was happening. An incredible turn-around began, with stalled wagons and field artillery pieces blocking for hours the muddy, narrow road. The army wagon trains stacked up along the roadside, while the 43d Regiment observed the mess from the woods, waiting to take up its marching position in the column.

In the middle of this juggling process, Key heard muskets rattling and cannon fire to the north. Evidently, Grant's army was attacking. Key was worried—there had been no link-up with Johnston's army. The regiment was ordered to take up positions with the entire brigade to protect the wagon trains.

About 2:00 P.M., the battle sounds swelled to a new high around Champion's Hill. When it grew dark, the news spread that Pemberton had suffered a serious defeat, that the other brigades of Stevenson's division had broken and were fleeing. Now the 43d received orders to constitute part of the rear guard.[9]

Early the next morning, Grant's forces again struck the retreating troops. About 9:00 A.M., General Vaughn's brigade of Tennesseans broke; some of the men rushed to the bridge across the Big Black River, and others tried to swim across; stampede set in. Key's regiment was among those assigned to restore order and to protect the wagon trains on their way back to the Vicksburg lines. Along the tortuous way, Key and his weary men often had to stop to help with broken-down wagons. Much of the time they were under fire and had to skirmish with the enemy. Key and Colonel Gillespie were in constant action among their men. They could not forget that General Vaughn's troops had brought disgrace upon the state; the 43d's conduct had to be exemplary. Finally, their contact with the Union troops was broken, and on May 17 they approached the hills before Vicksburg.[10]

The construction of new fortifications, which had begun last August, had made great progress these last weeks. Key was glad to see the high, 20-foot-thick earthen wall of the fort and the deep, wide ditch in front of it. This would force advancing Federals, even if they took the ditch, to climb a steep almost vertical slope to get to the fort. As he came closer to the defense line, he scrutinized the line of rifle pits and entrenchments that stretched northward. Here the cliff dropped suddenly down a steep fall of almost 150 feet. Below was a dense jungle of vines and cane. On a second cliff perched another fort guarding the ridge running westward toward the Mississippi.

Could Pemberton's forces hold out until General Johnston rescued them? Key looked southward along the continuous level ridge; this area was also well fortified. On the approaches, great felled trees were lying across the path, hindering the advance of the Yankees. Obviously, the Federals would have to attack in narrow columns along these main roads to Vicksburg and face these strong fortifications. The felled trees, steep ragged slopes, and rivers would be too great an obstacle. These fortifications extended out from the main line of resistance in salients. Salients and redoubts had been placed at intervals of about 200 yards. Thus, the cleared area facing this entire trench line—through which an assailant would have to pass—could be subjected to devastating cross fire.

Key's feet ached, he felt the weakness and chills of a fever, but he had to control himself. He had to stay alert. His men had to do well. The 43d now came to a road junction and turned south behind the lines, where the regiment was guided to a reserve position. Along with five companies of the 3d Tennessee Regiment, the 43d was assigned to the reserves. They were to defend the ridge line that would serve as a secondary defense should the Yankees break through the outer front lines.[11]

Empty supply wagons and ambulances had to be arranged so that they could easily be set on fire if the enemy broke through. Some of the horses were turned loose to forage for themselves; food was becoming scarce and could no longer be spared for them.

Even in these reserve positions, there was no time for the men to rest. They were immediately ordered to take up spades and shovels to dig holes and bombproof shelters. When the limited supply of tools ran out, men were ordered to improvise with bayonets and makeshift tools. When it was time to eat, they were given meager rations of bacon, rice, peas, and salt pork.[12]

But the Yankees were busy too. There was distant rumbling as Union artillery was being placed into position and soon the rounds began to fall. In the fierce fire, men sought shelter in ravines, bushes, and between the rocks. After a false alarm of a major enemy attack during the night of May 19, there followed two days of comparative quiet. Now Key's men had a chance to dry out, sip a bit of the fast diminishing supply of coffee, and sample and discuss the quality of the newly introduced mule meat. At night, the men watched enemy gunboats lob shells into Vicksburg—13-inch mortar shells with blazing, sputtering fuses forming arcs across the sky.[13] However hot he had been during the day, Key got the shivers every night. His feet ached; he felt weak and knew his fever must be rising, but he did not speak to anyone of his illness. This was no time, he thought, to pay attention to minor complaints.[14]

The morning of May 22 dawned fair and clear and was greeted with mortar rounds from the Yankee gunboats. The sun soon burned down on the parched fields and on the soldiers of both causes. Soon the Union batteries joined in with their gunboats. The pace of enemy fire steadily increased until it seemed that every Union gun had joined in one thundering cannonade. "Nothing could be heard," one soldier said of that day, "but one continual shrieking of the shells as they came cutting through the air, the sharp fizz of minie balls as they came by the hundreds whizzing past."[15] Horses and mules sprawled bleeding on the ground. About 11:00 A.M., the barrage reached a crescendo, the muskets rattled without ceasing, the sharpshooters became increasingly accurate, and the ferocious firing continued unabated until one o'clock. In their holes or shelters, Key's men were alert, ready to move and listening to every sound of the fierce combat to their left.

Ordered to reinforce the main line of General Stephen D. Lee's brigade, the 43d rushed forward through the artillery rounds. To the left of Key's men was a redoubt that had been decimated by artillery earlier and hence abandoned. As most of the Union troops were falling back, a lieutenant colonel yelled to the Federals around him and led about sixty men forward and into the trenches at the base of the redoubt. There the Confederate lines had been breached, and two Union flags were waving from the trenches. The Confederate general sent orders that the position had to be retaken, and before reinforcements could be brought in, a lieutenant colonel of the 20th Alabama Regiment, with forty men from Waul's Teal Legion, volunteered. They rushed the works, took back the position, and prepared to kill the surrendering Union soldiers with hand grenades.[16]

Key's men had little time to watch that episode, for assaulting Federals were moving in upon them. Perspiring, lips dry, and hearts pounding, the Tennesseans remained alert behind the breastworks as mortar shells and artillery continued to land close to them. Out front lay the dead like harvested sheaves of wheat. Any moment now the command would be given to rise in the trenches to the attack. The order came. Despite grapeshot and musket and canister fire, Key stood on a parapet, shouting, encouraging his men. Nearby a man was hit and called out for help. The surgeon made his way toward him as Key gave orders. Then he again fixed his attention on the approaching Federals and shouted to his men to keep up the fire. All could see his big frame rising above the trench line.

Dust flew as several rounds of Minié balls peppered the ground in quick succession. Somebody cried that the colonel was hit, that someone had to get the surgeon; but the surgeon was wounded too. Colonel Key lay bleeding in the trench, where the men had pulled him to safety. His pain increased, throbbing heavily, drowning out the roar of battle. His body was convulsed, doubled up, on the stretcher now. Then all went dark.[17]

On that day, Grant's assault failed. Immediately, he laid siege to Vicksburg to starve out the Confederate garrison. General John-

ston did not try to relieve Vicksburg. For forty-seven days, as Key
was later told by a comrade, Key's men stayed in the lines of battle.
These were days of burning sun, drenching rains, thick fogs, and
heavy dew. There was incessant firing by enemy pickets, and there
were heavy mortar rounds at intervals throughout the night. To
the men of the 43d, the word was passed—as rations became even
more meager and as their ranks thinned to half—that Colonel Key,
at the hospital, was going from bad to worse. It was not just his
wounds; he had a rampant case of malaria.[18]

On July 4, 1863, the once beautiful banner of the 43d, chris-
tened by Key at Mount Stirling but now shredded with musket
holes, was lowered in surrender. The terms paroled all the men;
but Key, malaria-ridden, lay wounded. On the previous day, Robert
E. Lee had been defeated at Gettysburg. It seemed that Key's death
hour, like that of the Confederacy, was drawing near.

# 6

## Surrender

Several months later, when the leaves once more were turning red and yellow, Lizzie Key sat at a secretary in a bedroom of the Lenoir plantation sorting a group of letters. Occasionally she raised her head and looked pensively out of the large eighteen-paned window across the fields and hedges. She stared at a charred building with two big stone chimneys that had been the Lenoir's furniture factory. Some of the fields were dotted with army tents. A few gray-clad soldiers were washing clothing in a nearby creek; others clustered about little fires, propping up their kettles and preparing supper.

The ruins of the furniture factory recalled the awful day the Yankees had come to the house a year ago and spent an hour ransacking it. She would never forget the burly, blond-haired Federal, standing halfway down the grand staircase, laughing and mocking her mother at the bottom of the stairs. He carried a huge knapsack filled with Lenoir possessions, and on his head perched Lizzie's brother's straw hat with its fancy blue ribbon. Lizzie's brother had died of typhoid fever during the Kentucky campaign, and seeing the Yankee soldier with her dead boy's hat on made Lizzie's mother hysterical, which merely amused the Federal. Albert Lenoir, ill and infirm, and unable to defend the Lenoir women, had trembled with rage. Supporting himself against a table, he had flailed the Yankee with a torrent of words. Standing by, supporting and calming the Lenoirs, was Aunt Clarsie, who had sassed the Federal as "poor white trash" and cried that if her husband were here, he was one colored man who would punish the Federal to an inch of his life.

The drunken Federal then came abreast of Aunt Clarsie. "Woman, you don't need to bow down to her nor none of these white folk any more!" he shouted. "You're free, woman, you can go. Ain't you heard? We freed all the slaves on this plantation hours ago."

"You're the one who better go, Yankee. Get out of here!"

It had been Lizzie who had drawn their attention away from the Federal, crying out that the furniture factory and the mill were on fire. At that, the Federal had swung open the front door, swaggered onto the porch, where two other soldiers stood, and gleefully pointed to the flames across the field.

"Your slaves are free free, free," hollered the Yankee, going toward his horse with the child's hat still stuck on his head.[1]

All this had happened a year ago, but it still made Lizzie shudder. She remembered her father's prophecy that the war would make his children paupers and his wife a widow. Not long after that Yankee invasion, the remaining slave women had hummed in low tones, and Albert Lenoir was put to rest in the family grave as the tearful Lenoir women watched. Now there were no men left. At the lowest moment, Aunt Clarsie and her husband had proudly walked up to the remaining Lenoirs and announced that they were moving to the town of Loudon to work. With the money earned by their labor, they would take care of their late master's family.

And so they did. The great Lenoir family, Tennessee aristocracy, was now beholden to these generous Negroes. The Lenoir slaves had been set free. There had been no insurrection, no violence, and no looting but for that by the Yankee invaders. Who was more civilized—the Negroes or these Yankees? Lizzie had her answer. Who had killed, stolen, and desecrated? Not one Negro, but dozens of Federals—and all in the name of bettering the lot of the Negroes!

Old Bill Lewis in Chattanooga was a finer citizen than those rogues would ever be. But Southern independence would come one day, as bleak as the cause looked now, and these Yankees would be done with. Lizzie prayed for a few more victories like that at Chickamauga.

She glanced out of the window at the busy encampment. Lizzie had kept herself active every day preparing what appetizing foods she could scrape together for the soldiers. Toward evening she would help prepare dinner in the mansion, for General Longstreet and his staff had been the Lenoir's guests now for several nights.[2]

Longstreet told the Lenoir ladies of the great victory he had helped win at Chickamauga, just outside of Chattanooga, when his forces had arrived just in time to reinforce Bragg and defeat the Union troops. The federal forces there would have been entirely destroyed had General Thomas not stood firm as a rock. Thomas' stand had been made possible by a native Tennessean who knew the terrain—a fiery redhead with the Union Army named Bill Crutchfield.[3] But despite Crutchfield's and Thomas' efforts, the Federals now were bottled up in Chattanooga, so securely, Bragg figured, that Longstreet's forces could move to Knoxville and lay siege there too. Maybe Knoxville and Chattanooga would turn into Vickburgs in reverse!

Vicksburg, Vicksburg—that fateful name was awesome to Lizzie. Vicksburg had seen the final chapter in Colonel Key's military career. Lizzie did not know where her David was now, but she could not believe that he was dead. He would return someday. Her thoughts were with him every day and every hour, and she often recalled the happy day of his last furlough, which seemed so long ago.

She was distracted by a knock, a faint call at the front door. It would be one of Longstreet's soldiers. She went down the staircase, across the hall, fumbled at the latch, and swung back the heavy door. There stood a broad-shouldered, bearded, hollow-eyed, bony man, with a great mass of unruly curly hair, in a torn and muddy uniform. The stranger stretched out his hands to her. She stepped back in fear. Only when he spoke her name did she recognize her husband.[4]

Key had not been home long when Longstreet's army moved forward toward Knoxville. He was aware that a rebel colonel was always a target for Yankee raiders or for embittered Tennessee Unionists. Andrew Johnson, now military governor of the occupied portion of the state, talked of stringing up ex-Confederate officers like Key. So, despite the wintry weather, it seemed safer for Lizzie, Dave, and the children to journey over the mountains to North Carolina's Happy Valley, where the Lenoir relatives lived. Lizzie's mother provided the wagons, and one of Colonel Key's men volunteered to serve as a driver. Young Albert, Emma, and Kate piled into one wagon along with the weak colonel, and a second one of Key's men followed with another wagon and the baggage.

That night, in sleet and cold, they camped in a tent at a crossroad. Lizzie was fearful that the children would catch pneumonia and that her husband, shaking with fever, would take a turn for the worse. The next day they forded cold rivers, rode the railroad for some distance, met their wagons again, and struck out on the frozen roads across the mountains. They told the children to count the huge icicles on the cliffs when they complained of cold or boredom. The frozen road became slippery, and the mules pulled the wagons with difficulty. The mountain streams churned with ice, and at sunset the temperature dropped still lower, the winds cut more sharply, and the youngest baby was crying.[5]

At the next bend in the road, they saw several cabins. The windows showed light, and smoke poured out of the chimneys. Lizzie insisted that they stop, warm up, and ask for something to eat. Key shook his head. Freezing or not, he would not risk the safety of his family by entering the cabin of Unionist mountaineers. He would remain in hiding with his two men. Finally, Lizzie agreed. She drove one of the wagons up to a cabin, descended, and knocked. The door opened, and a rawboned mountaineer invited Lizzie and the cold children in. He offered hot food and later played with five-year-old Albert while he questioned Lizzie about her political sympathies. Lizzie gave no clue, for she dared not challenge a mountaineer mind like Bill Crutchfield's. But young Albert, bouncing on the big man's knee, gave it away when he spied a rifle over the mantle.

"I want a gun," he cried.

"What would you do with it?" queried the mountaineer laughing.

"Shoot a damn Yankee," answered the little boy.

Lizzie's heart pounded; seconds passed like hours. But the alerted mountain man only smiled. After all, his side was winning anyway. Had the lady heard the recent news? While Longstreet's forces were far from Bragg's army, Grant had taken command in Chattanooga, built up his forces, and delivered Bragg a crushing blow. Now Bragg's army was retreating into Georgia. In Tennessee, only a few isolated spots remained in Confederate hands. Andrew Johnson, the military governor, was taking stern action to bring Confederate men to justice, and there was no need to take it out on women and children.

After a short rest, she thanked the mountaineer for the supper and returned to the wagon. Now Colonel Key and his men could eat more of the bacon they had brought along. But discouragement seemed as endless as the winding, ice-glazed mountain road ahead.

During the Christmas season of 1863, the party arrived in Happy Valley at the old mansion of General Lenoir, who had been Lizzie's grandfather. Lizzie's cousins gave the Keys a warm welcome. The house had a beautifully appointed parlor covered with fine English paneling, and the dining room was crowded with antiques. Three stairways led to the many detached bedrooms. This house was indeed a reminder of happy days now past and a time about to die.[6]

When spring came, beds of tulips, hyacinths, and jonquils bloomed in the spacious gardens amidst the giant spruce trees. It all reminded Lizzie of happy girlhood visits. Here spring seemed to portend hope, but all the news was grim. Sherman was marching into Georgia; unwilling to retreat like his predecessors, Grant was locked in mortal struggle with Lee in Virginia; General Stoneman was raiding North Carolina, his soldiers requisitioning cows, chickens, and provisions; and the bushwhackers were becoming more plentiful and dangerous, burning and ravaging the land. Rewards were now being offered for Confederate colonels captured alive.

Stoneman's men were soon all over the area, and Key's friends and cousins set up a watch around the house to alert the colonel should they approach. For Key, there came days and nights of sudden escapes, of hiding in the hills while he was shaking with a recurrence of the fever. And he worried that Lizzie might be taken hostage or mistreated.

One cold night, Lizzie was up late caring for Sarah, her new baby. Suddenly, she heard the heavy front door swing open and bang shut. She started toward the stairs but was met halfway down by one of her cousins, who breathlessly reported that General Stoneman's raiders were burning the cotton factory; some of them would surely come to the house at any moment. Lizzie scurried into Key's room, shook him awake, and helped him dress. He left quickly by the back door.

No sooner had Lizzie made up his bed and returned to the fire in the living room than she heard sabers tapping on the railing of the porch. Two Union officers demanded Colonel Key by name, but she replied that he was not there.

"Did he hear our approach?" responded one officer.

"Yes," Lizzie replied, steadily returning his gaze.

"Where is he?"

"I don't know, but I don't think you will find him."

After a futile search of the rambling house, one of the officers said coldly, "Well, Mrs. Key, tell Colonel Key that we will be back in about two weeks and will take him for a trip north for his health."

Two fearful weeks began. Stoneman's raiders scavenged the neighborhood for horses, cattle, and provisions. And they searched for Colonel Key, who had remained across the river, hiding at a relative's house. During this time, Lizzie and her cousins found a sick Union soldier on their porch. It seemed strange to take in one of Stoneman's men, but they did so. The man was too weak to be moved even after Colonel Key's return.

A few nights later, three Federals again were at the door, and Lizzie could not help asking about the bleeding hand of one of the soldiers. He had fallen and run a knife into his hand.

The other soldier asked, "Who are you, the wife of the rebel colonel?"

Lizzie replied, "Yes." Turning again to the soldier's bleeding hand, she added, "That wound must be fixed." She went to a little chest and took out bandages. By the parlor fire, she matter-of-factly dressed and bound the hand.

As one of the soldiers watched the woman work by the red glow of the fire, he asked, "Where really is the colonel?"

Her eyes not moving from the hand, Lizzie replied that she did not know. She knew a search would soon follow. They would not find Colonel Key; he was far across the river by now. But in another room, they would find the Union soldier, who knew Key would have to return, who might even have heard where the colonel's hideout was across the river. Trusting in his charity, she told her listeners of the Federal from Stoneman's army in the upstairs bedroom.

The soldiers mounted the stairs to rouse him. They talked for an hour while Lizzie rocked baby Sarah by the fire. Finally, the bedroom door opened, and the men descended and announced that they would sleep there.

The next morning, Lizzie had the young Negro get up early and prepare a big breakfast for all the Federals. After the soldiers had eaten heartily, they played with the children, and the wounded leader turned to Lizzie and said, "Mrs. Key, you need not hide the colonel any longer. Your hospitality will be thankfully accepted, not demanded, from here on."[7]

Only bad news of the Confederacy came to Happy Valley. Any

talk of a compromise peace had ended after Lincoln's re-election. Andrew Johnson had been elected Vice-President, and Parson Brownlow was the new military governor of Tennessee. Dave Key's brother, Summerfield, was back with the army, in General Vaughn's brigade. Morale, as reflected in his letters, was extremely low among the soldiers fighting in the Shenandoah Valley. They went into one battle with 1,200 men and came out with fewer than 600, many of them without guns. Colonel Gillespie had been wounded and captured. Shortly after the new year, in 1865, Summerfield wrote:

We have no news. Things are going badly here. General V. [Vaughn] takes no seeming interest in his command. He remains at Bristol, gives no direction at all to his Brig. The men are destitute and dissatisfied—need clothing and pay. They [recruits] . . . disappear nearly as fast as they come in. Most of the men who go away say they are going to join some of the numerous scouts that are prowling over this country and stealing from everybody. . . . Col. Bradford . . . is dissatisfied and talks of tendering his Resignation. . . . Capt. Aiken has a parole and says he is unwilling to go on duty until he hears from the Sec. of War.[8]

As the months of the year 1865 passed, the situation grew worse. Sherman's army had marched all the way to the sea, and Union troops moved into Savannah and Charleston. Richmond was occupied. Lee and then Johnston surrendered. Jefferson Davis was sought as a war prisoner. Parson Brownlow, the governor, was determined to make the Confederates pay. It was a crushing defeat.

On top of this came the news that Abraham Lincoln, who had taken a charitable attitude toward the South, had been assassinated. His successor, Andrew Johnson, sought justice and retribution; he felt no charity for those who had led the South to secession.

Lizzie and Dave sat under a giant mountain spruce, looking toward the valley where the little Yadkin River cut through the North Carolina mountains. It was dusk. Key was hunched forward, his bony elbows resting on his knees, his big hands supporting his head. What would become of his family? Every cent they had was gone, even the house in Chattanooga. The Lenoir plantation was worthless now—a lot of land but no help, no capital. And Key, a lawyer, as a former Confederate would be disbarred from practice. He doubted whether it would even be safe for him to return to Tennessee. Every day, his neighbors brought news about an ex-Confederate or his family almost beaten to death or driven from the state, all under the reign of Governor Brownlow, who sanctioned and encouraged this terror.[9]

The colonel sighed, seeing no end to his worry and frustration. But this day as every day, Lizzie found consolation reading her Psalter. The mountaineer that cold night of their trek had shown mercy. Stoneman's soldiers had shown mercy. And Andrew Johnson was President, with the right to pardon. He had been one of David's close friends, and Key knew Johnson far better than most men. Surely, many men, even in the old days, had called him cold and selfish, but Key had said that Johnson was at heart warm and generous. Perhaps Key should turn to Johnson? Or had Johnson changed? Did he really plan to carry out all the threats that were attributed to him? And would they ever be able to return to their old home? Of course, the Unionists were running Chattanooga. Lizzie had heard through her cousins that Key's one-time friend Bill Crutchfield was a man of great influence now and that the town was full of Yankee settlers.

David McKendree Key swallowed his pride, not just for himself, not just for Lizzie, but for the children—for seven-year-old Emma, six-year-old Albert, four-year-old Kate, and one-year-old Sarah. They had the right to a future. Perhaps a rebel colonel could be barred from citizenship, from the right to vote, from the practice of his profession, but children must not be excluded from life. However difficult it might be, Key would seek mercy. He would appeal to the President himself, hoping that the common sense of earlier years was still alive in Andrew Johnson.

That evening, Key addressed a letter to the President at the White House. Because he felt that Johnson would probably never reply, Key wrote coldly, asking whether he, as a rebel colonel and secessionist leader, was to be hanged. If so, would the President please let him know "at what time, and if the ceremony is to take place in North Carolina"? Then, with desperate candor, Key pointed to the total futility of his existence and his future, and he asked what the President expected men like himself, across the South, to do with their future. Could his sometime friend give advice?[10]

Early the next day, the letter was in the mail. A part of Key's life was over. His future, as well as that of many other Southerners, would depend upon the answer from the former resident of the familiar house in Greeneville, Tennessee, who now opened mail in the Rose Room of the White House.

During that summer, D. M. Key received two extremely important pieces of mail. One was a full pardon signed by President Andrew Johnson; the second was a letter written by Bill Crutch-field, who had been informed by mutual friends of Key's wish to return to Chattanooga.[11] Crutchfield, so he said, had heard that, during the war, Key had treated all men kindly and courteously, regardless of their political opinions. Such a man, even though he had been in the rebel army, had nothing to fear from a high-minded, intelligent community like Chattanooga. Of course, there would be many difficulties in Key's path. But whatever help could be "rendered by me and mine and all your old friends shall be freely, frankly, and cheerfully given." So spoke the man whom Key had once driven out of Chattanooga.

The man who read these words spent the summer in North Carolina raising a crop of corn, which he harvested and sold in August. With the money he bought a high-bowed wagon, drove Lizzie and the children over the mountains to stay with her mother at the plantation, and set out eagerly to see what had happened to Chattanooga since the Yankees had come to settle.

# 7

# Reconstruction Politics

David McKendree Key was now a stranger in Chattanooga. The ex-Confederate colonel found only Lookout Mountain unchanged, and it watched the federal settlers like a lion couchant. Missionary Ridge was now bare, sheared of its trees after thousands of boys in blue had charged up the steep slopes and shattered Bragg's army. Seven forts now stood on the hills surrounding the town, and a great wooden bridge spanned the Tennessee River. At one end of town loomed a federal rolling mill, built to make rails to support Sherman's march to the sea. Bordering Market Street were government corrals for army mules, wagon sheds, and magazines; the city now had a big military prison, marked by stockades, with plank guard walks around the top. Newly arrived Negro soldiers proudly patrolled the prison and the streets, awesome reminders that Key lived by the courtesy of his conquerors. More than 3,000 Negroes had settled in a refugee village across the river, and the population of Chattanooga itself now totaled only about 5,000 people of both colors. The year after Key's return, the Chattanooga Negro received the right to vote and hold office, and a Negro was elected alderman.[1]

Poverty-stricken and frail, Colonel Key longed for Lizzie and the children. Whenever possible, he visited them at the Lenoir plantation. He now lived rent free in a house lent him by a friend. The neighbors overflowed with kindness, one offering the ex-rebel the use of his milk cow, another giving him breadstuffs from his mill. Bill Crutchfield, as good as his word, helped Key get a loan to buy a tract of land. After a year of hard work, Key was able to write jubilantly to Lizzie: "Yesterday I paid up for our new farm, but it will require some hard work and economy to raise the means to furnish our house, erect the necessary buildings and make repairs. Then we will have to buy a wagon and team, our farming implements, cows, pigs."[2]

He also returned to his law practice, such as it was. Many penniless former Confederates, pressed by Northerners, sought him out. He wrote to Lizzie: "While I bow to the conqueror and accept his terms, yet I defend the poor conquered Rebel. It may have been through my influence that he engaged in the cause, and how shall I fail now to extend to him a helping hand?"[3] The helping hand, however, had to be unrecompensed.

Competition was stiff in every business, for federal soldiers mustered out in Chattanooga settled in droves. One, signing his name in the Crutchfield House register book, added, "age 21, occupation, carpet-bagger." A rakish young man, a former federal captain who had first seen Chattanooga as an assistant commissary officer, presided over millions of dollars' worth of war-surplus stores—an assortment of Colt revolvers, Enfields, mules, horses, wagons, food supplies and railroad equipment—shipped to Chattanooga storehouses from all over the South.

The new Chattanooga entrepreneurs recognized that they needed more than just get-rich-quick carpetbaggers who exploited federal stores at bargain sales or in back-room deals. They hoped to attract carpetbaggers with outside capital, whether from Massachusetts or Illinois, and a remarkable advertisement appeared in the Chattanooga *Republican:*

WANTED IMMEDIATELY ANY NUMBER OF CARPET-BAGGERS
TO COME TO CHATTANOOGA AND SETTLE
The people of Chattanooga, no longer wishing to stay in the background and feeling the necessity of immediately developing the vast

mineral resources surrounding them, by which they can place themselves on the high road to wealth, prosperity and power, extend a
GENERAL INVITATION to all CARPET-BAGGERS to leave the bleak
winds of the North and come to CHATTANOOGA.

It is unnecessary to repeat what is universally known, that our
climate is mild and healthful; our soil fertile, and our mineral resources and railroad facilities unequalled in the world.

Those who wish to come can be assured they will NOT BE RE-
QUIRED TO RENOUNCE THEIR POLITICAL AND RELIGIOUS TENETS,
as the jurisdiction of the Ku Klux and other vermin does not extend over these parts.

Persons wishing to immigrate will be furnished detailed information concerning any business, by addressing Box 123, Chattanooga,
Tennessee.

                         VOX POPULI

P.S. Those having capital, brains and muscle preferred.[4]

Carpetbaggers with capital, brains, and brawn did flock in. New
banks sprang up, one of them built of brick and organized by a
Union officer. An ironworks company was established by two federal officers, Captain Hiram Chamberlain and General John T.
Wilder, former commander of the Union forces that had fired on
Chattanooga when Key's regiment was defending Cameron Hill.
Some of the Union officers had an arrogant bearing when they met
men they had fought and defeated. They dressed nattily and flashed
from their lapel the Loyal Legion button, symbol of membership in
an elite society of Union Army officers—easily equal, in their estimation, to George Washington's Society of the Cincinnati.

As the years passed, those who acquired wealth moved up onto
the terraced hills overlooking the city. As decades passed, they began to build homes with Victorian cupolas, towers, and steep roofs
—quite different in taste from the clapboard houses of former Confederates that stood in the valley below. The "terraces" represented
Northern status, especially to the women. While in business meet-

ings and courtrooms Southern men sat side by side with Northerners, Southern women could not muster such a businesslike attitude.
Southern ladies ridiculed the way Yankee women walked, criticizing
them for lifting their feet too high and prancing like stallions in
the Austro-Hungarian royal court. Such Southern ladies considered
East Terrace the tasteless showpiece of *nouveau riche* Republicans
who had pilfered government supplies, foreclosed on Confederate
rebels, and sucked dry the disfranchised Southern Democrats.

One of the favorite stories perpetuated in the parlors at the
foot of the terraces was the tale of an East Terrace matron
known as "Bloody Mary," who had slandered the Confederate flag
and supposedly carried much of her husband's allegedly ill-gotten
money strapped to her leg under her petticoats. One gossip claimed
that she had spied it strapped there when the woman lifted her skirts
to take out some money to make a purchase. "Bloody Mary" was
said to be too snobbish to receive Southern ladies in her home and
preferred to entertain Negroes. Not that she lost any love for them,
sniped the Southern ladies. But the Republican men were lining up
the Negro vote to ensure continuation of their power after the
Democrats regained the right to vote.

Soon the Republican politicians of Chattanooga developed such
respect for the legal ability of ex-secessionist leader D. M. Key that
they chose him to represent them in a decisive suit. Key accepted
the case and fee as a business proposition. Although Key could not
completely overcome the barrier between his kind and those cocky
types who wore the Loyal Legion button, he was happy to see how
quickly men like Crutchfield and Clift banished enmity. With the
passing years, Bill Crutchfield grew as a man. The character of his
new dry-goods store symbolized his popularity with both new-
comers and old-time Southerners; he carried an assortment of both
Yankee notions and Dixie goods. Bill Crutchfield was a naturalist by
avocation and was happiest when studying the birds and leaves of
the mountains surrounding Chattanooga. Key shared this interest,
and they often rode out together to observe the flora and fauna.

They both enjoyed the peace and beauty of the mountains and no longer harbored extremist emotions.

Key found many of the newly settled Northern Democrats to be easygoing, friendly people who had never been too keen on the war policies. Most of them had come from the states along the Mississippi and Ohio rivers. And many of them detested the radical Republicans who had disfranchised the Democrats in Tennessee by passing a strict registry law that allowed the county clerks, all Republicans, to decide who should be allowed to register for voting in Chattanooga. Politically, Chattanooga's Northern Democrats were forced into an alliance with Key's group in order to try to upset the Republicans' power.[5]

Key found the native Negroes who had won voting rights far less arrogant than the Negro troops stationed in the town at the close of the war. Some of Chattanooga's Negro citizens became justices of the peace, deputy sheriffs, policemen; some went to the legislature; one was a county-court clerk. Many sat in the jury box. True enough, many of them were eager to demonstrate their newly won freedom.

Lawyer Key felt that since most of the Negroes lacked education, they would have to learn to respect the law. There was, for example, an illustrious justice of the peace called "Squire" Kirk, whose jurisdiction included the Negro suburb of Stanleytown. A good friend of the Squire's, driving a public conveyance that broke down one icy morning, slipped and hurt his hand. This hack driver let go such a tirade of cussing that some good sisters from the Squire's church swore out a warrant charging him with "blasphemy, sacrilege, and all degrees of impiety; of combining, conspiring, confederating and ageeing with himself and the wicked one to profane and destroy all that is good and pure and seemly." The hack driver, who always let the Squire travel free, looked at him with confidence. But in court, confronted by the sisters and many other members of his church, the Squire fined his astonished friend $50. After the triumphant sisters had left the court, the Squire calmed the defendant by throwing all the court records into the fire. He then called the case "squashed." The good Squire now happily noted that he was satisfied, the sisters were satisfied, and that his friend the driver was satisfied too. "Dat's de way to do bus'ness; make ev'ybody sa'sfide," said the Squire, and the case was dismissed.[6]

To attorney Key, men like the Squire seemed neither mean nor vicious, but void of education and unprepared for office. Key theorized that this was all the more reason why Negroes should retain the rights they had been given at the close of the war and should be provided with the means of a good education. He knew that many Negroes paid more attention to business than to politics, and he realized that any attempt to restrict and penalize the Negroes as a race would drive them into extremism, which would be food for demagogic politicians.

The growing agitation about the Chattanooga Negroes was not directed against them as such but, rather, against the Chattanooga Republicans who were manipulating the Negro vote to stay in power. Negroes viewed the Republican organization not as a party but as a redeemer—"a collective Moses leading them out of and beyond reach of bondage."[7] Yet, there were many Negroes like the now deceased Bill Lewis, conservative and business-oriented. In Chattanooga, all barbers and hack drivers were Negroes; many of the retail stores were run by Negroes; many of the leading Negro citizens were skillful masons. Before a decade had passed, many Chattanooga Negroes had attended and graduated from Fisk University, and one toured Europe with the Fisk Jubilee Singers, who were received by princes and by Gladstone. The Democrats whom Key heard talking about the day when they would regain power and put the Negro in his place derived most of their antagonism from the Republicans' use of the Negro. The color line had to be taken out of politics, Key believed; it would be disastrous and explosive for Democrats and Republicans to let this issue become the major difference between the parties.

For the Democrats in Tennessee and for Key personally, 1870 was to be a decisive year. The radical Republicans were swept out of office, and Key's close friend John C. Brown was elected president of a constitutional convention. At this convention, Key represented his district and aided in the drafting of a constitution that ended restrictions on Tennessee suffrage and enabled former Confederates to return to power.

Back home in Chattanooga, Key was elected chancellor of the Third District. Now Chancellor Key, dressed in his long frock coat, rode over the lonely mountains to hold court in the various county seats. He often amused himself en route by filling his saddlebags with chinquapins and apples for the children. Wherever he went, he tried to help people overcome the bitterness of the war. But this was not an easy task for ex-Colonel Key; people remembered well, after all, that he had been a secessionist leader.

During the campaign of 1872, Chancellor Key's name was placed in nomination—without his consent—as the Democratic candidate for Congress. Chancellor Key was alarmed by the vast support he received from the extreme element of former Confederates. It was rumored and hoped that Key, if elected, would wrest all power from the moderate Union Democrats. These rumors grew, moving Chancellor Key to write a letter to the party leaders. He told them that the war had settled his quarrel and that he would not champion rebel animosities. He would get out of the way if his name amounted even to so much as a feather's weight "in the way of peace, pacification and good will." It was unthinkable to him now to stir up "sectional and rebel emotionalism to get elected to office"; he felt that "all pride, ambition, and self-interest should be sacrificed to the public good."[8] Thus, Key declined the nomination.

But the feuding party factions got together, combined with liberal Republicans, and agreed to Key's platform. They asked him again to run for Congress; Key accepted. His Republican opponent turned out to be Bill Crutchfield. As the campaign progressed, the factions in Key's party continued feuding. Under attack, Key spoke out for the rights of ex-rebels to run for office. Unfortunately, this fanned rumors that he had agreed with the extremist wing of the Democratic Party to put back into office all the former Confederate rebels. This split enabled Bill Crutchfield to defeat Key, who was learning that it was easier to form coalitions than to make them work in the wake of mutual suspicions.

Chattanooga was an unusual town in the Reconstruction period, but David McKendree Key was rapidly becoming an unusual public figure even for Chattanooga, and he made some party regulars rather suspicious. Key argued that the city's business progress was being hindered by the attitudes separating the Yankees who lived on the terraces from the old Southerners who lived below—attitudes expressed when the Loyal Legion, on one side, and the Confederate Veterans Association, on the other, rekindled the spirit of strife by the respective celebrations they held every year. Key maintained that the issues were no longer the Virginia and Kentucky resolutions of 1798, Calhoun, secession, or even the war. The real issues now were how to build up Southern commerce and industry, how to help the Negro become a useful citizen and intelligent voter, how to make Chattanooga's sanitary system work and get the sewers underground, how to establish a better fire department and get steam engines, how to make the Tennessee River more navigable, and how to make Chattanooga the railroad center of the South.

At a memorable ceremony in 1870, when the soldiers' graves in the big Confederate cemetery were decorated with flowers, Chancellor Key spoke his mind. He did not eulogize Civil War battles, did not worship the past and conjecture where the South might have gone if Johnston had united with Pemberton early in the Vicksburg campaign or if Pickett's charge had succeeded at Gettysburg. Each side, Key reiterated, believed itself right; each side was imbued with "consistency, integrity, and devotion to principle." It merely stirred up antagonism for the future to believe and charge otherwise. Chattanoogans must overlook the past faults of one another, and all should acknowledge "one flag and one country, knowing neither North nor South" but only a "common destiny."[9] So spoke Key on a clear May day, his voice ringing out over the heads of hundreds of Chattanoogans standing silently before rows of white Confederate tombstones. Perhaps some of the ladies grumbled under their parasols, disapproving of the direction Judge Key's talk was taking. But, after all, he had been selected by the Republicans to represent them in court; had they, some wondered, purchased his soul?

Chancellor Key realized that Chattanooga's destiny and reconstruction was inextricably part of the rebuilding of the entire South. And much of the South's future depended on Key's former friend President Andrew Johnson.

After Key's pardon, he had not seen the President. But in 1867, he and Lizzie had taken a trip to Washington. Key then was still so poor that he had only recently been able to afford to bring Lizzie and the children back to Chattanooga to live in the new house he had bought. On that trip to Washington, the Keys lodged at an inexpensive boardinghouse. The landlady greeted Key disdainfully and treated him like a rebel backwoodsman, obviously of no importance in the capital. On the off chance that the President would see him, Key had written to Johnson, and that evening the White House coach-and-four arrived to take the Keys to dinner with the President. The landlady stood gaping as the elaborate coach headed for Pennsylvania Avenue.

At the Executive Mansion, the Keys were received by Mrs. Martha Patterson, Johnson's daughter, who served as the White House hostess, since Mrs. Johnson was an invalid. She was eager to show Lizzie the White House, which she had just redecorated, and the two went off after the Keys had been welcomed by the President. Key was greeted warmly by his old friend Andrew, whose eyebrows were more furrowed and whose lower lip was more protruding than Key remembered. Washington, with its scheming politics and its Civil War aftermath, had not treated Andy Johnson kindly. The President asked Key to sit down, and the two talked as they had so often in the old house in Greeneville.[10]

Johnson told Key how he had steadily lost power as the radicals had gained it. He was now like a stranded man on a sand bar in a rising tide. They spoke of the position of Tennessee, the only Confederate state readmitted to the Union; the radical Republican Congress had sliced up the rest of the South into five military districts under martial law. In these other Southern states, civil government would be restored when a state had drawn up a constitution disfranchising those who had fought for the Confederacy and enfranchising the Negroes by ratifying the new Fourteenth Amendment. These measures sounded moral, but Key pointed out that this same year, 1867, the Northern state of Ohio had rejected extension of suffrage to its Negroes. It was a most difficult situation.

Johnson told Key that when the Northern radicals had returned to Congress in December, 1865, they had revolted against his plan of reconstruction, although it was based upon Lincoln's concept that the Southern states had never really been outside of the Union. The Union was indivisible, reasoned Johnson. Once the errant Southern states had set up a loyal government, they should be restored to the Union, just as Tennessee had been readmitted. While he was still Vice-President, Johnson had fiercely talked about hanging secessionists, but now that he stood in Lincoln's place as President, he was championing Lincoln's forward-looking reconstruction plan. Letters like Key's had also helped him think things through.

But the most powerful man in Congress, pock marked Thad Stevens, and Senator Charles Sumner, who walked with a limp and seemed to curse life itself, both rejected Johnson's theory. The Confederate states had committed suicide, they claimed, and were nothing more than conquered provinces; only by the mercy of Congress could they be readmitted to the Union.

That night in 1867, in the Johnson's private living room at the White House, Key observed Johnson's tense, tough face and realized how Stevens and Sumner had hurt the old warrior. They had charged that Johnson was merely trying to shield with clemency people who were enemies of the Union. But to Key, Johnson's clemency but proved his courage and magnanimity. Even at the cost of losing political support, he had upheld this liberal policy toward the South. Now Johnson stood alone. His abilities lay, Key felt, in preserving the best of the past, not in creating a new road for the future; this was his tragedy. His early struggle with poverty and for self-education had left him little time to develop some of that charm and worldliness needed in political life.[11] Johnson had few friends now. The Republicans hated him, even those in Tennessee who controlled the state. Brownlow, the governor, once had wired to a friend in Washington: "Give my respects to the dead dog of the White House."[12]

Johnson's battle with the radicals, Key knew, was now centered on a new issue: the joint committee of fifteen congressmen and senators that threatened to usurp the power of the Presidency. As Key and Johnson talked that night in the White House, Key came to realize that Andy was giving his life's blood to keep fifteen would-be dictators from taking over the power the people had invested in their President. While the two men talked, Key looked at the books that lay on the table. They reflected Johnson's favorite reading. He still thought and read about how Rome had slipped from republic to empire, how the people of Stuart England saw the crown enlarge its prerogatives at their expense.

It was late when the Keys drove back to their boardinghouse that night. Lizzie now knew almost every detail of change Mrs. Patterson had made in the White House, and she had heard of Mrs. Andrew Johnson's longing to return with her husband to the clear air and good life in Greeneville at the foothills of the Great Smoky Mountains.

Not long after this visit, the House of Representatives impeached Johnson. The Senate tried but failed to convict him; however, it did smear his name. There was gossip that he was a drunk. But Key admired his old friend. He knew that Johnson had won the victory of preserving the Presidency.

Undaunted, Johnson returned to Greeneville. He ran for Congress and was defeated. But in 1875 he was elected to the Senate. Key was wild with joy, unaware that this Senate victory would in time change the character of his own life and would pass to his own back the heavy cross Johnson had borne.[13]

# 8

---

# Grantism

A sunny July had given way to a rainy August in 1875, when Chancellor D. M. Key learned of the death of Senator Andrew Johnson. Key received a telegram asking him to join James Porter, the governor of Tennessee, en route to the funeral. Key was heartened to have the company of his old friend Porter, who, like Key, had been a secessionist leader and rebel colonel, but was now a man of moderation in these days of political extremism.

At Greeneville the scene was mournful. Andrew Johnson lay in his coffin, his body wrapped in an American flag, his head resting on a copy of the Constitution, as he had requested. The black-draped bier moved slowly through the streets to the burial place on a steep knoll overlooking the town and the Great Smokies beyond. From the workshops and fields of North Carolina, Virginia, and Tennessee the common people had flocked sadly into town. Key could see few people of high office or wealth in the crowd, but a sea of poor folk, white and Negro, young and very old, had come in hacks, farm wagons and carts. There were few buggies, but many people were riding broken-down mules. Most of the mourners had weather-beaten faces and work-hardened hands. They all had come to pay homage to one of humble beginnings who had fought for the common people. When Key saw a country boy and his mother coming in a wooden cart pulled by a broken-down horse, he remembered that eighteen-year-old Andy Johnson, illiterate and poverty-stricken, had arrived this way in Greeneville with his mother and had supported her as a tailor's apprentice.[1]

After watching the casket lowered into the tomb, Key raised his eyes to the Smokies, purple mountains that spoke of immortality. His throat tightened, for he had never felt such sad empathy for this much maligned man, one who had remained unbowed before the gods of political greed.

The governor too had been much moved. On the train back, Porter and Key spoke much of the Great Commoner. In Chattanooga, the governor's party had to wait for the Nashville train, so Key ordered his carriage and drove the party across the river to a lovely spot in the Chattanooga countryside. They rested beside a clear spring under the boughs of great white oaks amid grass and wild mint.

Suddenly the governor turned to his host. "Colonel Key," he said, "as soon as I get to Nashville, I am going to send you a commission as United States senator, to sit until the meeting of the next legislature."

Key was speechless. He had not in the least sought this office—though the *Chattanooga Times* had editorially advocated the choice in his absence. He was caught by surprise and mixed emotions. Only recently had he succeeded in restoring his finances, and he would not have the means to move Lizzie and the family to an expensive place like Washington. Yet, in all conscience, he could not refuse Porter's offer, even though it meant months of separation from his family. Before the governor departed, Key agreed to accept the position of senator, but he made it clear to Porter that he did so without political promises or obligations.[2]

But Chattanooga was wild with joy—everyone from ex-Federals on the terraces to ex-Confederates in the valley below. To all of them, Key's appointment meant more influence for their town. A Knoxville paper quipped: "The village of Chattanooga is as proud of her new Senator as 'a negro with a new shirt.' "[3] That night the town mobilized the band, and the Light Guards marched to Key's house on Chestnut Street carrying blazing torches, compelling the new senator to speak. When his big frame was silhouetted on the front porch, everyone cheered, and everything he said produced thunderous applause, even when it was something about not being a politician, not being a partisan, but for the interests of the entire country. Such platitudes were expected, but nobody seriously entertained the idea that he might not put sectional interests above all else. The South and the Democrats had been the underdog; the South could not afford to have generous politicians. The band struck up "Dixie," and everyone joined in, singing enthusiastically.

From all over the state came many editorial reactions. The *Memphis Avalanche* said: "Chancellor Key belongs to the new generation of public men in Tennessee. . . . While it will not be expected that he will come up to the dead Statesman . . . the people of the whole state will rejoice to know that their new Senator will be as far removed from jobs and rings as the great Commoner was."

The *Dresden Democrat* expressed the thoughts of many who, having heard enough about Key to suspect his party loyalty, insisted that the choice "was not the fortunate one. . . . The Key unlocked the Governor's heart, but there are many hearts all over Tennessee of a combination that *Key never can fit.*" Most displeased was the *Memphis Appeal,* a staunch supporter of the other Tennessee senator, Isham Harris, former war governor, former secession mentor of Key, but now suspicious of some of the Key's soft talk about the Southern cause.

Congress was not in session when Key received his appointment, and the flurry of excitement soon quieted down, at least until one evening in October, when Key prepared to move to Washington for the session that was to begin in December. A reporter knocked on the senator's door, was warmly received in the parlor, and treated to some shockingly candid answers to a series of leading questions. The panic of 1873 was still being felt, and when asked about its causes, Key pointed the finger at Jay Cooke and other speculators. Since the Civil War, there had been a mass of greenbacks floating around. Key said that even though he was a hard-money Democrat, he was against resumption of specie payments until the states had paid off the bonded debt. The reporter then asked Key for his opinion on the national bank question, a controversial issue since Andrew Jackson's day. Key declared that he was against abolishing the national banking system, explaining that this would only worsen the depression. This position was directly opposed to that of the state's Democratic platform. Key wanted the states to be allowed to permit the establishment of local banks whose issue could be redeemed in greenbacks and national bank notes. In his opinion, the trouble was that all the money ended up in the large commercial centers, but local bank issue would provide currency for home use.

Then the new senator unloaded another bombshell. He felt the state should start to pay off its indebtedness, and he announced that he was against the solution of the old line Democrats, which was repudiation—repudiation of debts regardless of whether it ruined Southern credit in the North and in Europe, regardless of whether it would drive away Northern trade, capital, and industry.[4]

The reporter joyfully scribbled down these remarks. He had his story. This green politician had committed an unpardonable sin by differing with the Democratic platform of the state of Tennessee.

The story was published, and the reaction was swift. All over the state, one Democratic paper after another chastised Key, charging that he talked like a Republican and demanding that he change his program or hand in his resignation. At the Governor's Mansion in Nashville, Porter's embarrassment was partially relieved when some of the more liberal Democratic papers pointed out that Key had not said that he was in favor of the national banking position, but merely that he did not want it to be abolished abruptly.

Key's foray into political controversy alerted the entire Bourbon Democratic political machine. They called themselves Bourbons because they aimed to restore the old regime of the South. The Bourbons were led by Isham Harris. Unlike Key, Harris had changed little since the fiery days when he had hijacked Tennessee into secession. But Harris was not too upset, for Key's appointment would last only through January. Then he would have to stand on his own for election before the Tennessee State Legislature, a legislature controlled for the most part by Isham Harris.

After this interview, even some of Key's political supporters were suspicious. His loyal friends warned him to remember that he would be closely watched in Washington and that his election was already in the balance. Key sensed that a coldness had come over some former friends across the state; he realized that he had an arch opponent in Isham Harris.[5]

December rain and fog, ice and slush welcomed Key in the capitol on the day he was sworn in as a senator. It was a trying ordeal. In Tennessee, he had been accused of being inadequately imbued with the ideals of the secessionist Solid South—now he found himself sniped at in Washington as being a rebel still wearing Confederate gray. It seemed as if every senator and every visitor in the packed gallery bore down upon one who wore the brand of rebellion. He strode down the Senate aisle, a stranger to everybody, an unknown in politics, the successor to the controversial Andrew Johnson. Later in the day, when Key tried to mix with the other senators, he found his assigned seat surrounded by radical Republicans and brass spittoons. He tried small talk about his only claim to fame—his family of seven. To this, one senator retorted that he had nine children, another that he had ten. The wind thus taken out of his sails, he relaxed. Soon, the barriers broke down, and he began to get on well with the senators. They grew to like his candid and unassuming attitude and easy humor.[6]

Some days later, heart pounding, he delivered a eulogy honoring his predecessor, Andrew Johnson. Key presented Johnson as a conservative who was, nonetheless, so devoted to the common people that his statements were often misunderstood and taken as radically agrarian demagoguery. Key admitted that Johnson was strange and peculiar, but called attention to his courage in politics, his devotion to the Constitution. He called Johnson a marvel in history and added that the country had never lost a more loyal and fearless defender of its people, a more devoted friend. After this speech, Key was complimented even by some of the radical Republicans.[7]

The winter weeks sped by. Key settled in a boardinghouse run by Mrs. Shedd, a short, thickset woman who was a self-styled doctor, or "medical electrician," and used Turkish and Russian baths in her curative processes. In a letter to Lizzie, Key promised that he would stick to the baths at the Capitol and said that for $35 a month he was eating at the Imperial Hotel.

Over the Christmas holidays, Key caught the train to Salem Academy in North Carolina to visit his two eldest daughters, Emma, now a brown-eyed beauty, and Kate, who was just recovering from a case of shingles.

In Washington, the homespun Tennessean entered the society of the gaslight era. He visited rooms crowded with ornate gold-leaf mirrors, gilded chairs and sofas, fashionable paintings, and chandeliers with frosted bulbs and dripping with long crystal hangings. Senator Key emerged at Washington parties in his best country dress coat from his chancellorship days, but without gloves—amid the stylish gentlemen in swallow-tailed coats, white vests, and white gloves. Inevitably, he would get wedged in, not by young beauties, but by a sea of fat rosy older ladies whose low-necked short-sleeved dresses flashed with gaudy jewels. They were much amused at the "backwoodsman," as they called him. Key said that these parties reminded him of menageries—though here splendor and feminine flesh were exhibited. Why elderly and corpulent ladies wore low-cut dresses with short sleeves, more suited to a woman like the gorgeous wife of the Spanish ambassador, was more than he could understand.

The Tennessee senator eventually purchased a swallow-tailed coat, although his friend General Dibrell of the Tennessee congressional delegation would have none of it. Key did persuade Dibrell to go with him to the opera, where the Spanish mode of dress was so glittering, the singing so beautiful that they stirred even the senator. But Dibrell preferred listening to a darky's banjo;

he yawned so audibly that dresses, feathers, and ribbons rustled, and Key realized that everyone in the theater was looking at them. Deciding some explanation was needed, Dibrell said, loudly and distinctly, "I am sleepy." Key feared that they had carried "backwoodsman" behavior too far and that the whole event would appear in the morning paper.[8]

One February evening, when the icy wind moaned around the corners of Mrs. Shedd's boardinghouse, the senator busily put on his newly purchased finery in preparation for a reception given by the Secretary of the Interior. He looked out of the window to see whether the storm was still rocking the steeple of President Grant's church. At a safe distance, a crowd had gathered to watch its fall. The steeple seemed to symbolize the present state of the Grant Administration, for Grantism was now so corrupt, so top-heavy that it too soon had to fall.

There came a loud knock at the door, and upon answering it, Key found two unexpected callers—wiry Andrew Kellar, publisher of the *Memphis Avalanche,* and a Mississippi steamboat-line representative.

Key greeted these two constituents and invited them to sit down for a brief chat. But the gentlemen remained. The clock ticked away hours, the grate was refurbished, the room grew dense with cigar smoke, and the wind outside continued to howl. Kellar had been a secessionist leader in western Tennessee and later a rebel colonel. After the war, like Key, he had broken with Harris and the Bourbon machine. Kellar was both a philosopher, analyzing the sickness of Southern politics, and an activist, seeking to find ways to overthrow the present political leadership. In search of a specific scheme to change it all, Kellar now wanted to throw off the yoke of New York's Tammany Hall, whose loquacious Northern Democratic leaders babbled about being for the South but in a pinch always deserted it. The government had spent millions to improve rivers, build canals, and help the railroads in the East—but not in the South and Southwest. The three men agreed that Tammany congressmen would not vote with Southern Democrats for Southern internal improvement. Key himself was planning to propose a bill for one appropriation for improvements in Tennessee.

The three men also discussed "radical Grantism," which empowered federal troops to occupy the so-called unreconstructed states. The army had often cracked down on the South with a conqueror's whip. Had Andrew Johnson's proposal for reconstruction been adopted, it would have restricted this tyrannical rule by curbing the power of the radicals in House and Senate, as well as the dictatorial Committee on Reconstruction.

The corruption in the Grant Administration was nation-wide conversation. Washington was full of tales about William Belknap, Grant's Secretary of War, a handsome, vain man who was fond of display. His extravagant, pleasure-seeking wife gave the gaudiest parties in town and sported the most expensive dresses and jewelry. But more sensational than the Belknap parties was the gossip about how Belknap had amassed his "fortune" from the proceeds of the sale of army trading posts. When impeachment proceedings were instigated against him, the Belknaps' gay days came to an abrupt end. Key later observed that "the gay butterflies which had flitted around Gen. Belknap [and his wife] in the days of their glory crowded the galleries and corridors of the Capitol that they might witness their fall. . . . Alas! Abandoned by friends, denounced by all, they are fallen so low there is none to show them reverence. He who two days ago had control of our armies can, today, scarcely command a servant."[9] And this man had been the head of the army whose bayonets ruled the South. This scandal had rocked the rotten Grant Administration, much as the angry wind rocked the steeple of Grant's church on that cold February night.

Although Key was indignant about such blatant thievery, he was far more upset about the foolish "hotspur" Southerners in the House and Senate. Key raised his voice and waved his big hands in agitation as he complained to his visitors about the gullible Southerners who were so easily baited by Tammany or Republican tactics. This game was called "waving the bloody shirt." The so-called stalwart Republicans would distract attention from Belknap-type incidents of corruption by stirring up such heated Civil War emotions that Northern Democrats and Republicans would unite against the South. Senator Morton of Indiana and Congressman Blaine, who were both trying for the next Republican Presidential nomination, were now trying to outdo each other in the waving of that bloody shirt.

Blaine, a born and practiced actor, was ahead. Upon the introduction of an amnesty bill that proposed to waive all remaining legal disabilities of former Confederate officers and officials, he dramatically demanded an amendment that would exclude Jefferson Davis, "the author, knowingly, deliberately, guiltily, and willfully of the gigantic murders and crimes at Andersonville." In the name of his kinsmen, his friends, and his countrymen, Blaine dramatically declared, he protested "against calling back and crowning with honors of full American citizenship the man that organized that murder." Key had felt sickened by the excitement Blaine's demagoguery had elicited in the gallery. Key felt that Davis, to the last, had favored peaceful secession. He felt humiliated and powerless as he listened to Blaine raging on, declaring that the massacre of St. Bartholomew's Day, the deeds of the Duke of Alba in the Low Countries, and the thumbscrews and engines of torture used by the Spanish Inquisition could not compare with the atrocities of Andersonville.

It was good bait every time, noted Key. And again the ex-Confederates bit hard. On this occasion, Congressman and former Confederate General Benjamin Hill had jumped up and violently rushed to the defense of the Confederacy with such sectionalism that all Northerners united to defeat the bill. This show conveniently stole the headlines, diverting public attention from scandals of corruption in the Grant Administration.

On that day, after Blaine's victory and the defeat of the important amnesty bill, Key had gone to a party. In the crowd of guests he had observed Congressman James Garfield greeting Blaine, shouting enthusiastically, "Oh, you're glorious, Jim!" Garfield had declared that never in his thirteen years in the House had he seen such a brilliant victory.

When Key finished telling the men from Memphis about Washington politics, the embers had burned low; outside, the wind still howled. Kellar and his friend had listened attentively, occasionally interrupting Key with eager questions. They shared many of his worries and hopes. They agreed with him on the need for more appropriations for shipping and railroads for the South, despite Tammany opposition to such proposals. But the most important issue was, the three men agreed, to find a way that would rid the South of the military overseers and regain an effective voice for the South in the nation. The Southern hotspurs and the Northern radicals both were still refighting the war and making political use of the racial issue, obstructing the more positive course Key and his visitors hoped to follow. A bond of understanding had been established when the visitors finally bade the senator good night.[10]

During the following months, Senator Key spent much of his time sitting in the Senate chamber, half listening to verbose speeches, writing letters to constituents and to Lizzie, and giving much thought to his conversation with Kellar. On some days, his reveries were interrupted when the handsome, ebullient senator from Georgia, General John B. Gordon, took the floor. Key would groan, shake his head, and tell himself that the South had been trapped again. For days, Senator Morton of Indiana had been working to get the Senate to pass a resolution accepting the credentials of a mulatto carpetbagger from Louisiana named Pinchback. But Morton was unable to get the necessary number of Republicans to back the resolution, for carpetbaggers were becoming increasingly unpopular with Republicans. Now Morton resorted to the bloodyshirt technique. He claimed that Robert Toombs of Georgia had admitted that the Democratic Party achieved political control of Georgia "by carrying the black vote by intimidation and bribery." Day after day, Morton had spoken on the floor, repeating similar charges and watching Gordon squirm in his seat. One day, Morton raised his voice, persumably quoting Toombs again: " 'We carried the election by bribery and intimidation; I confess it; I was a party to it.' " Why, Morton asked, was the senator from Georgia so quiet?

Gordon's face flushed in anger. As if the battle bugle had blown, he jumped to his feet. He retorted that no doubt Morton had given money for every election in Indiana.

"Ah, Mr. President," cried Senator Morton, "that will not do. Mr. Toombs did not say that he had given money, as men can do legitimately to carry on an election, but he said he had given money to buy votes. I never did that." Morton added that Gordon had recently referred to "the world, the flesh, and the senator from Indiana." Senator Morton smiled and added, "He carefully excepted from among the enemies of Georgia democracy the devil, [for] they are friends and allies."[11]

Now Gordon answered Morton furiously. Some seats away, throughout the skirmish, Key was writing a letter to Lizzie about some shrubs he was to send her for the yard. As Key realized that Morton's stratagem had been successful, he added to his letter: "I am writing under difficulties. Gen. Gordon is making a furious speech. . . . I fear some Republican will come back at him. . . . These Georgia hotspurs do or will do us harm, I fear. . . . P.S. Just as I expected. Morton is pouring hot shot into Gordon."[12]

# 9

## "Senate Gas"

During the Senate sessions, Key watched senators fire away at the brass spittoons, trying to distract himself from what he called the Senate "gas." Gordon and Hill were trapped again and again in this "gas" by the Yankee Stalwarts. Gordon, an illustrious, intelligent General, should have been able to recognize a decoy. Yet, like Hill, he rose to the bait and was made to howl like a child by Morton's and Blaine's skillful taunts. And each howl on the Senate floor, written up in the newspapers, distracted public attention from the scandals in the Grant Administration.

Soon, the Stalwarts developed a new decoy, way down in Mississippi. It seemed that in the 1875 elections, which had been accompanied by violence and disorder, a Republican majority of 25,000 had curiously been converted into a Democratic majority of 30,000. Late in December, during Key's first year in Washington, Morton laid out before the Senate so-called evidence that armed revolution had produced that Democratic majority; he moved that a select committee investigate the Mississippi election. Senator Bayard, a Democrat, protested loudly that the Senate had no right to intervene in matters of state jurisdiction. Most Democrats closed ranks behind him, and Morton jubilantly charged this proved that the guilty Democrats knew his accusations were true.

One January day after another, Key watched Morton expostulating in the Senate, straining his stentorian voice. Key found distraction in reading over his colleciton of newspaper clippings. He looked at the excerpt from the *Yazoo Herald,* which had advocated shooting Republican voters on the spot. He picked up the *Yazoo Democrat,* which recommended "try the rope." The correspondent of the reliable *Cincinnati Commercial* reported that 100 persons had been killed in political quarrels. On the Senate floor, Morton held forth without letup. After two months of constant tirades, he collapsed, physically exhausted. But Morton was not a man to give up. After his recovery, he was at it again, attacking the South. "The Democrats seized the legislature by fraud, murder, and intimidation," he cried. And his friend Senator Boutwell chimed in, "Slavery, the spirit of slavery, is and ever has been the enemy of the Union, and it is today. . . . Trust no man who was brought up under the influence of slavery. . . . The Southern senators dominate the country, defy the laws, oppress, persecute, and murder the citizens."[1]

Tension came to a climax the following day. Senator Bruce, a handsome, educated, and able Negro from Mississippi who sat two rows in front of Key, was usually quiet and contemplative. But now he rose to deliver an impassioned speech, as if playing the crescendo of Morton's fortissimo. He too claimed that Democratic victories in recent elections had been unfair and dishonest.[2] Bruce was an effective speaker. His verbiage hit hard, and everyone looked to Gordon, expecting his counterattack.

But instead, David McKendree Key rose. All eyes turned to observe his heavy-set features. In the gallery, members of the press leaned forward to take in whatever this homespun backwoodsman could add to the act.

Soon, the resonant Tennessee voice with the Southern twang resounded in the chamber. Key noted that much had been said about the conditions and purposes of the Southern people, that there had been "fearful utterances" in heated debate; but nevertheless, he was quite confident that proper regard would now be paid to what Southerners had to say. For it would be a "mistaken magnanimity which would permit us seats on this floor and yet allow us to present nothing but deceit, treason, falsehood, and hypocrisy." The Tennessean said that the issues of the late contest between North and South had been decided, for all time, against the people of the South and that the South must abide by the decision and not question it.

Then the hefty senator gave his hindsight philosophy of the Civil War. "Property in slaves existed long before our government was established. Our Constitution recognized this. . . . This generation inherited this Constitution and slavery." The South, unfortunately, "became the heir of slavery; to the whole country belonged the Constitution." Basically, he said, the conflict was not black and white, but a conflict of ideas taught to each side by their ministers, statesmen, and schoolteachers. "It was a war of education." A part of the Southern education was to look upon the colored man as inferior, and Southerners still were reluctant to acknowledge the Negro's political equality. This attitude toward Negroes, Key firmly insisted, was shared by Southern Unionists and rebels alike. The colored man "has the sympathy of his former master, and deserves it." The slave, knowing both that the war involved his freedom and that he deserved freedom, nevertheless in most instances "remained true and faithful to his master's fortune and family. . . . Though there were four million of these people in the slave states, yet there was no insurrection, insubordination, or incendiarism. History furnishes no other example of such forbearance under such circumstances." No doubt, he must have thought of the Negroes of the Lenoir plantation, of Aunt Clarsie and the rest.

Naturally, the new relationship between the races, so contrary to their habit, would lead to mutual distrust. "Tardy progress the North should understand, for really the South is progressing more than hoped," Key continued. "A great societary revolution such as the South has undergone . . . demands time, study, experience, and use before there can be an adjustment of the various disturbed, disordered, and scattered elements involved in it."

Persuasively, Key added, with almost naïve candor, "I have no quarrel with the terms given" after the "victory over the rebellion was complete, [but] I want amity that is heartfelt." That word "rebellion," carefully chosen, caused heads to turn all through the great chamber, now quiet except for the Tennessee voice. On this jubilee year of the centennial of independence, the speaker asked, why could not the North celebrate by exercising a magnanimity surpassing any in history? "Sir, American genius, industry, energy, and perseverance, properly directed and encouraged, can and will overcome anything which men can subdue, and erect anything which man can build."

So much for Key's philosophy. It sounded strange to Southern ears because of its admissions of Southern guilt, its praise of the Negro, its use of the word "rebellion," and its supplication to the Northern conquerors.

Key's voice grew intense as he came to the point—the Mississippi elections. He declared that true Southerners wanted law and order. Those who violated the law should be punished—but not the entire South. Key made an astonishing announcement: he would vote for the Republican resolution to investigate the Mississippi elections; not that the investigation was deserved, but because opposition to the investigation could be construed as an admission of guilt.

Republican lips stretched in suppressed smiles. The Mississippi shift in votes, Key continued, had not been as great as a recent Massachusetts shift, which had not produced charges of corruption. Key said that he respected Morton and Boutwell. Although their denunciations of the South were unmerited, he was aware that the senators believed they were true. The trouble with Senator Morton, said Key, was that he lived too far away from what was happening in Mississippi. The colored people were unalarmed and were disrespectful only to those former officeholders who used to dupe them. Key closed by saying that any Southerner who "stirs in the hearts of his people the fires of hate and disloyalty is a much worse enemy of his section and of his people than he who rails at them from a Northern standpoint." Any Southerner who forgot this, Key added, was foolishly and inexcusably furnishing his opponents "their most effective means of war."[3]

When the Tennessee orator sat down, senators on both sides of the aisle left their seats and crowded around, shaking his hand and congratulating him. It was as if a bridge had been built between the factions. Even Senator Gordon grasped the hand of the conciliatory Tennessean. Key momentarily was a hero that late afternoon in the Senate room. It looked as though he had swayed the Democrats to change their minds on the issue of the Mississippi investigation.[4]

Then came the surprise. When the vote on the Mississippi resolution was taken, Key alone among the Democrats voted for it.

The next morning, Key left Mrs. Shedd's boardinghouse early and briskly walked down E Street to take his breakfast in the Imperial Hotel dining room. He sipped the good coffee while he examined a stack of newspapers that lay on the table before him. Many Northern papers carried complimentary remarks about his speech. *The Capital* commented: "Ben Hill and such as he would do well to imitate it." The *Washington Chronicle* maintained that "the really able Senator from Tennessee made a most excellent speech, in admirable temper," and that "Hill, Gordon . . . and other Southern fire-eaters ought to profit by the example." The *Chicago Times* editorialized about the refreshing difference between Key and the "irrepressible cussedness of Toombs, the Calhounism of Tucker, or the Jeff-Davisism of Hill. . . . When the Keys of the Democratic Party become sufficiently numerous . . . the 'bloody shirt' will be buried."

But as Key suspected, much of the Southern press roared like a lion with a yanked tail. The Bourbon *Whig and Tribune* put it succinctly: "Senator Key has rendered doubtful, by this single speech, his return to the Senate. No faltering tones will suit" the Democratic Party in Tennessee. The *Jackson Sun* said that Key had committed a miserable blunder in supporting the resolution, that he had eulogized Senator Boutwell just after he had insulted the whole South, that in this maiden effort he had "dug his own political grave exceedingly deep." The *Memphis Appeal,* which idolized Isham

Harris as the best of Southern manhood, told readers to read Key's compliments to Boutwell and Morton after their insults to the South—if the reader had the stomach to. "Faugh! It makes us sick." The *Brownsville Democrat,* which had supported Isham Harris for Key's Senate seat, said that "the only reparation he can offer to the people of the State he has outraged and misrepresented is to resign . . . come home, Key, come home."

But Key's presentation of what he considered to be truly the attitude of the South was endorsed by other Southern papers. An Alexandria, Virginia, paper praised Key for condemning the whining tone of the South. The *Cairo Bulletin* commented that "the press and people of Tennessee, instead of denouncing him, should congratulate themselves that they are represented in the Senate by so wise . . . a man." Eastern Tennessee's *Morristown Gazette* said that Key had struck a chord in the hearts of Southerners that would not stop vibrating. It added that "both Radicalism and Bourbonism must die, that with proper management Conservatism could live."[5]

The staunchest of Key's defenders was Colonel Andrew Kellar, the publisher of the *Memphis Avalanche.* In his editorial, Kellar sarcastically quipped that the rebel soldiers who disapproved so violently of Key had war records "prior to 1861 and since 1865"; that these types would have been delighted only if Key had shaken his fist at Morton and Boutwell and called them hyenas. If Key had so conducted himself, "then those who think a man has reached the most elevated plane of statesmanship when he rises in his place and calls somebody a liar, and ferociously shakes tangled masses of hair at him, would have shouted 'Bully for Key.' "[6]

These were lonely days for the Tennessee senator. At the very hour that he was delivering his oration, Lizzie was in labor. Chattanooga seemed far away, and Key longed to be home with his wife now, longed for his family. And he missed his Chattanooga friends. Instead, he had the company of rough General Dibrell, the proximity of the motley group taking Mrs. Shedd's "bath" treatment, and the social life of the capital. He enjoyed his walks through the capital, but each April day brought showers of condemnations upon the Tennessee senator, who had dared to stand alone. Key's intention had been to do the statesmanlike thing, to represent a forward-looking South—and thus to deprive Morton, Boutwell, and Blaine of their target.

Yet the loud noise of condemnation resounding from the Bourbon press was echoing in the North. Morton was greatly enjoying it, reading extracts from Tennessee papers that condemned Key. Of course, he maintained that these vicious extracts, not Key's speech, represented the true spirit of the South. This maneuver got under even Key's tough Tennessee skin. But he still believed that the most effective way to counteract the political power of the radical Republicans was to make clear to the North that the clamor of a few noisy Southern politicians was not the true voice of the South; that the majority of Southerners wanted to cooperate for peace, economic development, and progress. The best tactic, he felt, to convince Northerners of the Southerners' sincerity would be to recognize openly that the Negroes were free citizens, that a state cannot secede, that a Yankee who had fought against the South might have done so out of dedication and conviction, that both sides now had to overcome their hostility.

To Key, these attitudes, all expressed in that fateful speech, were truly the attitudes now developing in the South. Yet every day, the impression his speech had made in the North was counteracted by hotheaded Southern newspapers, especially in his home state; these papers were convincing Northerners that Senator Key had misrepresented the true temper of the Southern people.[7]

Yet, Key was learning a lesson in politics, one he pondered well as he took his walks through the streets and along the pathways of Rock Creek Park. He thought about it at Washington parties, in the rooms lit by gilded chandeliers, where he found himself wedged in by the crowd of guests. The lesson he was learning was that in the Senate, each politician was really a double man. One was the senator who knew Key personally, swapped jokes with him, warmly shook his hand after his speech, and gave him lavish and genuine praise. But there was another man in that senator. When it came to voting that man was busy obeying not Key's logic, not the grass-roots people of his constituency, but the political machine that had backed him. One of the rules of that machine was to operate in unison, and not the way the junior senator from Tennessee operated. Thus, many so-called leaders of America's political destiny were only followers. The men who paid the piper and called the tune were often the political manipulators back home, parochial and narrow men, isolated from national problems and even the debates in Congress, busy building up their political empires, and fighting to preserve them, often with racist slogans and a lost-cause mythology.

Throughout the spring, Key watched this muddy process of machine politics. By the time the proposal to investigate the Mississippi election reached the House, Key's speech and stand had so ventilated the issue that the Democrat-controlled House, unlike the Senate, voted to appropriate the money for it. The Southern Democrats in the House now stood united on the issue, supporting the investigation. And yet, Key and his friends noted, they were not condemned for having changed their stand, because they had done it together under orders. They were not called traitors, not censured for this alliance with the Republicans. The press was hushed. The difference was that the ostracized Key had dared to stand and vote alone. Colonel Kellar's paper editorialized:

> The *Chattanooga Times* asks the *Nashville American* and the *Memphis Appeal* why they do not denounce the whole Southern Democratic delegation in the House for permitting the House, without a word of opposition, to appropriate $10,000 to pay the expenses of the Mississippi investigation. Why, bless your unsophisticated soul, Mr. *Times,* you certainly don't think those great Democratic organs would have "pitched into" Senator Key if the other Democrats had also voted for the Mississippi resolution? It was his solitary vote that made him a traitor in their eyes.[8]

And yet Key realized that by stepping forward and forcing the issue, he had gained a victory for moderation in the South. He was receiving many complimentary letters from all over Tennessee. These letters proved that the machine did not represent the temper of the people. But it was the machine, not the people, that usually won elections. Key had predicted that he would be attacked, that this lonely stand might lead to his defeat. But now he was disturbed by the probability of that defeat. To explain his position, he permitted Kellar to publish in the *Avalanche* a letter in which he made this determined statement: "I trust that I have courage enough to fall if my fall is necessary to save the people I represent. . . . I must not ride anchor."[9]

# 10

## A Stolen Election

Many of the lawmakers, like Key, once in Washington, could not afford to bring their large families there and hence left them at home. For the "pure" ones, this often made for a boring life. For the less pure—and most of them were less pure—it made for plenty of free entertainment provided by the lobbyists, and the most delightful of all was that offered by the lady lobbyists. By the 1870's, the great vested interests of the growing United States of America had learned that an attractive, clever beauty in the District of Columbia was worth far more than many male firebrands. Many of the nation's lawmakers frequently took a few blocks' stroll from their hotels to visit the salon of a lady lobbyist. There they would encounter a circle of other distinguished legislators, join in the warmth of the great wits, and enjoy feminine smiles, elegance, music, and dancing. As the clock struck midnight, the hostesses would escort the group to a formally set overfurnished dining room, where vintage Burgundy or iced champagne was served, accompanied perhaps by broiled oysters and cold game pie, mixed salads, and appetizing vegetables. As Mark Twain had written in the *Gilded Age,* a novel quite popular in the 1870's, "who could blame a Congressman for leaving the bad cooking of his hotel . . . to walk into the parlor web which the cunning spider lobbyist weaves for him?" And as the entertainment continued until dawn, cunning influence was exerted upon the nation's business.

We do not know that Senator D. M. Key, devoted family man, succumbed to the cold game pie, winsome wines, and wooing women. Nor was the Tennessean a regular customer of the bars and gambling parlors in the basement of the Ebbitt House. He was, however, an avid poker player during the war, and it is likely that the habit of winning at poker remained with him in Washington.

As the May sun burned down on the granite steps and asphalt avenues, the marble columns and green-copper domes, Key became restless. He longed for relief from the depressing Washington heat, from politics, from the everlasting Belknap impeachment, and from Mrs. Shedd's noisy house, with its steady stream of customers. That summer he allowed himself the luxury of a plush train ride to the International Exposition in Philadelphia. On this trip, Key was the guest of Senator Cameron of Pennsylvania, one of the great railroad moguls of the country. Key thought of this trip as another way of demonstrating that Northern Republicans and Southerners had put the hostility of the war behind them. It was indeed a pleasant trip, and there was much good food and convivial drinking going on in Cameron's special club car.

Upon arriving in Philadelphia, Cameron smoothed the way for his guests through the crowded station and on to the opening of the famed exposition in Fairmount Park. They heard a Methodist bishop's invocation and President Grant's address, which officially launched the exposition. As the President closed, 100 guns roared in applause, and Key, for a moment, thought himself back at Vicksburg. With the grouped Republicans, Key trooped from one ornate building to another. He greeted the beautiful wife of Don Pedro of Brazil and her pet monkeys and visited the zoological gardens. He viewed four acres of machinery in a superstructure of wood and glass with eight miles of shafting, heard hundreds of machines banging away, and examined Gatling guns, sewing machines, and a gadget a fellow named Bell had invented that was said to transmit electrically the sound of the human voice. As marvelous as was

this display of the machine age, the Cameron party happily returned to the marvels of their special railroad car for more tasty
morsels and good liquor.[1]

Perhaps this taste of high life convinced Key to improve his
dwelling place. Anyway, soon after this journey, he abandoned Mrs.
Shedd's boardinghouse, with its "Russian" and "Turkish" baths,
which, he insisted to Lizzie, he had never used. He now moved into
the more aristocratic Imperial Hotel on E Street. This hotel, within
view of Pennsylvania Avenue, was not up to the Willard or Ebbitt
House, but neither was the junior senator from Tennessee. Now
that Key had more adequate living quarters, he invited Albert, his
oldest son, to visit him in Washington. His two comely oldest
daughters, Emma and Kate, were attending Salem Academy, a
school for young ladies in North Carolina. Key had hoped to visit
them during the summer months, but he feared that the Harris
machine would make much of his absence from the Senate and
decided to stay through the session. Furthermore, Albert had expressed great interest in visiting Washington after reading in his
father's letters about the recent raid the Treasury Department girls
had made on the Capitol, where many a distinguished Senator had
been trapped amid skirt bustles and had been forced to listen to
demands for an extra-pay appropriation.

Albert was trusted to escort the two girls to Washington, with
Lizzie's blessing. She thought that a taste of home life would be
good for her husband in his strange Washington surroundings.
When the three young Keys arrived at the B & O Station, Albert
rented a hack, and they headed for the Imperial. En route they
passed Judiciary Park and saw the cannon being placed that soon
would be first to bring the news that the Republican Convention in
Cincinnati had nominated their candidate for President. During this
happy visit, Key took his teen-age children to the Smithsonian Institution and on a trip down the Potomac to Mount Vernon. And
he gave the three young Keys a taste of the campaign excitement
during this national election year.[2]

The Republican candidate, Key suspected, would be James G.

Blaine, the man from Maine who was a perpetual waver of the bloody shirt and had often stirred up strong sectional feelings. By June, the smooth Mr. Blaine was in hot water, having been charged with taking $64,000 against worthless collateral in a Little Rock railroad. Blaine said that Democrats merely were trying to malign him. But later, while Blaine was sitting in a session of his railroad committee, someone whispered the name Mulligan to him—and Blaine's face was said to have turned ghostly white. Blaine was told that Mulligan was about to testify against him, that he possessed letters Blaine and his former law partner had written—letters proving Blaine's guilt.

The roar of charges against Blaine swelled. Gossipers said that Blaine later met Mulligan at a hotel to plead for mercy. It was told that he begged Mulligan to consider the disgrace the scandal would bring to Blaine's innocent wife and children and that Blaine induced Mulligan to send him these letters. Blaine persuaded Joshua Caldwell, one of his associates, to telegraph a statement exonerating Blaine to the chairman of the committee, Proctor Knott. Knott, a handsome Kentucky Democrat, did not realize that Blaine had manufactured this telegram and conveniently kept it a secret. This afforded Blaine the opportunity to plan the dramatic incident he hoped would save him. Before a hushed House, he announced that former Confederates on the Judiciary Committee were trying to ruin him, that he was unashamed to read the controversial Mulligan letters for all his 44 million countrymen to hear. Cloaked in humility and emotionalism, his hand noticeably trembling, he confessed his sins by reading portions of the letters; the hushed people in the gallery listened, convinced that Blaine was innocent. Then Blaine deliberately strode down the aisle and confronted Knott, who did not know what to expect. Everyone in the chamber and in the gallery was breathless as Knott looked up at Blaine, who was towering over him.

Blaine's voice broke the silence as he turned his self-abasement into a thundering attack, demanding to know whether Knott had received the telegram from the "missing witness."

"How did you know I got it?" the surprised Knott said in a guilt-tainted reply.

"I heard you got a dispatch last Thursday morning at eight o'clock from Joshua Caldwell completely and absolutely exonerating me from this charge, and you have suppressed it."[3]

The chamber broke into wild excitement. Blaine rushed before the Speaker's desk, waving the dispatch, and the gallery broke into an uproar. His victory was complete, an astonishing and sickening spectacle to Senator D. M. Key.

The next scene, the following Sunday, was not planned by Blaine. Under the pressure of the Washington heat and his heavy campaign schedule, he slumped, unconscious, into the arms of his wife just after entering church. The *New York Sun* ran the headline "Blaine Feigns a Faint," but sympathy piled high for the martyr from Maine.

Blaine's acts were a prelude to the Republican National Convention. There Colonel Robert G. Ingersoll, the golden-throated atheist orator, nominated Blaine. To Key, it was an emotional appeal that typified the worst in radical Republicanism. Ingersoll declared that Blaine, the man who had "torn from the throat of treason the tongue of slander," needed no "certificate of moral character signed by the Confederate Congress." He had, said Ingersoll,

> snatched the mask of Democracy from the hideous face of the rebellion. . . . Like an armed warrior, like a plumed knight, James G. Blaine marched down the halls of the American Congress and threw his shining lance full and fair against the brazen forehead of the defamers of his country and maligners of his honor. . . . In the name . . . of those who perished in the skeleton clutch of famine at Andersonville and Libby, whose sufferings he so vividly remembers, Illinois—Illinois—nominates for the next President . . . James G. Blaine.[4]

The convention hall reverberated with cheers and song; and in the initial balloting, Blaine soon moved ahead of the other two leading contenders.

Undoubtedly, Blaine would have won, as Key had predicted, had not some clever politicians, desperate to stop Blaine, got the convention adjourned for the day on the pretext that there was not enough gas available to light the hall for the evening meeting.

During that decisive night, a motley but brilliant group of Ohio politicians, appropriately called the Ohio Gang, met long and talked hard over cigars and liquor. They were determined to stop Blaine. Their behind-the-scenes chief of staff was General William Henry Smith, general agent for the Western Associated Press, whose ally and friend was General H. V. Boynton, another powerful newspaperman. Smith convinced Boynton that their candidate, B. H. Bristow, did not have sufficient business backing to win the nomination and that the Bristow people should switch to Rutherford B. Hayes of Ohio. Meanwhile, other members of the Ohio Gang persuaded Conkling and Morton to support Hayes in order to stop Blaine. Thus, on the following day, the new coalition worked, and the nomination went to the tall, handsome governor from Ohio, former Union General Rutherford B. Hayes. Hayes looked very proper with his high silk hat, plaited linen shirt, black shoes and tie, along with his most proper wife, who wanted to bring every drinking man in the United States to temperance. Hayes was indeed very different from the typical Grant Republican.[5]

In Washington, the cannon in Judiciary Park boomed, the bands played, and the Key children chided their father about his unfulfilled prophecy that Blaine would unfortunately get the nomination. No one was more delighted to have been wrong. Key was much relieved at not having to live through a Presidential campaign during which demagogue Blaine would wave the bloody shirt, stir up sectional and factional hatreds, and make constant references to Southern prisons and Northern dead.[6]

The Democratic Convention met at St. Louis in the heat of July and nominated wealthy Samuel Tilden, the sixty-two-year-old, tall, slender bachelor who lived among fine art objects, classical books, and imported wines in his elegant Gramercy Park town house in New York City. Tilden was a corporation lawyer with rare intellect and aristocratic manners. It was indeed amusing to contemplate the contrast between the brilliant, intellectual Tilden and the stodgy Hayes.

Many Southern Democrats, and no doubt Key himself, were antagonized by the nomination of a Tammany man. For years, Key had resented how Southern Democrats were being manipulated by New York politicians. At the convention, Key's friend Colonel Andrew J. Kellar of the *Memphis Avalanche* had declared vehemently that Tammany still controlled the Democratic Party and had neither empathy for the plight of Southern Democrats nor interest in furthering improvements in the South, such as better riverways, harbors, railways, and local self-government. All these were issues Kellar and Key had discussed that windy night in Washington.

But still, to Key, Tilden was the candidate whom he had to support—the best alternative among bad choices. Although Key believed in placing country above party, he said he did not admire those who easily switched party affiliations, perhaps forgetting about his controversial Senate vote. He believed in working to make his own party the best possible means of serving the nation. So the junior senator from Tennessee intended to champion Samuel Tilden along the campaign trail as was the duty of a loyal Democrat. Kellar's loyalty, however, was more profoundly shaken.[7]

That autumn, Key returned to Tennessee. He rode through the familiar countryside of eastern Tennessee making speech after speech. He exhorted Tennesseans to support Tilden rather than the unknown Hayes, whom Key called a front for Republican stalwarts. As the national campaign progressed, Republican demagoguery increased, and principal Republican orators like Morton, Conkling, Blaine, and Chandler stirred up Civil War memories and sectional hatreds—apparently with Hayes's consent—in an effort to distract public attention form the current economic hardships. In response, Senator Key struck out harder and harder against Hayes, who seemed no different from James G. Blaine.

When it appeared that Republicans would not carry critical states like New York, Ohio, and Indiana, the desperate stalwart

leaders renewed their attempts to win over the carpetbagger vote of
the South. In the middle of October, when riots broke out in South
Carolina, President Grant sent thirty-three companies of federal
troops to three Southern states—South Carolina, Florida, and Lousi-
ana. Thus, on election day, Union bayonets would be on hand to
"supervise." The South was bristling with suspicion, denunciation,
and hatred.

On election day, Key was back in the Chestnut Street house in
Chattanooga. Early returns indicated that Tilden would win, and by
the time Key retired for the evening, this outcome seemed a certainty. Hundreds of miles away, in his Gramercy Park home, Samuel Tilden retired to his luxurious bedchamber to dream pleasantly
of victory and inauguration. In his rented house across from the
State House in Columbus, Rutherford B. Hayes went to bed dejected, certain of impending defeat. He had already heard that New
York and then, in quick succession, New Jersey, Connecticut, and
Indiana had fallen to the Democrats.[8]

While the two Presidential candidates slept, a politicians' trick
reversed the course of history and swept Key's life into strange new
channels. It all began because the fiery-tempered Republican editor
of *The New York Times* did not sleep that election night. During
the war, John Reid had spent nerve-racking days and nights in the
dingy, cold cells of Libby prison, and he never learned to sleep well
after that. Never would he forgive the rebels, nor would he ever
want to see a Democrat occupying the White House, even if that
Democrat were from New York City.

About midnight, after all other newspapers had conceded Tilden's
victory, Democratic National Chairman Abram Hewitt asked the
*Times* by what majority it conceded Tilden's victory. Reid retorted
vehemently, "None!"

About 6:30 A.M., newsboys were selling the early edition of the
*Times* along Broadway, shouting the headline: "A Doubtful Election." No other papers gave such a report; there was no foundation
for the headline. High above Broadway, in the *Times* editorial

offices, Reid's assistants squirmed and fidgeted uneasily. How would Reid justify this reportage?

Reid did not know himself, but then he was handed this message from the Democratic National Committee: "Please give your estimate of the electoral votes secured for Tilden." Why did the Democrats bother to ask at this hour for his opinion if they were so certain of victory? Electrified, Reid, who had grasped at straws, found a big one. Oregon had apparently gone Republican, he told himself. And South Carolina, Louisiana, and Florida were under the control of carpetbaggers and federal occupation troops. Surely, if he could "arrange" for those states to go Republican, Hayes would win the election. He grabbed his coat, rushed into the street, grabbed a hack, and bolted into the empty headquarters of the Republican National Committee in the Fifth Avenue Hotel. There he found the previous day's newspapers and vote tabulation sheets scattered about. No one was there; the Republican workers, conceding victory to Tilden, had gone to bed.

As Reid spun on his heels to leave, he practically fell over a strange little man wearing an immense pair of goggles, hat jammed down over his ears, bundled up in an enormous coat, and carrying a gripsack. Reid stared and then recognized Bill Chandler, who handled campaign funds and had just returned from a field trip. Chandler, whose hatred of the South and the Democrats was equal to Reid's, walked with the *Times* man past dozing bellboys to an empty lounge. There Reid excitedly outlined a plan. They lost no time. Together they burst into the bedroom of the fat, sleepy chairman of the Republican National Committee, Zachariah Chandler. While he still sat on his bed, clad in his nightgown, they convinced him that the Republicans should immediately claim the votes from the three occupied Southern states—and thus the national election. Next, William Chandler and Reid hurried out to the Western Union office. They wired the carpetbagger governors of South Carolina, Florida, and Louisiana that Hayes could be elected if they would ensure that their states reported a Republican victory. The governors read and complied.

Later that morning, Zachariah Chandler boldly announced: "Hayes has 185 electoral votes and is elected."[9]

Within a few days, emotions ran high throughout the nation. Between Republicans and Democrats a barrage of fraud charges was hurled back and forth. The real test, however, would come when Congress met in December to determine which electors and returns from Florida, Louisiana, and South Carolina were legitimate and proper. But Congress consisted of a Republican-controlled Senate and a Democrat-controlled House. A terrifying echo of the crisis of 1861 grew louder and wilder in Key's ears as he prepared to return to Washington, and he prayed that history would not repeat itself.

# 11

---

# Brink of Danger

December 2, 1876, was a cold, gray Friday. Senator Key chatted with fellow passengers as he relaxed beside an ice-covered window in his creaking railroad car on the way back to Washington. Now and then he looked out into the wintry landscape. He saw the snow-covered Virginia mountains, thick icicles hanging from bridges and craggy railroad cuts, and streams jammed with ice floats. The frozen road winding up the mountains reminded him of a winter journey thirteen years earlier and of the cruel, icy roads over which he, Lizzie, and the three tiny children had made their way through the North Carolina mountains to Happy Valley. What a bleak time it had been. In those days of war, uncertainty, and despair, he had been tormented with questions about the future of the South and about the wisdom of their sinking cause.

Now Lizzie and the smaller children—Sarah, Margaret, and Frank—were comfortable in the house in Chattanooga. He imagined them sitting by the cozy living-room hearth roasting chinquapins. Emma, Kate, and Albert were safe and happy in school, preparing for useful lives in one united Republic. Key fervently hoped that the children would always live in peace. One mistaken war was enough in a generation. It seemed inconceivable to him that hotheads on both sides could come to forget their common stake in the Union and again destroy the happiness of thousands of families, from Maine to Florida. A difficult, dangerous situation confronted the nation. To settle the election, would the governors, the majority of whom were Democrats, really call out their militia and fight President Grant's regular army? And if force of arms were used to settle this election, would this not set a dangerous precedent for the next one?

In Mexico, this method had become the norm, and every few years there occurred in that country such a settlement by force of arms. Recently, when the incumbent again had violated the Mexican Constitution, the people had revolted. Within a time span of a little more than a half century, Mexico had had two so-called emperors, three dozen presidents, nine or more provisional presidents, and ten dictators. In the United States, this was the centennial year of the birth of the Republic—1876; perhaps it would also be the year in which its citizens would destroy their free method of election. As the train rolled past such Virginia stops as Culpeper Station and Manassas, all battlegrounds of the war, these thoughts disturbed Key. These were not wild exaggerations, but something that might soon become reality.[1]

In Washington the following morning, the worried senator made his way to the Imperial Hotel. The city was bristling with suspense; the crisis was about to come to a head. In the bar of the Imperial Hotel, in the large, elegant dining room of Ebbitt House, wherever the worried Tennessean greeted returning congressmen and senators, he found wild talk about what might happen the following Wednesday. On that day, the Presidential electors of every state would meet to cast their votes officially. The attention of the nation would be riveted on Louisiana, Florida, and South Carolina. Tilden had received 184 uncontested votes; Hayes had received only 163 uncontested votes. If the twenty-two votes from the three disputed Southern states were Republican, Hayes would win the election by one vote. And those states were controlled by carpetbaggers and occupation troops.

The chairman of the Democratic National Committee, Abram

Hewitt, decided to respond to the Republican attempt at stealing Southern votes by stealing the Oregon vote. There, three Hayes electors clearly had won. One of them, J. W. Watts, was a deputy postmaster; as a government employee, he was clearly disqualified as an elector. On November 15, Hewitt secretly telegraphed the Democratic governor to choose a new elector, and the governor chose the Democratic elector E. A. Cronin. The two remaining Republican electors were indignant and refused to serve with Democrat Cronin. The governor, undismayed, accepted their resignation and appointed two more Democrats to fill their places. The electors, however, were two-thirds honest. They sent to Washington two votes for Hayes, one for Tilden. This strategic maneuver would give Tilden the 185 votes needed for victory. But even if this vote were contested, it would force the Republicans to demand that Congress investigate the Oregon returns. This would set a precedent and enable the Democrats to force Congress to examine the results in the Florida, South Carolina, and Louisiana election boards. Complicated enough, the issue became even more confusing when Watts resigned as postmaster, thereby claiming he was entitled to be an elector. He joined with the two other Republican electors, and together they sent in three votes for Hayes.[2]

Key reached his own painful conclusions. He differed with the Democratic Party line and reasoned that the Oregon majority had voted for Republican electors; that regardless of the postmaster's eligibility, the Democratic governor had not acted within the "spirit and intention of the general law" when he appointed a Democratic elector. It was a partisan move "against the will of the people." At a time when a dangerous crisis threatened the foundation of the Union, there was no room for partisanship.

He believed it was wrong to add to the explosive, complicated controversy over the Florida, South Carolina, and Louisiana election returns the Oregon controversy. How to resolve the dispute over these states? The path to settlement was not clarified by the Constitution. The Twelfth Amendment says that "the President of the Senate shall, in the presence of the Senate and House of Representatives, open all the certificates, and the votes shall then be counted." Counted by whom? The Constitution does not say. If they were to be counted by the president pro tempore of the Senate —a Republican—the disputed Democratic returns might well be rejected, and Hayes would be elected. If, however, both houses jointly determined which returns to accept, Tilden would be elected by the Democratic majority in the House.

Key feared that a deadlock might occur. Hothead Southerners might beat the tom-toms of rebellion, the Northern Democrats might feed this Southern bellicosity by sounding the old refrains against the South, and emotions would spiral on both sides to create another crisis such as that of 1861. If the South again committed itself to secession, Key believed Tammany Hall and other Northern Democrats, at the eleventh hour, would abandon the Southern Democrats as they had in 1861. On the other hand, if Northern and Southern Democrats remained united and staged a military march on Washington, the Grant Administration would bring in the army. In either event, the Republic would die.

Petty, shortsighted politicians, like hungry dogs, were yapping for scraps of meat, willing to tear apart this Republic for their personal gain; this thought infuriated Key. After his speech on the issue of the Mississippi election, the favorable response from grassroots people of both North and South had convinced him that the small vocal minorities who represented political machines did not speak for the majority of Americans.[3]

As Key sat by his window at the Imperial, gazing across Pennsylvania Avenue toward Judiciary Square, he analyzed the many letters he had received after his Mississippi speech, letters that had helped him to understand the attitudes of the people and his own duty to them. A letter from Memphis was particularly meaningful to Key:

I was gratified to see you do just what you had the moral courage to do. . . . We have too many men in public life who don't know the sentiment or what controls the sentiment of the people. It has been the mistake of the politicians for the past twenty years. They have gone off in a line while the people took the opposite direction. The fault lies in sending weak-kneed, time-serving *politicians* to do the work of patriotism & statesmanship. Had the statesmen ruled, the war would have been averted; and had they had control since the war, there would to-day be no Radical party in power.[4]

Such responses led Key to the decision to speak before the Senate, to make clear that the attitude of the majority of the Southerners was not that of their spokesmen. He felt compelled to declare that the people of the South were for peaceful and constitutional settlement of the present crisis. After all, only a few party leaders, eager for patronage and power, were driving issues to the brink of war. Thus, Key would speak out for the real people of the South and chastise the extremists on both sides, who did not represent their constituents, but merely fostered their own selfish ambitions. He would speak his mind. If the speech cost him his Senate seat, so be it.

The senator from Tennessee watched closely the day-by-day developments, and daily he saw more portents that the things he feared might turn into reality.

Congress convened on December 4, 1876, amidst surging tensions and accusations. Debates grew hotter, and many members began to carry arms. One of Tilden's advisers pressed for him to adopt a more aggressive, warlike course, to call for Democratic rallies and meetings in every city, town, and hamlet all over the country to discuss the situation. This seemed a clear prelude to military action. Another adviser counseled Tilden to move quickly and forcefully before the Republicans militantly seized the initiative, and another urged him to take his seat in the capital, "though it be at the point of a sword." A high-spirited descendant of Ethan Allen wanted some patriot to lead the way in crushing "the foes which now threaten to engulf us." The Democratic press printed stories slanted to excite Democrats to arms and circulated rumors that plans were afoot for General Sheridan to take command of the Department of the East and, if necessary, to direct troops and warships to "bulldoze" any opposition to the Republicans in New York City.[5]

The Republican press reprinted circulars claiming that the Democrats were calling on Southern rifle clubs to marshal their forces in the capital to ensure Tilden's election. Each accusation set off new suspicion and rumors, and more and more people were driven to take extreme sides.

The Democrat-controlled House had dispatched committees to the three disputed Southern states to conduct an investigation. The Republican-controlled Senate sent out its committee too. These two sets of committees were soon releasing conflicting reports on the same situation. Senator Sherman, especially, was spreading many vicious stories about Southern atrocities in the recent election— stories that Key felt were entirely unfounded and that upset him deeply.

Key now had formed a more definite opinion about the election controversies. Quite clearly, the Republican-controlled election boards in the three states had acted reprehensibly. In Louisiana, for example, he observed that the law required the board to be drawn from both political parties; yet no Democrat was on the board. In all three states, the partisan boards produced vote counts that defeated the Democratic gubernatorial candidates by suspiciously meager majorities. Was it, perhaps, more than coincidence, Key wondered, that these boards managed to disqualify just enough Democratic votes to obtain a Republican victory?

On December 3, Grant told the Democratic National Committee chairman that he would maintain an impartial position on the controversial elections in the three Southern states. This amounted to an admission of his doubts concerning the Republican election claims. The suspicious conduct of the Republicans in these states was too much even for Grant to stomach, Key noted. The Tennessee rebel now developed a respect for the former commander of the Union Army that he had not felt earlier that year, when he had called on President Grant at the White House.

If the will of the voter had been thwarted in three states by such corruption, Congress had both the right and the duty to investigate the operations of these election boards, reasoned the senator from Tennessee.

The Ohio Gang relentlessly pursued their strategy to place Hayes in the White House. When President Grant announced that he would remain impartial, which meant that the army would remain impartial too, the Ohio Gang almost panicked. Where could they possibly gain the additional congressional strength to ensure that the "vote count" ended up in favor of Hayes? The only possible windfall might come from disillusioned and discontented Southern Democrats, and there seemed to be plenty of them, as Democrat Colonel Kellar had noted during the Democratic National Convention. The problem was to reach that group of Southern dissenters and to form a new entente. A member of the Ohio Gang, Murat Halstead, a Cincinnati newspaperman, made a first try by approaching Democratic Congressman L. Q. C. Lamar of Mississippi, implying that Hayes, if elected, would make certain concessions to the South. He asked the congressman to talk to Hayes. Lamar refused but was willing to send his representative, W. R. Roberts, of the *New Orleans Times*. Hayes told Roberts little more than that he saw the justice in Southern complaints about carpetbaggers and that he wished in the future to consult with Southerners like Lamar and Gordon. But such mild overtures were not enough to get Southern Democrats to break party ranks.

Nevertheless, the news of this meeting broke in the *Cincinnati Enquirer*, setting off rumors that Hayes had tried to buy Southern conservatives by offering them "power, place, and emoluments in return for support."[6] Chances for an entente collapsed, giving way to suspicion. Neither faction dared even negotiate for fear of criticism from the press, the public, and each party's politicians. No one was willing to risk the brand of party disloyalty.

Dejected, newspaperman Murat Halstead told Hayes, "I confess I do not know what you can do now."[7] But one member of the other gang, William Henry Smith, still had hope, for he remembered a conversation he had had with Colonel Kellar at the Democratic

Convention. Murat Halstead had tried to gain contact with the Southern conservative politicians, but could not the matter be handled better by first approaching Kellar? Smith wrote Hayes about Kellar:

> . . . he has been fighting the Bourbon Democrats. . . . It is his earnest desire to aid in building up a Conservative Republican party in the South, that shall effectually destroy the color line and save the poor colored people. In my judgment much can be done with the help of such men, between now and February, to secure a good understanding with the better class of White Southerners.[8]

While Smith had been pondering the advantages of getting together with Kellar, Kellar had thought of contacting Smith. Kellar decided to spend a December vacation with William Henry Smith in Chicago. He believed, so he wrote Smith, that the two of them could work out their separate troubles together, that the "thinking men" in Southern business circles, at least in Tennessee and Arkansas, would be favorably disposed toward cooperation with Hayes forces. Kellar recalled Macaulay's maxim that "compromise is the science of politics."[9]

While Smith and Kellar were meeting, another member of the Ohio Gang, Congressman James Garfield, was chatting discreetly with several Democratic congressmen. Congressman Cassey Young of Memphis, Tennessee, felt that Garfield should make a speech proclaiming the liberal policies Hayes planned to follow toward the South, that this might lead fifty Southern congressmen to join in support of Hayes. But these Southerners would need some assurance —a kind of *quid pro quo*. Never too concrete about what the *quid* or the *quo* should be, the Southerners apparently were aiming for Republican support of greater subsidies for internal improvements in the South and withdrawal of federal troops from the three occupied states.

While Garfield was putting out feelers, Kellar and Smith journeyed to Cincinnati, where Smith had arranged a conference with Richard Smith of the *Cincinnati Gazette*. After the three men had

talked in the editorial room of the *Gazette,* Richard Smith produced
three letters from his Washington correspondent, General Henry
Van Ness Boynton, one of Washington's outstanding journalist-
politicians. Boynton had a brilliant faculty for working shrewdly
and secretly; his deft touch was on the political pulse of both
parties.

The three letters revealed much. Boynton agreed with Garfield
on the opportunities for inroads into the Southern camp. The next
step was for Boynton and Kellar to meet and work together in
Washington. William Henry Smith agreed to travel to the capital
with Kellar to introduce him to Boynton and perhaps also to Garfield. The leading personalities of the Western Associated Press
would now be quietly used to shape an alliance between the Hayes
forces and the dissident Southern Democrats. The newspapers of
that association could mold publicity to aid the plan, while Kellar
and Boynton would direct operations in the capital. William Henry
Smith wrote enthusiastically to Hayes about the plan.[10]

In those colorful days of Washington lobbyists, discreet meetings
of great importance were often arranged at the Willard Hotel before some vital caucus on the Hill. "To meet at the Willard at
night" was almost a byword. Under the vaulted, frescoed rotunda
ceilings of the hotel, by the soft light of the crystal chandeliers,
gentlemen of importance rendezvoused. After a game in the billiard
room, the host would escort the intimate group over thick rugs into
the saloon and then into the world-renowned Willard dining room.
The cuisine was noted for its imported delicacies from Europe—
Frankfurt sausages, Dublin marmalades, London pickles and gingers
—and for the most excellent Florida winter shad, Chesapeake blue
points, and diamondback terrapin.

Here, or at a similar place not far from Newspaper Row on F
Street, courtly William Henry Smith introduced tweedy-looking
Kellar to the meticulous Boynton, whose thin beard nevertheless
had a tendency to look slightly moth-eaten. On a festive December
evening, when the first Christmas decorations had appeared on

Pennsylvania Avenue and the sound of caroling was in the air, the three gentlemen lingered into the night over food and wine as they plotted a Presidential victory. Kellar and Boynton, alike in mind and method, formed a warm bond of understanding and mutual admiration over their glasses of Christmas cheer.

It was essential to their plan that Southern leaders turn away from warlike election solutions and publicly announce that they now stood for peace. And a Southern spokesman of great national esteem had to speak out on this issue.

We do not know exactly how the conversation went, but obviously, Kellar must have argued enthusiastically that his good friend Senator David Key was the right man. And he must have reminded his companions of the senator's speech on the Mississippi elections. Boynton expressed interest in meeting Key, and Kellar told him it could easily be arranged. Key lived only a few blocks away, at the Imperial Hotel. Kellar told Boynton that he saw Key frequently and that he believed Key would be of great help to their project. He added that he believed Key was planning to speak out on these issues shortly. Thus, Key might be the ideal man to persuade other Southern conservatives to break away from Tammany influence.

The meeting with the Tennessee senator was arranged. The moment Boynton shook Key's big hand, he was captivated by the senator's steady, good-humored manner and his determination to cut a straight furrow no matter how rough the sod.[11]

During the next few days, Boynton frequently saw Key talking with his Southern conservative colleagues, and he seemed to be most persuasive in turning their sentiments toward peace. Boynton and Kellar were delighted to learn that Key was determined to declare publicly in the Senate that the people of the South hoped for a peaceful and lawful solution to the election. When they warned him of the consequences of making such a stand, Key made light of the threat of such political retaliation.

No doubt Boynton realized that there was a difference between the thinking of Kellar and that of Key. To Key, a constitutional, peaceful solution to the election was most important. At every opportunity, the Tennessee senator insisted, in his puritanical way, that will of the majority in each of the disputed states must be respected and that suppression of such democratic decisions by the majority was the road to civil war, military government, and dictatorship.

Key fervently hoped for a realignment of parties and for the end of Tammany Hall's domination of the South. He hoped for a realignment achieved in an open and legal way. Whether a Republican or a Democrat would enter the White House was of secondary importance to Senator Key. His primary concern was the preservation of the constitutional process. He now remembered well the lessons his early mentor Andrew Johnson had taught him in Greeneville long ago, and the battles Johnson had waged while in the White House.

Kellar also wanted the South to take a stand against the forces of war and dissention. Boynton, Kellar, and Key all agreed that the first step toward this aim was to bring about an alliance between the Hayes Republicans and conservative Democrats. But once Hayes was committed to this alliance, Kellar—unlike Key—wanted Hayes to win, regardless of the methods that would have to be used. Kellar hoped that the outcome of the elections in Louisiana, Florida, South Carolina, and Oregon would be in doubt long enough to force Hayes to commit himself to this alliance. And Kellar would resort to any lobbying necessary to help push these disputed votes into the Republican camp.[12]

Thus, Key's constitutional puritanism was clearly reflected in his political comportment, be it at Ebbitt House, at the Imperial, or in the Senate. He spoke out forthrightly for a nonpartisan alignment in which the South would make a peaceful stand for law and order in order to preserve the democratic heritage of the Republic. Nevertheless, Key still felt strong loyalty to his party—while the Machiavellian Kellar would do anything to destroy the old Solid South, in which he saw the roots of another civil war. Despite these differences, Key, Kellar, and Boynton worked effectively, making call after call during this Christmas season, and many a vote began to change.

# 12

## Speech of Peace

Early in the morning on December 18, a stocky figure clad in night-gown and slippers pulled back the curtains of his hotel window, yawned, and blinked at the blanket of fresh snow on the adjacent roofs. D. M. Key looked down on ice-covered Pennsylvania Avenue, where struggling horses were tortuously pulling along a streetcar. Key shivered and turned to the washstand and found a layer of ice in the pitcher. He lit a fire in the small grate and warmed the pitcher, poking at the ice as it began to melt.

On this day, he would speak out on the Senate floor. He dressed with care, bundled up in his long coat, pulled his beaver hat down snugly over his big head, and briskly strode out of the Imperial Hotel. It was a very cold morning, and Key crossed quickly at the corner of Ninth Street and Pennsylvania Avenue to catch the streetcar that had just pulled up at the stop. He paid his nickel to the driver and sat down to enjoy the leisurely eight-block ride along Pennsylvania. As the car bumped along, he looked out of the ice-flowered window to watch the passing sleighs pulled by strong horses in blazing harness. This was still an unaccustomed sight for the Tennessean, who enjoyed the festive Avenue—the jingling of passing sleigh bells and the red and green Christmas decorations dis-played in the store windows.

At the slippery foot of Capitol Hill, Key stepped off the car and gingerly started the long trek up to the Capitol. The path approached the main entrance of the sprawling building at a slight angle and afforded a striking view of the massive sandstone structure and its new marble dome, which glistened with a thin coat of ice. Key started up the eighty-odd ice-covered, slippery steps leading to the terrace. He cautiously moved along the iron bannister, for several rotund senators had already slipped and fallen.

Key paused at the landing, grasped the railing to steady himself, and turned around to take in the view of the stunning white-carpeted mall. Out of the sparkling snow rose the Washington Monument and the towers of the Smithsonian, and racing red and black sleighs dotted the mall. Key took a big breath of the invigorating air; he felt exhilarated by this winter beauty. He finished his climb, crossed the terrace, and entered the Capitol through the big bronze center door. He cheerily greeted the young pages as he shook the snow out of his heavy coat and warmed his big red hands.[1]

He hung up his coat in the elaborate cloakroom outside the chamber, pulled out of the inside pocket the notes and sketchy manuscript for his speech, and seated himself at his Senate desk. More than two hours later, at noon, the senators strode in from the downstairs restaurant. The president pro tempore called the Senate to order, and the chaplain recited the invocation. Routine petitions and memorials were introduced. Then Senator Wright introduced Bill 1082, which was to establish a court to conduct the proceedings that were to decide the contested elections. Next the Senate passed Senator Edmunds' resolution proposing to appoint a committee that was to confer with a similar House committee to formulate a proposal for the procedure of counting the electoral votes. Key caused some eyebrow raising among the Democrats by supporting this resolution. He reasoned that the procedure outlined in Edmunds' bill might break the deadlock, that it might circumvent further disruption and violence. Key felt his speech would indeed be timely today. Now that he had cast his vote for the Edmunds resolution, whatever else he might say in his speech could not possibly put him in more disfavor with the Harris machine. As with his vote on the Mississippi election, he had again opposed the party line, and he knew that this would also count against him.

At this point, Senator Cameron, no doubt wanting to make use again of his luxurious club car, proposed a long Christmas recess, and another senator asked for a resolution to mend some worn-out wood-paved streets in the District. Then a bill was discussed that proposed to continue the U.S. President's salary at $25,000, despite President Grant's complaint that Congress had raised the salaries of members of both Houses but never the salary of the President. Later in the day, the Senate turned to the issue of the electoral vote in Oregon.[2]

Key was on his feet, his 215-pound frame erect, requesting recognition from the president pro tempore. In a resonant, steady tenor, the gray-haired Tennessean reminded the forty-four senators present that the Constitution provided that the people of the country—not the politicians—select their government and that the voice of the majority be heeded. The senator warned that when this voice "fails to have force and expression, under legal authority—when it is or shall be suppressed by power or subterfuge or other means— our greatest fears should be excited and strongest apprehensions aroused." Such a serious threat to republican institutions should be everybody's concern, for it jeopardized "the interests of the present and future." But if the voice of the majority were to be stifled and disregarded, "the nod of faction or beck of the tyrant would take the place of the people's voice."

"We at this moment stand on the brink of danger," Key warned his colleagues of the Senate, "and we should pause long and consider well before doubtful steps are taken." Perhaps as he drawled the word "pause," he recalled the saloon argument between Crutchfield and Davis on the eve of the Civil War, when Key himself failed to pause, when he had followed the line of the Harris machine without question. He now poured the experience of a lifetime into his speech.

"I am no alarmist," he called out, gesticulating with his big hands. Surely the nation would not choose war. "The lessons of our late struggle are too fresh, its events are too recent, its scenes of carnage and death too vividly impressed . . . to permit another and similar contest." Key did not want his audience to forget Pickett's fatal charge at Gettysburg, the blood-soaked Chickamauga cornfields, or the high mounds of Union dead at Cold Harbor. "Our widows are yet mourning," he continued. "The orphans' tears are not yet dried, and all around are the lame and the wounded."

The South was shorn of power, declared Key. It must submit to whatever reproach and injustice were heaped upon it. But the North had a grave responsibility toward the vanquished, for the people of the South would be "without remedy for wrongs if the Constitution and the laws of the land fail them."

"If our voice be disregarded, our valid elections set aside," Key continued, "we may complain . . . but we cannot, will not, resort to violent measures. It were madness in us to attempt it." He then reminded his listeners that this was the centennial year of the Republic's first Presidential election. The country was 100 years old; the eyes of the world now turned upon this American nation to see how the disputed election would be resolved. America must remember its heritage. By law, said Key, the election belongs "to the will of the majority, and its will must be respected and obeyed."

How should this precept be applied to the specific disputes in Oregon, Louisiana, Florida, and South Carolina? Of course, if an election were conducted contrary to legal procedure, it should not be sustained, regardless of how clear the voice of the majority might seem to be expressed. But the controversy was over the interpretation of the returns and over who were the lawful electors. Key reasoned that when the law is ambiguous as to the procedures and interpretation of an election, the greatest weight should be given to the decision of the majority. Oregon, he said, had voted for the Hayes and Wheeler electors by a majority of about 1,500 votes. Had he been governor, said Key, he would have carried out the verdict of the people when the postmaster disqualified himself and appointed a Republican elector, for on election day the majority of Oregon voters had declared their desire that Hayes be President. "Under our electoral system," he continued, "it does not follow that these gentlemen have been elected to these offices, but in the determination of doubtful questions affecting the electoral vote, the doubt should weigh in favor of the voice of the majority." The majorities in Louisiana and Florida, however, had apparently favored Tilden; but the election boards in these states "adjudged illegalities in the votes . . . to reverse the majorities" in favor of the Republicans. Thus the voice of the majority had been squelched.

Then Key pointed out that pure partisanship was leading some senators to great inconsistencies and illogic in their arguments. Republican Senator Sherman, the general's brother, had asserted that the states alone had power over the election of the Presidential electors, for the Constitution of the United States declares that the electors shall be elected according to state laws. Applying this line of reasoning to Louisiana, Sherman had concluded that Congress could not nullify the action of the Louisiana State Returning Board and could not reverse its decisions, in favor of the Democrats. But Sherman would not apply this logic to the Oregon question. Thus, political expediency was producing inconsistency of argument and emotionalism.

Senator Sherman stroked his pointed beard; he seemed surprised by Key's attack, for the two men were cordial, casual friends. "But sir," continued the Tennessean, "we should take a broader view of the subject." Plainly, the Democratic governor of Oregon and the Republican-controlled election board in Louisiana each had "decided in favor of its own political party, and in doing so has changed majorities . . . to meet party necessities in the hour of party extremity." Each partisan tribunal "decided in favor of the party when each understood that its party triumph could not be assured without the decision it has given." It was a weak government, indeed, that could not rectify "the fraudulent decision of a returning board or governor . . . to protect and defend the privileges and franchises of free men and our public liberty."

Now Key turned to the many atrocity stories of rape, murder, and mayhem that had been circulated, especially by Senator Sherman. These lurid tales about ruthless pressure exerted by the Democrats in the Louisiana elections, he declared, had been told by former slaves, and such testimony was "not of the highest character of credibility." Slavery demoralizes the slave, Key asserted. The slaves' close associations had been entirely limited to people of their own race—and only those in bondage with them. Although there had been some glorious exceptions, Negroes who had achieved freedom and distinction, the slave environment had made it impossible for many of the simple Negroes of the South to understand the implications of sworn testimony. Key immediately added that the Negro was not to be blamed for this deplorable lack of freedom and education and that there had been astonishing progress since the recent emancipation.

While Key spoke thus, Senator Blanche Bruce of Mississippi had entered the chamber and taken his place two rows in front of Key's. Blanche Bruce was one of the few Negroes in the Senate, an elegantly dressed, well-educated man—and a former slave. Composed and polite, Senator Bruce listened to the speech of the former rebel.

Key charged that woolly tales were being used by men like Senator Sherman to discredit the South. Citing an example dating back to 1866, Key told of the testimony of Frances Thompson and Lucy Smith before a congressional committee investigating the Memphis riots of that year. The committee had described Miss Smith as of "modest demeanor and highly respectable in appearance" and had reported that both she and Miss Thompson, who was on crutches and supposedly suffering from cancer of the foot, had been subjected to the cruelest and most brutal violations during the riots. Frances Thompson had testified before the House that she and Lucy Smith lived together and that their home had been invaded by seven Irishmen. Four had violated her, and three had attacked Miss Smith.

The congressional committee chairman had been so touched by

the story, continued Key, that he had wrathfully scolded Southern whites who "breathed vengeance against the Negroes" and shot them down like dogs—yet were never deterred by their skin prejudice from acts of rape. This committee had accepted all the testimony of helpless Frances Thompson and decent Lucy Smith. But the story had a sequel. Some years later, it was discovered that "Miss" Thompson was a man and that this fact had been known to the modest and "highly respectable" Lucy Smith.

The senator from Tennessee said he believed that Lucy Smith's testimony, fondly cited by the Ohio senator, was no more true than that of Eliza Pinkston, now cited by Sherman. Eliza had claimed that white men had rushed into her house, grabbed her baby and cut his throat, then shot her in the throat, the leg, and the breast; they had dragged her outside, got her wood-chopping ax, struck her head so hard that the ax was broken at the eye, and then had hamstrung and raped her. Yet, after all that, she had managed to cross the cotton fields for short stays with various neighbors. "And on this testimony," cried the Tennessean, "a state is to be disfranchised and a President whom the people never elected is to be placed in office. My friend from Ohio lets his heart run away with his head." Such crimes could be committed only by savages, continued Key, or those with the instincts of savages, not by white people. At this, Senator Bruce winced and turned gravely toward Key.

These supposed crimes, continued Key, occurred in a state under Republican, not Democratic, control. If these accusations were only half true was it not strange that no warrants were issued, no offenders arrested? Should we not make our government one of law, not of force?

Key concluded with the main thrust of his argument.

The peace, the harmony, the liberty of the people are of far greater importance than the question as to who shall be the occupant of the Presidential chair. Neither party should seek the advantage under technical theories or by force of physical powers, but the right should be reached by honest, nonpartisan, and peaceful methods and the country, the whole country, be uppermost in all minds and hearts."[3]

As Key sat down, Bruce rose to his feet, his tall figure towering over the Tennessean; he was aroused and hurt by Key's reference to Negroes.

"Mr. President," said Senator Bruce, "I wish to ask the senator from Tennessee simply one question. Does he believe that the outrages committed on Mrs. Pinkston must have been committed by black men because of the revolting and atrocious character of the outrage?"

Key answered, "I will say to the senator from Mississippi that I did not say they were committed . . . by white men or committed by black men. The expression I used was 'savages or those with the instincts of savages.'"

Bruce said sternly, "I am somewhat surprised at the senator from Tennessee . . . he casts a gross reflection upon a race that certainly does not deserve this censure."

Key replied with finality, "The senator is mistaken in what I said, as I have remarked."[4]

Key was taken aback by Senator Bruce's reaction; he had intended no such offense to Negroes. If this were Bruce's attitude, he wondered just whom his speech would please. Obviously, he had antagonized many Democrats with his views about Oregon and many Republicans with those about Louisiana. And he had pricked the sensitive Bruce. How could the senator from Mississippi have so misunderstood his intentions? Bruce had a short memory. Where in any postwar speech had any other Southerner in the Senate spoken up for the Negro cause as Key had done less than a year before on that very floor? Or when during that year had a white Senator worked more diligently to obtain full citizenship for the Negro?

The Senate now turned its attention to routine matters until the gavel banged out adjournment at 3:25 P.M. Key carefully made his way down slippery Capitol Hill, facing the setting sun and an icy wind coming across the mall. He took the streetcar home and again

enjoyed the Christmas atmosphere on the busy avenue. The tinkling
of the sleigh bells accompanied a group of early Christmas carolers
singing of peace on earth and good will toward men. Despite all the
confusion, Key's heart felt lighter. He had done his duty, he had
voted for the Edmunds resolution, and he had spoken out against
both Southern extremists and Northern Republicans who were
spreading farfetched stories about the South. He had made his plea
for law and order and had made a stand for the South on the side
of peace and good will toward men.

And yet, Key knew he would have to face a bitter dilemma. In
Tennessee, his speech for peace would be so twisted by the Harris
machine that it would lead to Key's defeat in the coming senatorial
elections, which would take place in about four weeks. When, tired
and hungry, Key entered his room at the Imperial, the winter sun
had disappeared behind the Arlington hills, across the Potomac.
And Key's exhilaration had given way to a more somber mood.

On that freezing-cold evening, Kellar returned to his house at
1209 F Street glowing with optimism over Key's speech. Kellar and
Boynton visited Congressman Garfield of Ohio. Garfield pledged
his help; he promised to speak to Congressmen Young of Tennessee
and Hill of Georgia, as well as to other influential Southerners, to
convince them of Hayes's positive attitude toward the South. Jubilantly, Kellar wrote to William Henry Smith, telling him about
Key's speech, about the progress of their peace plan, and about the
speeches Congressmen Young and Hill proposed to make as a
follow-up to Key's. Kellar reported that at least thirty members of
the House now supported their plan and that "the situation in
Washington has changed immensely, from the war-like to the most
peaceful."[5]

Even Key's eyes flashed with exaltation as he discovered sign after
sign indicating the victory of their peace plan. How glad Key was
to hear ex-Confederate General John Shelby say, "I was for rebellion once, but I am not now. . . . If actual war should occur between
the two parties and President Grant should call for volunteers, I

should not lose two hours in responding."[6] Another famous wartime leader of the South, ex-Colonel John Singleton Mosby, declared that he too stood with Shelby. And the once fiery *Richmond Enquirer* proclaimed that if war came, the South must remain a passive spectator. Indeed, the *National Republican* hit the mark when it editorialized: "The Bourbon Northmen, up to within a few days ago, intended armed opposition. . . . Their steeds of war now stop prancing. . . . Southern leaders since the election have been consulting their constituency . . . and have fully determined on a summary separation from the Southern doughfaces."[7]

As Key happily boarded the train to spend the Christmas holidays in Chattanooga, he knew that much had been accomplished during a few short weeks in Washington. At last the country seemed most eager to achieve peace. The man who bade him farewell, Andrew Kellar, realized that the Southern Democrats' support of Key's peace policy did not necessarily mean their support of Hayes. Kellar believed that something else, a pay-off such as government construction loans for the South's industrial development, might be needed to reach that objective.

Key, for example, had reported to Congress that in his section of eastern Tennessee the production of iron ore from five furnaces could be increased about 30 per cent if only more and better railroads were built. Key had also asked for better waterways in his district and had introduced an amendment to the Rivers and Harbors Appropriation Bill to obtain $12,000 for such a project on the Clinch River.[8] As a member of the Senate Post Office Committee, he had seen the South and the West repeatedly neglected in arrangements for mail service. This was especially true in the matter of rural and star routes, which serviced isolated areas that the railroads and waterways did not reach.

Forward-looking Southerners were aware of the enormous progress and changes going on in the country's industry of their day— the height of America's industrial revolution. Thus, men like Key desperately sought the government subsidies needed to develop Southern industries, railroads, and waterways. These men were becoming increasingly restless, eager for results. They were fed up with the Tammany Hall Democrats' empty promises to support legislation authorizing subsidies for the South. Southerners resented bitterly that of the $104,705,173 doled out to build roads, canals, and railroads in the years from 1789 to 1873, only $4,430,192 had gone to the South. Where were the promised subsidies for the Southern Pacific and the Texas Pacific railroads, which would give Tennessee a southern route to the West Coast? Key was bitterly disappointed when, in December, 1875, the chairman of the House Appropriations Committee, a powerful Indiana Democrat, pushed through a resolution against granting further subsidies to private corporations. It was a double standard, aimed against the South.[9]

Andrew Kellar had shrewdly watched the Southern senators—Key, Lamar, Young, Hill, and Atkins—as they saw the dreams of the South shattered by Northern Democrats who would not support their appropriations proposals. Would not a serious promise of such support be the very *quid pro quo* he and Boynton needed to gain Southern support for their plan? Could not the Hayes Republicans offer to give the Southern Democrats what Northern Democrats were denying them? In exchange, Southern Democrats would give their support of Key's policy and refrain from a filibuster that would block Hayes's inauguration.

During the next few days, Kellar and Boynton were busily arranging meetings in the Ebbitt House bar, hosting dinners at the Willard, and entertaining special guests at Welkers', Washington's most exclusive restaurant. But the problem was to make their scheme work. The railroad lobbyists they wanted to utilize were fighting among themselves. One of these powerful men behind the scenes was handsome, dapper Tom Scott, railway czar of the Civil War years, who was an associate of Senator Cameron in his Pennsylvania Railroad. Scott was president of the Texas and Pacific Railroad Company, which had been formed in 1871. The company had two brilliant lobbyists—John C. Brown, former governor of Tennessee, who was the company's vice-president, and General Grenville Dodge, its chief engineer. But their lobbying efforts were being directed against the other railroad camp—the Central Pacific Railway Company of the Union Pacific and its subsidiary, the Southern Pacific Company. The upshot of the work of all these busy lobbyists was a stalemate between the two lobbies.

Kellar and Key both were close to John C. Brown, and Kellar and Boynton now threw their weight behind the Texas and Pacific. Two days after Key's speech, Boynton wrote to William Henry Smith that it was essential to their plan to be certain of thirty to thirty-six congressional votes. Where could they come from? "West Tennessee, Arkansas, a large Kentucky element, Louisiana, Texas, Mississippi, and *Tom Scott* wants to help for the Texas & Pacific Railroad." If Governor Hayes would agree to make these promises of subsidies for industrial development in the South, "Scott with his whole force would come here, and get those [Southern] votes in spite of all human power, and all the howlings which blusterers North and South could put up."[10]

Now that his work in Washington was done, Colonel Kellar packed up to return to Tennessee for the holidays. On his way home, he detoured and made many stops to ensure that the various publishers in the Western Associated Press would support his scheme. He stopped off in Cincinnati to gain the backing of the publisher of the *Cincinnati Gazette,* and he asked him to enlist the aid of the publisher of the *Chicago Tribune.* Kellar was well aware that the Western Associated Press was a powerful vehicle for shaping public opinion; it could also help to camouflage backstage maneuvers.

But Rutherford B. Hayes was deeply disturbed by the plan Boynton and Smith proposed to him. Puritanical Hayes recoiled from the back-room schemes hatched by gentlemen of the press in the bars along Washington's Newspaper Row, for little did he seem to know of the activities of the Ohio Gang, of *New York Times* editor Reid, or of Zach and Bill Chandler. Hayes wrote to Smith that he did not want to be committed to this plan, that he mistrusted the forces that were to become part of this scheme. "We must rely on our own strength to secure our rights," wrote Hayes to chagrined William Henry Smith. "With firmness it can be done."[11]

Thus, the plan was held in abeyance over the holidays. During that time, it almost died, for railroad lobbyists were busy fighting one another, Southern congressmen did not trust Hayes, and Hayes was suspicious of the lobby forces he needed to win the election.

# 13

## Reckoning

David McKendree Key was U.S. senator by the grace and choice of
Tennessee's statesmanlike governor, not by election. His recess
appointment would extend until the state legislature met in its
regular session in January, 1877. Then the seventy-five representatives and twenty-five senators of the state of Tennessee were to
select the man who was to fill the senatorial seat for the remaining period of Andrew Johnson's term. This election, some said,
would be the Tennessee maverick's day of reckoning. One of Key's
closest advisers was tweedy, perceptive H. V. Redfield, a politically
attuned reporter for Murat Halstead's *Cincinnati Commercial*. Redfield said Key might have easily won the election on the very first
ballot—except for his record of having cast three maverick votes
in the Senate. And how would Key explain, in the brief time available, to these Tennessee farmers and hillbillies why he had voted
with the Yankees to investigate the Mississippi elections or why he
had sided with the Republicans to set up an electoral commission?
The worried Redfield arrived in Nashville, satchel in hand, to join
Key's other advisers—railroad lobbyist John C. Brown, Colonel
Kellar, and Colonel A. S. Colyar, another ex-Whig and gallant Confederate regimental commander. Colyar, a brilliant businessman
who soon was to develop the Tennessee Coal, Iron, and Railway

Company, was the spokesman for most of the Tennessee industrialists of Whig origin whom he had marshaled solidly behind
Key. Colyar, Brown, Kellar, and Redfield—Key's staunch supporters
—discussed their fears and the tragedy of the situation.

"He is a patriotic man," the reporter moaned, "and would rather
be right than senator."[1]

But more must be said about Redfield's attitude toward Key. For
as much as Redfield loved Key—and he first had got to know him
years earlier, when he was stationed as a correspondent in Chattanooga—he did not consider Key a man of exceptional political
ability. But Redfield stubbornly admired Key's character and insight into the needs of the country in this time of mounting crisis.
Redfield believed that character and insight, more than genius, were
lacking on the national scene. In this regard, Redfield maintained,
no one could fill Key's shoes.

Ex-Governor Brown shared Redfield's concern, but it was Kellar
who was most upset and most worried. Only he and General Van
Ness Boynton fully knew of Key's crucial role in the inside events
of the Presidential election in Washington. Keller feared that it
would be catastrophic if Key were to be eliminated from the Washington scene at this time. Kellar and Boynton needed Key—a man
who was untainted by lobbyist maneuvers, a forthright spokesman
in the Senate. To save Key, Kellar was willing to pledge all possible help. He volunteered as his campaign manager and for the time
being dropped his work in Washington to remain in Nashville, the
Tennessee state capital. Kellar and Redfield both knew that it would
be a tough fight for votes, that they would have to meet the full
brunt of the bristling, disciplined Democratic machine politicians,
led by Key's erstwhile friend Isham Harris.

From a spacious window high in Nashville's Maxwell House,
the grandest hotel in the entire South, Isham Harris, master machine politician of Tennessee, watched the crowds bustling in the
streets below. There was the clatter of hooves as the hacks pulled
up before the elegant entrance, bringing in dozens of legislators.

Some of them looked rather slovenly, others were well dressed, and most of them were carrying in their bags ample supplies of Tennessee whiskey, from good bourbon to mountain dew, to last them for the entire session. Out of that motley group, Isham Harris was determined to get two results: first, his own election to the Senate for the next six years; second, the election of a suitable junior senator—a trustworthy member of the machine, a man who knew how to take orders, certainly a type unlike that eccentric, undependable D. M. Key, who was always breaking party ranks.

Harris left his comfortable chair for a better view from the window. Below, the cobblestones reverberated with the noise of carriage wheels and horses' hooves and the calls of the liveried young Negro boys rushing about to receive the guests. At fifty-eight years of age, this pugnacious, stormy Tennessean was of rather humorous appearance. Throughout his frantic public life, the more hair he had shed atop his now shiny pate, the more the halo of grizzly, curly growth that remained around the edges stood out. His wide mustaches, like two enormous quarter moons, swooped out beyond his cheeks. But there was nothing even slightly comical about Isham Harris's political impact. When this curmudgeon in black bow tie and broad-winged coat stood on a podium, he breathed condemnation, like a dragon spewing fire, upon all who dared defy the sacred tenets of the party of the Solid South or question the morality of the color line that knitted it together.

Isham Harris, who had already been a Tennessee congressman when Key was but a college lad, had the same combative streak that had distinguished early Tennessee pioneers like David Crockett. All these men had been orators with resonant voices, capable of eloquent profanity and knifelike sarcasm, and once they deemed themselves right, no force, however powerful, could shake them. Opposition on the stump, as one Tennessean later declared, "was like waving a red banner at a bull." The defiance of Key and Kellar was indeed like waving two red flags in Isham Harris' face. He would speak against these turncoats all over Tennessee. As he thought of them, he grew angry, and his curly locks stood out straight from his bald pate like the horns of an angry, charging bull.[2]

Harris had a political memory that never forgot or forgave. In 1861, he had politically seduced Key away from his mentor Andrew Johnson. And Key had been disloyal to Harris when he slipped back to Johnson's attitudes. For Key, the war had ended in 1865; yet for Harris, a second war had just begun. Perhaps this second war was Harris' compulsive compensation for things that had happened during the real war. What had happened to Harris during that war indeed made a strange story.

In 1862, Harris had vacated his governor's post to become military aide to General Albert Sidney Johnston, then considered a far greater hero than Robert E. Lee. When things had seemed bleak for the Confederacy, Johnston's armies had marched to Shiloh, burst upon Grant's sleeping soldiers, and sent his battalions reeling backward. Only in the sector known as the Hornet's Nest had Grant been able to slow up the ferocity of the Confederate victory. If the South could exploit its advantage, Grant's army might be driven into the river behind the lines. But here history played its trick on Harris. After General Johnston had personally led a column of faltering troops to clean out the Hornet's Nest, he returned to the rear, and while he was momentarily alone, a bullet whined through the air and lodged deep in the back of his right thigh. Some moments later, Isham Harris came upon the general, his face ashen, his body swaying in the saddle and about to topple.

Harris cried, "General, are you wounded?"

"Yes, and I fear seriously." With that, the reins dropped from Johnston's hands.

Supporting the sick general, the great hope of the South, Harris was unnerved and rattled. He guided their horses to a protected position and lowered the unconscious Johnston to the ground. Only then did he frantically search for the general's wound, tearing off blouse and shirt, beginning to panic when he found nothing. Fatal moments passed before Harris saw the blood streaming from Johnston's boot. By then it was too late for the simple tourniquet that could have saved the general's life.[3]

The great leader, the bright hope of the South, was dead, and the initial victory at Shiloh was never followed up. Many Southerners would believe forever that Grant's army would have been routed and destroyed and the war won had Johnston lived. There had been whispers: who had lacked the presence of mind to save Johnston's life? It was ironic. As the war wore on and the South suffered one reverse after another, Tennessee passed into Yankee hands. There was a quip, a bitter one, passed on by the disgruntled men in the Confederate camps. "Tennessee," they said, "never seceded. Isham Harris seceded and carried Tennessee along." Yet Isham Harris, who had carried the state into war, never commanded troops in battle during that war; and in that one fateful moment, some said, he failed to save the best commander the Confederacy ever had.

The year after the collapse of the Confederacy, the distraught Harris had moved to Mexico, then to England, a lonely expatriate. When he finally did return to his old law practice in Memphis, he had regained his old fanatical determination. He lived for the day when the South would rise to fight again; then he would make his atonement and lead the avenging sons of the South into battle. At any rate, Harris prospered, making both money and political capital. Soon, he gained an iron grip on the cotton and tobacco planters of the Democratic Party in Tennessee. He and the other machine politicians knew that a solid one-party South was a prerequisite for their schemes and that a fully developed two-party system would be fatal to their plans. For then, the ballot box would give a voice not only to those emotionally inflamed by memories of the past, but also to people who wanted to work for a more fluid future. The best way to avoid this loosening up was to keep alive the lost-cause theme, the importance of fortifying the color line. Thus, Isham Harris had kept racism and sectionalism rampant.

There was an obstacle in Harris' path. In that thriving, sunny cotton city of Memphis, this hindrance was personified by Colonel Andrew Kellar, able regimental commander during the war. Kellar's paper, the *Memphis Avalanche,* came to represent all that Harris hated. It galled Harris no end when Kellar and Key—one in western Tennessee, the other in eastern Tennessee—teamed up and pushed the theme that the fire-eaters (that meant, among others, Harris), who seemed so eager to start another war, were not generally those who had gallantly fought in the last war. Harris was most distressed to see Kellar, slowly but surely, win support in Shelby County, right around Memphis, which was the heart of the cotton area. Now Harris himself had to run for office to maintain his grip on the party.

Despite Harris' forensic attacks on anyone who dared to threaten his dream of a machine-controlled Solid South, he was an astute politician and able to switch ground temporarily if necessary. Harris did not overlook the favorable grass-roots reaction to Kellar's campaign in the *Memphis Avalanche* championing Key and praising him as "not sectional, not narrow in his view of public measures, not an ultra partisan, but yet thoroughly identified with the Democratic Party." Kellar was calling Key the choice of Tennessee conservatives, of the successors of the old Douglas Democrats and Bell-Everett Whigs, and of the late Andrew Johnson's admirers. Quite a combination, thought Harris. "The real Conservatives, the old-time Union element in Tennessee," the *Avalanche* editorialized, "have chosen Judge Key as their representative now that Andrew Johnson lives on in their hearts."[4] Kellar, appealing to all elements in Tennessee politics who might revolt against Bourbon Democratic rule, was attempting to achieve on the state level the kind of coalition he was hoping to align nationally. All the more reason why Harris had to disrupt that coalition now.

Across the state, the strong controversy about Key's Senate speeches had produced a more moderate climate among the grass-roots voters in contrast with the hysterical mood of the power-grasping machine politicians. It was even becoming fashionable in Tennessee to talk about broad national aims that would reconcile sectional strife. In this climate, Harris switched his political tune too. Upon being serenaded at his home by his political followers, he

piously pledged patriotic conservatism "far above sectional prejudice."[5] Not for a moment would he now allow himself to be
represented as the partisan extremist and Key as the wise statesman.
He prepared to mimic Key's general philosophy and thus to destroy
Key's campaign issues. At the same time, Harris pointed an accusing
finger at the Chattanoogan as unpredictable and unwilling to stick
with the Democrats in a crisis. From forums, in the caucus, and
before reporters, he played this theme over and over again. Soon
the combined Bourbon-dominated press of Tennessee was catapult-
ing Key with articles calling him the most unreliable Democrat
in the state. And more and more people began to believe it.

In the forthcoming election, Harris planned to get himself elected
to the full six-year term as U.S. senator. With his powerful machine,
he envisioned no obstacles to accomplishing this aim, but to defeat
Key and place a member of his machine in Andrew Johnson's old
spot seemed not that easy. Harris had designated as Key's formidable opponent round-faced, affable, benign James Bailey. Fifty-year-
old Bailey was the brother-in-law of the more aggressive Colonel
Burch, who was managing editor of the powerful *Nashville American*. A former Whig and not an original secessionist, Bailey was
not the perfect Harris-machine man. But Bailey, who was not
strictly of the Bourbon mold, was the ideal pawn for Harris' maneuver to defeat Key. This mild, innocuous candidate would rob
Key of the issue of extremism and yet was a safe party choice.
Harris knew that Bailey would be dependable and would not play
the maverick in Washington. Unlike Key, he was a member of the
"state credit" or "high tax" wing of the party. And yet, most of
Key's supporters would think of Bailey as their second choice.[6]

For the real extremists, there was General Bate, an old-timer in
politics, a last-ditch Bourbon who dreamed of battle every night.
Bate had been the first Tennessee volunteer to rush to the front in
the Mexican War, that grand war in which Tennessee had been
dubbed the "Volunteer State." During the Civil War, Bate had
been wounded three times, and six horses had been shot dead
from under him. Unlike Harris, Bate could not be charged with

never having been in the thick of it; he had been in the midst of combat far more often than D. M. Key.

The Republican candidate was Horace Maynard, a New Englander who had been educated at Amherst and transplanted to eastern Tennessee. His striking dark complexion, hair, and eyes gave him the appearance of a Cherokee Indian. Harris knew that Key could count on the support of nearly all of Tennessee's Republicans if Maynard dropped out of the race.

On wintry January 10, Key, Kellar, Colyar, and Redfield trudged up the two flights of marble steps to the three-storied, colonnaded portico of the sandstone capitol, the pride of the state since 1845. Legislators and lobbyists swarmed through the marble halls, and Key greeted many friends and acquaintances among them. He finally sat down with his companions near one of the Ionic columns in the gallery of the House of Representatives to watch the balloting. On the floor below, the legislators were pouring in, back-slapping, lighting cigars, pulling out snuffboxes, and adjusting the position of the spittoons, trying their range and aim.

Senator Key eyed the assortment of people seated below. Most of them were fairly young men. Redfield pointed out that thirteen of the twenty-five state senators were farmers and that about half of the group consisted of ex-rebels. Since the state constitution allowed legislators compensation for seventy-five legislative days only, Redfield explained, this election would be over in a hurry, for other matters had to be considered too during the session. "The idea of working for nothing was never attractive for Tennessee legislators," observed the *Cincinnati Commercial* correspondent.[7] This lack of decent remuneration led many of these lawmakers to accept money for voting the "right" way. Although Key probably did not realize it, neither Kellar nor Harris was strictly above buying votes.

The gavel brought the noisy chamber to order, and soon the balloting was under way. General Bate took an early lead with thirty-three votes, followed by Bailey with twenty-four, and May-

nard with twenty—while Key was trailing with only thirteen. A
majority of fifty-one votes was needed for election. Kellar was not
upset by Key's lag, for he hoped to receive Maynard's votes when
he dropped out of the race. By the twenty-seventh ballot, though,
Bailey, who had captured some of Bate's votes, had a count of
thirty-eight. The gallery was tense; if the Republicans could be
induced to switch their votes to Bailey, he would be elected. But
rumor still had it that the Republicans were waiting for Key to pick
up thirty votes and then would switch to him. Suddenly, a few
party leaders scurried around, and a Democratic caucus was held.
Something apparently had gone wrong. Harris for once lost control,
and the caucus exploded. Kellar was jubilant; if Bailey and Bate
could stay in the running for a few more ballots and if neither
could break the stalemate, the Key forces would be able to make
their all-out bid for victory. Thus, victory was almost within Key's
grasp.

The victory indeed would have been clinched had not State Senator Thompson, a Bate fanatic, decided to copy Colonel Ingersoll's
bombast on behalf of Blaine. Thompson now spoke for his "plumed
Ivanhoe." Thompson was not Ingersoll, and his speech ended in a
ludicrous gush: "A vision of the past rushes before me," he cried.
"I see a great battle . . . I see a grand hero in strife; I see his white
plume, like that of Ivanhoe . . . I see him reel and fall. . . . This
is General Bate, fighting for me, fighting for you." The legislators
were bored, gaping, or laughing. Thompson's speech had misfired.
In the next two ballots, plumed Ivanhoe's vote count dropped from
thirty-three to twenty-six.[8]

Kellar anticipated the catastrophe. The stalemate had been
broken too soon, before Bailey's political support had dissolved.
By the forty-fourth ballot, Bailey's count, fattened by Bate's votes,
had risen to forty-four. Key stood at twenty-seven, having gained
some Republican votes in a premature attempt to stave off his defeat. The forty-sixth ballot made it painfully clear that not even
the Republican votes could give Key a majority.

Key now made up his mind. Despite Kellar's protestations, he sent a message to his floor manager, T. C. Lowe of the Shelby County delegation, and instructed him to withdraw his name from the ballot without delay. He added that he was about to leave for home.

Lowe rose to carry out the senator's wishes. With a ringing voice, he pointed out that the career of Key in Washington had been meteoric; it had lasted scarcely a year and yet had made an impact on the whole nation. During that year, Key, who had been an unknown, had "placed himself in the front rank of those great statesmen who adorn the Senate." In a national crisis, he had been the man who had seen the need to take a broad view. Yet, when he spoke out in the Senate for moderation and claimed that the South —the real people of the South—were on the side of peace and the Constitution, the bloody-shirt Northern Republicans had retorted that Key might be a moderate but that his moderation was not representative of the South. He had been *appointed,* they had said, not *elected.* They had sneered that he would be repudiated in the first Tennessee election.

Lowe's voice reached a peak as he cried, "They were right!" The charges of the Northern radicals were now borne out tragically by the defeat of Senator David McKendree Key at the hands of the Tennessee legislature, which was elected by the people of Tennessee. Lowe challenged all Democrats to ask themselves whether they had allowed personal prejudice to outweigh party and public interest. Was it that no man could receive the endorsement of a Southern state who dared to rise above sectional prejudices? Lowe looked challengingly around the chamber, stood up straight, and said, as if weighing each word, "Now let each member here . . . answer for himself this question: For which of these reasons have I refused to vote for Senator Key?" On that note, Lowe formally and indignantly withdrew Key's name and curtly sat down.[9]

Isham Harris could relax now; the deed was done. As a political figure, Key was dead. What did it matter if Lowe and such types, moaning their swan song, begged crumbs for the defeated?

There was just time enough for Key to catch the evening train to Chattanooga. At any moment, a new senator would replace him, and he had no taste for dawdling around. To Lowe, Colyar, and Kellar, to all his staunch supporters, he expressed his gratitude. To the end, he tried to maintain his characteristic lighthearted touch. But the stubborn Kellar was unwilling to admit defeat. As always, the Memphis Fox's speculative mind searched for a new angle. Would Key give him permission to place his name again in the race, quickly, even without contacting him in Chattanooga, if a sudden opportunity developed?

Key shook his head. No! He had had enough. He had already told a reporter that his name would not again be placed in nomination. But Kellar continued to argue; he would not give up. He appealed to Key's sense of duty. Had Key really rendered his full obligation to his party? Finally, Key was moved and smiled warmly as his big hand grasped Kellar's. He consented. He felt, however, that there was not going to be such an opportunity anyway.[10]

With that, he waved good-bye and with heavy steps strode out onto the capitol porch and down the marble stairs, pulling his beaver hat tighter over his head against the wintry winds. Soon he was on his train, traveling home along the bends of the Cumberland River.

In the next day's balloting, some of the Bourbons still withheld their votes. After all, now that the Harris machine had used the more moderate Bailey to defeat Key, why not now defeat Bailey with an all-out fire-eater? Such a thoroughgoing fire-eater was Washington C. Whitthorne. In 1861, as Speaker of the Tennessee State House, he had connived with Harris to secede and to take Tennessee along into the Confederacy.

On January 18, Whitthorne was nominated. Kellar, electrified, convinced that Harris had blundered, huddled with Lowe and Colyar. If Bailey lost out completely, if the contest became one between Key the moderate and Whitthorne the extremist Bourbon, then Key would win. Harris was getting too greedy for his own good, and now was the time to trip the old coot. So Kellar asked a senator, a Key supporter, to present Key's name again in nomination and to make clear that the presentation was being made without Key's consent.[11]

Kellar then produced his trump card—the entire Republican delegation switched to Key. Throughout the day, Key continued to gain votes. On the seventy-first ballot, Key's count had risen to forty-five; Bailey, Whitthorne, and Bate had rapidly dropped. Bailey's had dropped to thirty-four, Whitthorne's to nine. Bate's votes had rapidly shifted to Key. At sunset, the legislature adjourned for the day, and Kellar, Colyar, and Lowe jubilantly walked out of the capitol. Kellar was ready for a celebration; the following Monday, Key would surely be elected on the first ballot.

So thought Kellar. But while Key's friends celebrated, Harris worked ferociously. Obviously, Key could be defeated only by a moderate like Bailey and not by an extremist Bourbon. So Harris quickly whipped the machine into line behind Bailey. Over the weekend, evil seeds of suspicion were planted about Key. And that very evening, a new campaign was inaugurated. In the lavish Maxwell House Hotel, the Bailey-Harris forces rented dozens of rooms and brought in the liquor, food, and whatever other entertainment might satisfy the farmer legislators. Some said that more than $1,000 was spent over that weekend. In these luxurious smoke-filled rooms, where toasts were drunk and the liquor supply seemed inexhaustible, unsavory rumors were spread about Senator Key.

That weekend, Senator-elect Harris was at his political best. Some of the hosts passed around a letter from the *Nashville American* quoting from Key's December speech in the Senate. Had Key not said candidly that Watts, the Republican, and not Cronin, the Democrat, was entitled to the position of elector from Oregon? "In my opinion," read the letter "upon the construction given to this *one Oregon vote depends the next Presidency. . . .* I would today, without any reflection on Mr. Key personally, rather risk Roscoe Conkling uncommitted, then Mr. Key committed, and elected by Republican votes to the Senate." To Southerners, Roscoe Conkling was one of the most hated Republicans, a symbol of all that was despicable in Northern politicians.[12]

"Better to risk Conkling uncommitted than Key committed" made good wisecracking conversation throughout the weekend as the liquor flowed freely and the smoke thickened in the hotel rooms and saloons. No offense to Key personally—that fine, friendly chap —but any commitment by him was meaningless. Anyone who did not believe this had only to look at his record. What about Key's speech and surprise vote in favor of the investigation of the Mississippi elections? What about his shocking vote sanctioning the publication of Senator Sherman's falsified report on the Louisiana elections? What about his subversive support of the Edmunds resolution, a Republican resolution recommending that Senate and House confer jointly on the counting of the Presidential vote? When the listeners got sufficiently stirred up, more acid attacks were made. Last Friday, why had the Tennessee Republicans switched suddenly to vote for Key? The answer to every question proved that D. M. Key was disloyal, making secret deals, unworthy to remain in the Senate. Compare him with safe, affable, convivial Bailey. Yes, Key too was affable, convivial—but hardly safe.

The machine pumped out charges in its campaign of vilification, and the entertainment ran on into the night, Saturday and Sunday. The farmers were having a good time, and Harris was a jolly good fellow. The suspicions planted by Harris and his men were taking root in the liquor-soddened minds of the guests.

Shaken from their apathy, Kellar and his colleagues worked frantically to counteract Harris' efforts. Lowe buttonholed legislator after legislator to point out that the Harris people were only presenting one side of Key's December speech and falsifying its context. The letter they were showing around was not fair. Yes, Key had said that the popular vote in Oregon was for Hayes—but he had also declared that the popular will in Louisiana, Florida, and South Carolina had favored Tilden. He clearly had supported the Democratic position in these three Southern states.[13]

Kellar always concentrated his political efforts on the few "swing men," the heavyweights in the balance of power. He now tried to capture support from the very hotbed of Harris Bourbonism

—from former Bate supporters in western Tennessee. Kellar extracted promises from four Bate backers to shift to Key on the Monday balloting—and to declare that shift at the point when their four votes would swing the election to Key. This move would ensure Key's victory only if the wavering Shelby County delegation would stay with Key. The Shelby delegates had all subscribed to a low-tax platform. In tax issues, they were more closely allied to Key than to Bailey, who was a high-tax man. So Lowe and Kellar, who were from Shelby County, spent the remainder of the weekend seeking out each member of their delegation and conversing persuasively. Kellar was also not above paying people off.

Some of the Shelby County people were drinking both Kellar's and Harris' whiskey, quite willing to take the best each had to offer. The Harris machine singled out three of the Shelby County men for sumptuous dinners at the Maxwell House and lavish entertainment in the special hotel rooms. They were also subjected to a constant barrage of talk about Key, the suspect Tennessean who had voted with the Republicans on the Mississippi election issue, the maverick who had jeopardized Tilden's election with his December speech in the Senate.

On Monday, when the balloting commenced in the already smoke-filled chamber, Kellar, Colyar, and Redfield were bleary-eyed from lack of sleep but confident that they had Shelby County. On the seventy-second ballot, the Harris forces carried out the first step in their strategy. Whitthorne's votes were thrown to Bailey, thus placing Bailey in the lead. In the balcony, Kellar relaxed in his hard seat, unperturbed by the goings-on, watching representatives aim at their spittoons. Once the Shelby delegation had cast their votes for Key, he would signal the remaining Bate supporters to follow suit. That would clinch the election.

The big moment came. The Shelby delegation voted. Kellar was aghast at the double cross. Three of the men went for Bailey! Kellar, the Memphis Fox, had been outdone by his own county. Kellar sat speechless, unable to comprehend how he had been outfoxed by Harris. On the following ballot, Bailey was elected, and the chamber broke into pandemonium.[14]

That night the lights of Nashville shone upon two despondent and tired men trudging wearily toward Maxwell House. As they tried to rationalize what had happened, Andrew Kellar and H. V. Redfield both saw the irony in this victory of Tennessee's old-line Democrats.

Kellar felt, and would write in his newspaper, that the election of Bailey "was the work of the machinery of the Democratic party, supported by the high tax and bond and railroad influences." The Bourbon machine had defeated Key, Kellar would editorialize in his paper, for "his statesmanship was not only Greek to them, but a stumbling block and an offense." On this night in Nashville, Kellar became a stoic; he felt that even in defeat, there was a certain victory for Key. Whether he believed it or not, Kellar later wrote in the *Avalanche* that already Harris had indicated that "his course in the Senate [would] be an endorsement of Senator Key, and on the same high road of Statesmanship. . . . It may well be said, now as hereafter, that he [Key] marked out a new road for Southern Senators—a road which both Harris and Bailey must walk in."[15]

Back at the hotel, Redfield dispatched to the *Cincinnati Commercial* his eloquent article in defense of Key, an article in which he truly expressed what he believed:

Senator Key has paid the penalty of being more of a statesman than a mere party machine. Senator Key's course in the Senate has done much to disarm criticism against Southern Democracy. Extracts from his speeches were used by the Democrats of the Eastern States as an accurate gauge of Southern feeling and temper. Here is a Southern Democrat, they say, a rebel Democrat, if you please, but see how he votes and talks. And the other side replied that Key was not a representative Southern Democrat and that he would, in all probability, be ousted when the Bourbon Democrats got a fair chance at him. And they were correct. Not only is Key defeated, but Isham G. Harris is elected. All this the result of having fifty thousand majority [in the Democratic party in Tennessee]. Had the State been close they would not have done so.[16]

Throughout the state rose a chorus of voices expressing similar feelings. The *Knoxville Chronicle* remarked bitterly: "If he had consented to wear a political straitjacket, fitted to his person by such illustrious managers as the editors of the *Nashville American* and the *Memphis Appeal,* he would in all probability have been elected without opposition."[17] Thomas Lowe, traveling back to his home in western Tennessee, found all along the way tremendous popular support for Senator Key among the people of the state. He was astonished to find this support not only among the liberals of the party but also among many strict Bourbons. There was a vast chasm, indeed, between what greedy Southern politicians said and wanted and what the people of the South truly believed and hoped for.

In his next letter, Lowe offered Key one great consolation. "I was at home during the recess of our legislature," wrote Lowe. "I never saw a people as unanimously for any man as our people are for you. . . . Our people were so willing and ready to approve your course which I feel was pursued by you for the sole reason that it was right. There is a bright future for you in Tennessee. You are stronger by defeat."[18]

Not quite so sure, Key had returned to his Chattanooga law office with its view of Lookout Mountain and familiar, bustling Market Street. It was good to be home among old friends, with Lizzie and the children.

# 14

## Lobby Tactics

Andrew Kellar returned to the coldest winter Washington had suffered in decades and to dismayed associates who could no longer plan for a Hayes victory through an alliance of Republicans and Southern Democrats. Meanwhile, Northern Democrats had initiated a renewed campaign of inflammatory tactics. In eleven states they had enrolled "minutemen" with the motto "Tilden or blood," and in early January they had arranged seditious and stormy mass meetings. On Jackson Day, January 8, nation-wide rallies were held, and a chilling chorus grew, chanting, "Tilden or blood, Tilden or blood." At Ford's Theater in Washington, Henry Watterson, the voluble editor of the *Louisville Courier-Journal*, shouted for 100,-000 volunteers to march on Washington to demand Tilden's election. Not to be outdone, Joseph Pulitzer of the *New York World* offered "to bare his breast to the bullets of the tyrant and rush headlong upon his glittering steel."[1]

In this impassioned, blind rush toward national disaster, some Southern statesmen had to speak out boldly for law and order. Dejected, Kellar sat in his office on Newspaper Row, his usually darting eyes staring stonily at busy F Street below. He was not able to concentrate on the sheet of paper on his desk. He dawdled aimlessly, and brooded. D. M. Key had lost his seat in the Senate, and his policies had been repudiated in the legislature of Tennessee —the most moderate of the Southern states.

Kellar saw only one way out of the national dilemma. He and Boynton had to work again behind the scenes. They had to arrange conferences among Western Associated Press people, confidential meetings with Tom Scott, and secret conversations with Southern representatives on Capitol Hill. But it was most important to arrange for persuasive communications with Hayes—the only Republican who could make certain necessary promises to the Southerners.

And so Kellar and Boynton set to work again. As the February days passed, success began to attend their shrewd, patient efforts. Paradoxically, this bleak crisis forced Hayes, though reluctantly, to follow the Kellar-Boynton plan. Hayes knew that support, even within his own party, was collapsing. It was rumored that prominent stalwarts such as Conkling and Blaine, never too happy with the moderate Hayes in the first place, would no longer support him in a showdown.[2]

Meanwhile, the Kellar-Boynton group found additional strength in an unexpected compromise reached by two great railroad tycoons, Scott of the Pennsylvania Railroad and Huntington of the Southern Pacific. Scott and Huntington agreed to support each other's requests for government subsidies. Now Huntington brought a third member into this unholy alliance—Jay Gould of the Union Pacific. Few pieces of railroad legislation could have withstood the united lobby efforts of these powerful, and usually divided, interests. Boynton realized the extent of this coup when he entertained Dodge and Scott at his house in mid-January and received Scott's pledge that his powerful lobbying machinery would set to work at once and press for railroad subsidies for the South and the West. There was a setback, however, when the proposed railroad bill, after being reported out of committee, went to the bottom rather than the top of the House calendar. But nevertheless the lobbyists were confident that Hayes, once elected, would get their bill pushed through.[3]

The congressional debate over methods of settling the disputed election now reached a climax. Fortunately, on January 18, the resolution Key had supported—for which the Harris machine had scourged him—resulted in a compromise bill establishing the Electoral Commission. The bill shrewdly side-stepped the controversial constitutional issue as to who was authorized to count electoral votes, and it gave the commission the powers of the two Houses acting jointly.

The bill was a major step in the direction Senator Key had advocated a month earlier. The Electoral Commission, established by an act of law, was an adequate vehicle to settle the disputed election according to constitutional, peaceful procedures. Thus reasoned Key, comfortably seated at the head of his dining-room table as he discussed the latest reports in the *Chattanooga Times.*[4]

The two Houses and the Supreme Court would each have five men on the fifteen-member commission. The three Democrats and two Republicans from the Democrat-controlled House would balance the two Democrats and three Republicans from the Republican-controlled Senate. The Supreme Court named two Republicans and two Democrats. The fifth man that the Supreme Court was to send to the commission would be the fifteenth member—the one who could upset the balance. This man was to be chosen by the four Supreme Court justices already on the commission. For this crucial place, the justices chose Judge David Davis, who was an Independent.

But history played its trick. On the very day that the bill was passed in the Senate, the Illinois State Legislature upset the neat compromise by electing Justice David Davis to the U.S. Senate. This left only Republicans among the remaining justices of the Supreme Court. The Democrats were flabbergasted. The justice who finally was named to the commission was Joseph P. Bradley, indeed a Republican, but one who had written several judicial opinions quite unsympathetic toward the interests of stalwarts.[5]

On February 7, the Electoral Commission was to announce its first decision; it would rule on the Florida returns. Abram Hewitt, that powerful iron magnate and chairman of the Democratic National Committee, sent John Stevens, a mutual friend, to Bradley's house to find out how Bradley would vote. Shortly after dark, Stevens sat down in Bradley's comfortable parlor and read, with great nods of approval, Bradley's prepared opinion, which favored acceptance of Florida's Democratic electors. Stevens departed about midnight and dispatched the glorious news to "Ironmaster" Hewitt. This news meant that Tilden would be elected.

Long before the gavel brought to order the joint meeting in the House of Representatives the following morning, the galleries were packed, and even famous personalities such as General William T. Sherman and historian George Bancroft pushed and shoved in the crowd to get seated. Everyone waited impatiently for the main act: the commission's decision on the Florida vote. Only Congressman Hewitt seemed surprisingly calm, confident, and in strikingly good humor. Then came the reading. When Justice Bradley's opinion was to be read, Hewitt happily listened and looked as if he were about to be served the *pièce de résistance* at a superb dinner. He fondly thought of Stevens and his obliging report.

But no! Hewitt suddenly was dumb struck, and sounds of astonishment swept through the House. The conclusion of Bradley's opinion, which first had seemed to favor the Democratic electors, clearly came out in favor of the Republican electors.

Rumor had it that Bradley had changed his mind as a result of a midnight visit by several prominent Republicans, and some gossips even spoke of bribes. Republicans smugly argued that poor Stevens had been too dumb to know that an experienced jurist, when formulating his decision, commonly writes two opinions. Stevens had merely read the wrong one. But whatever the details, the Florida vote was now Hayes's.[6]

For the Northern Democrats, one blow followed another. The commission then voted, again eight to seven, in favor of the Republican electors from Louisiana.

Tilden now quickly devised a new strategy, reasoning that these open Democratic defeats would reunite the disparate wings of the Democratic party. A filibuster would be the perfect stratagem, and the Southern Democrats certainly could not resist a good filibuster.

If the electoral decision could be dragged out beyond March 4, Grant's term would expire, yet Hayes would not be President.

During these weary, wintry days, Andrew Kellar and Henry Van Ness Boynton spent much time together. Together they walked along the cold streets and avenues, sat in the press gallery of the House, and carried their news releases to the Fourteenth Street telegraph station. They constantly discussed the political situation and sought ways out of the maddening maze. Colonel Kellar, sensing the new Tammany Hall strategy, recognized Tilden's great ability "to handle men like a Chinese juggler does daggers."[7] Would Tilden really throw his weight behind a party filibuster—even if that meant that there would be no U.S. President on March 5? Tilden now designated Dudley Field as the real leader of the Democratic Party in place of Hewitt. Just what did the switch mean? Kellar wondered. And in a final showdown, how effectively could Tilden corral the Southern Democratic vote? What concessions could Hayes offer that might satisfy the South and induce Southern Democrats to break with their party? If the railroad subsidy promises were not enough to satisfy the South, what would? What offer could be made, and what offer would Hayes agree to? Could the inner circle of Western Associated Press advisers convince Hayes to make a workable offer that would satisfy Southern Democratic congressmen?

One evening, after dining at the Imperial, Kellar and Boynton returned to the Washington offices of the *Cincinnati Enquirer*. As they were talking, the worried look vanished from Kellar's face. That evening, the Memphis Fox regained his animation and optimism, and his pulse quickened in impatient excitement. He had the answer: the key to the dilemma was D. M. Key. Key, in the flesh, was the solution to the national stalemate! Hayes could make a secret commitment to place Judge Key and possibly one other Southerner in his cabinet if elected. Key's honesty, courage, and devotion to the Union were beyond question. In his outstanding Senate speeches, it had been clear that his concern for the nation as a whole transcended sectionalism. Key had made his stand for the general good despite the tongue-lashing of extremists. If Key were to support Hayes, Hayes's appeal would certainly grow.[8]

A Democrat in a Republican cabinet was unheard of; it would be highly unorthodox. In George Washington's cabinet had been men who later took up different party labels, but the distinction had not existed when the cabinet was formed. Unprecedented, unorthodox as it would be, nevertheless it was just the kind of startling step needed. It would heal the wounds of war, and it might get the votes needed to elect Hayes. Not many Southern Democrats, if any, would cross this Rubicon of party politics. Lamar, for example, had dared not go to see Hayes in December when asked to do so. And even though he had merely sent Roberts as his representative, Montgomery Blair's *Washington Union* had immediately charged Lamar with intriguing to throw the Presidency to Governor Hayes in exchange for a position in the cabinet.[9] Lamar had been infuriated almost to the point of dueling with Blair. All that recent publicity would make the path across this political Rubicon even more difficult for any Southerner. But Key would cross it, so Kellar stoutly maintained, if he gleaned that his action would benefit the South.

Key, a man who could not be bribed or bought in an age of bribing and buying, would be an ideal symbol to induce the Southern representatives in Congress to swing their support to Hayes. On a pedestal of alloy, placed there by the unholy combination of politics and lobbies, Key would be the pure gold embodying the dream of peace and decency. If Key consented to have Kellar use his name, Kellar would drop the word to some of his intimate associates in the House that Key was willing to be part of Hayes's cabinet. At the same time, Boynton would have the Ohio Gang work on Hayes.

Needless to say, essential to the plan was Key's formal acceptance of this crucial role. Kellar told Boynton that he would rush a letter to Key at once. The friends had talked all night. Their hope renewed, they left the newspaper office.[10]

At Crutchfield House, in Key's home town of Chattanooga, Key persuaded Jefferson Davis to become involved in the quarrel over Tennessee's secession.

The Chattanooga railroad crossroad became an important point in Confederate strategy. Key's regiment on Cameron Hill (foreground) took part in its defense in 1862. Lookout Mountain is in the background.

Chattanooga, shown here in 1864, was a carpetbagger town when Key returned there after the Civil War.

## DEMOCRATIC REFORMERS IN SEARCH OF A HEAD.

This cartoon shows the feuding within the Democratic Party and also portrays the nation, in late 1876, as verging on a second civil war.

The Democratic Party was not only split over monetary policy in 1876; it was also dominated by Tammany Hall in New York City—to the increasing disgruntlement of Key and other Southern Democrats.

## UP IN A BALLOON.

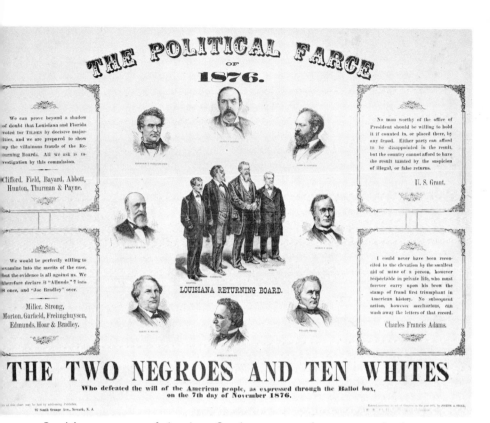

# THE POLITICAL FARCE
## OF 1876.

We can prove beyond a shadow of doubt that Louisiana and Florida voted for TILDEN by decisive majorities, and we are prepared to show up the villainous frauds of the Returning Boards. All we ask is investigation by this commission.

Clifford, Field, Bayard, Abbott, Hunton, Thurman & Payne.

No man worthy of the office of President should be willing to hold it if counted in, or placed there, by any fraud. Either party can afford to be disappointed in the result, but the country cannot afford to have the result tainted by the suspicion of illegal, or false returns.

U. S. Grant.

We would be perfectly willing to examine into the merits of the case, but the evidence is all against us. We therefore declare it "Allunde," 7 into 8 once, and "Joe Bradley" over.

Miller, Strong, Morton, Garfield, Frelinghuysen, Edmunds, Hoar & Bradley.

I could never have been reconciled to the elevation by the smallest aid of mine of a person, however respectable in private life, who must forever carry upon his brow the stamp of fraud first triumphant in American history. No subsequent action, however meritorious, can wash away the letters of that record.

Charles Francis Adams.

## LOUISIANA RETURNING BOARD.

# THE TWO NEGROES AND TEN WHITES
### Who defeated the will of the American people, as expressed through the Ballot box, on the 7th day of November 1876.

Louisiana was one of the three Southern states whose returns in the election of 1876 were disputed, involving it in charges of fraud.

Colonel Andrew Kellar, of Memphis, though a Democrat, had wanted to strike a bargain with the Hayes Republicans, but then Senator Key's moves became more essential to his plans.

The Electoral Commission, which Key and Kellar favored, was established in 1877, and a vehicle was found to validate votes without resort to war.

On March 2, 1877, former Union General Rutherford B. Hayes was declared President. Key's appointment to his Cabinet evoked charges of a secret deal.

The inauguration festivities of Hayes were resented by scowling Southerners who felt that Key was a Judas or Benedict Arnold.

The Hayes Cabinet, called a "bouquet of ugliness," did place Key with some strange partners. Left to right are: Secretary of State William M. Evarts, of New York; Postmaster General Key; Attorney General Charles Devens, of Massachusetts; Secretary of the Interior Carl Schurz, of Missouri; President Hayes; Secretary of the Navy Richard W. Thompson, of Indiana; Secretary of the Treasury John Sherman, of Ohio; and Secretary of War George W. McCrary, of Iowa.

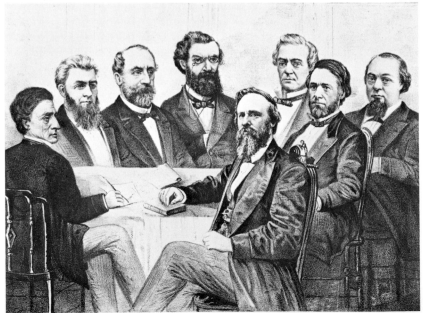

The above cartoon depicts the impossible task of any Democratic leader in the latter part of the nineteenth century. As a judge in Tennessee, and watching the growth of racism in politics, Key lamented the fate of the political parties.

The Republican Party was no better than the Democratic, but Key hoped in vain that it could find a leader to reestablish it in the South and offer a choice on racial and economic issues.

Key's last hope was in his unorthodox home town, where men like Adolph Ochs offered a vision for a new South.

General Van Ness Boynton, who had been an important behind-the-scenes lobbyist in the disputed 1876 election, is shown here in the 1890's, dressed again in uniform. He wrote Lizzie Key upon the Judge's death: "When the inside story of the policy looking to a more thorough reuniting of the sections becomes known . . . Judge Key will stand as one of the historic characters of an epoch in the life of the Republic."

# 15

---

## The Long Night

Chattanooga was on the main mail trunk line to New Orleans, and the train that puffed into Union Station about two days later carried Kellar's letter, which then was delivered to Key on the morning of the third day. Lizzie Key answered the friendly postman's knock, wished him a good morning, and walked with the mail to the sewing room. The sight of Colonel Andrew Kellar's return address made her speculate that the Memphis Fox must be up to some scheme involving her husband. What could it be? She could hardly wait for her husband to come home to find out what Kellar had written.

About 5:00 P.M., D. M. Key locked his tidy Market Street office and strode down the street toward home, cheerfully waving to fellow townsmen and tipping his beaver hat to the ladies. Suddenly, a mighty whistle blew, announcing that the "Last Chance," a riverboat, was approaching the dock. Key quickened his pace. He wanted to catch a glimpse of the busy crew as the gangplank was lowered and to exchange a few words with his friend Colonel Billy Nixon, the most colorful skipper on the Tennessee River. His lordly air and fancy gold-braided cap made a gaudy show for the townsfolk. Gregarious Billy Nixon always invited any of the "good fellows" who came down to the dock to his pilot's cabin for a glass of brandy from New Orleans. Panting heavily, Key reached Water Street. He called out a greeting to Billy, who asked him to come aboard. From a distance, Key heard the familiar calls of two little girls. He turned and waved to his youngest daughters. Elizabeth's blond braids and Sarah's red pigtails bounced and bobbed as the two little girls eagerly ran down the street toward him. They relayed their mother's message that he was to come straight home to read some important mail. With a talkative girl tugging on each arm, he dutifully turned toward the familiar red-brick tower of the Key house, visible across Fourth and Chestnut streets. Three abreast, they reached the spacious Key yard and marched down the walkway, bordered by ribbons of violet beds, now bleak with winter.[1]

At the door, impatient with curiosity, Lizzie Key held out the letter from Colonel Andrew Kellar. David chuckled about her inquisitive look, kissed her, and took the letter. He ran his finger along the top of the envelope and opened it. As he read it, the smile left his face. Waving the children off while still reading, he motioned Lizzie to follow him down the dark hall into the parlor. Key could not contain his astonishment. Again he read:

> I have not had an opportunity to write to you in regard to the liberty I urged upon your friends, after you left Nashville, in the use of your name in the Senatorial contest. I felt that a full tender had not been made to the party, and I desired one to be made. You were frank in your expression of confidence in me, and went so far as to say, the night before you left, that whatever I would do was right. Now, my dear Sir, will you permit me to exercise the same discretion again? The restoration of political good will, & the recognition of the South must go hand in hand. A reorganization of parties is inevitable, and in the interests of the Southern People, will you permit me to use your name? It is asking much, but I feel that I can do so, & will see to it that your public character will receive no hurt. Will you sanction my conduct to this extent? I may conclude by suggesting it will be desirable to have the South represented in the Cabinet and it may be in my province to aid in some degree to point out a representative. Let me hear from you both by telegram & letter. You may send a night message to 1209 F [Street] N.W. or letter to the same address.[2]

Most gentlemen of the Victorian age, as family heads, made their own decisions, ignoring their spouse; but between Key and Lizzie, there was a partnership uncommon to those times, although she habitually referred to him as "Mr. Key." So after rereading the letter, he handed it to Lizzie and turned to look out the big bay window, where the craggy peak of Lookout Mountain was basking in the red rays of the evening sun. On cold, clear February days, the wintry sky was deep-blue, and Chattanooga sunsets were well worth watching above Lookout's rocky peaks. There, thirteen years ago, Union soldiers had climbed about, preparing to attack the Confederate positions in the famed "Battle Above the Clouds," as it was called. Many an evening it seemed to Key that the light clouds, the sky, and the red sunset were still echoing the gray and the blue of the uniforms and the red of the blood of those who had struggled there and died.

Why had David McKendree Key lifted his musket against the cause of those Union men? Not simple, that answer. For the Confederacy? Something that now no longer existed? For principles— a theory of government, states' rights, the 1798 Virginia and Kentucky resolutions? This had been Key's easy answer in 1861, but what was it now, in 1877? Not that he considered the old theory wrong, states' rights false, the principles mixed. He still passionately believed too much centralization and dictation in Washington, too little power in the state and local government could rot the Republic. Vitally wrong about that war, Key had come to believe, was the evil way it had been provoked by selfish professional politicians and hotheaded extremists. They had not paused to consider the ill fate they would pass on to another generation. And "they" included Key, who had rejected Andrew Johnson's plea for the Union, willing to force fellow townsmen into the jaws of conflict.

Key still stood at the bay window. The colors had faded now, and night was falling. The mantel clock ticked on. Key could no more recall the details of those past mistakes than he could recall that sunset. But was the South on the brink of a new, worse mistake? Would there be no President on March 5, 1877? The Old World would look on and know that this experiment in liberty in the New World had run aground. Could Key refuse to lend his name as Keller had asked, when his acceptance might help break the deadlock and save the ship of state?

In accepting, Key might suffer political crucifixion. Congressman L. Q. C. Lamar, an honorable man, a conciliator in a partisan South for nonpartisan peace and justice, had refused to cross party lines as Kellar now asked Key to do.[3] And no wonder. For over a decade, the South had suffered under Republican tyranny and Northern injustice. The federal bayonet still was the law in three Southern states, and thousands of Southerners bitterly hated anything Republican.

Many of Key's best Chattanooga friends would be shocked to learn that he was contemplating a "deal" with Republicans. Many of them were staunch Southern Democrats, like the Van Dykes, who lived a block away from the Keys. Since 1872, Major Van Dyke had been one of Key's staunchest political supporters; but Van Dyke was a Democrat first, last, and always. His family still suffered from the ravages of war, and he would never forget that General Sherman had deported his grandmother to the North. Van Dyke would be shocked if neighbor David Key were to enter a cabinet in which Senator Sherman might also serve! Van Dyke would also recall that only last fall, Key, campaigning for Tilden, had told large Tennessee audiences that it was unreasonable to expect reforms under Hayes.

And so it would be whispered all over the neighborhood—a man of expediency, not of principle! A man who sold out to the East Terrace types who sported their Loyal Legion buttons in Washington and saw to it that the federal bayonet ruled the South! Key winced, thinking of these neighbors.

It would be hard to convince the majority of ex-Confederates that the Hayes Republicans might be setting out on a new course, a calm policy of moderation. To the permanently embittered, a man who would accept a position from the party of Thad Stevens, Charles Sumner, and Benjamin Butler would be considered a heretic and a turncoat. If he accepted Kellar's request, he would be called by these cursed names; from that there would be no escape, not even after his body rested in its grave.

Disturbed, Key shifted his weight in the hard mahogany chair. He was still gazing out of the window at the dark sky. His fears, his anxieties, hopes, and aspirations warred with one another. Key did not go to sleep that night. He paced up and down, pondering, thinking. At dawn, he knew what course he would take, regardless of personal consequences.

He would accept the offer of an appointment in the cabinet of Rutherford B. Hayes, Republican, former federal general—if there was going to be a cabinet. But on one condition: he would maintain his independent position and would not switch party allegiance. As long as the new administration pursued a liberal policy toward the South, he would support it and help to strengthen it. But if the administration failed to keep its promises of a progressive policy in the South, he would abandon it.

When the first sunbeams came into the east window, David Key wrote a letter to Kellar and scribbled out a short telegram. He walked briskly out into the morning air, and only a few moments later, the telegraph clicked off this message: "You may use my name as indicated provided no sacrifice of personal or political independence is required. Have written you."[4]

The long night of uncertainty was over; Key had made his decision, and many a Southern curse soon would plague Key's house.

The telegram from Chattanooga gave Colonel Kellar the needed authority to use Key's name in efforts to resolve the national stalemate that threatened to leave the United States without a President come March 5. The idea of appointing a Southerner to a Hayes cabinet, and even the thought of appointing D. M. Key, was not uniquely Kellar's. As early as January, one of Hayes's Harvard classmates had urged him to appoint Key to his cabinet, calling him "the best man from the South in Congress, and a very moderate man for a Democrat; but he is a Democrat."[5] With such recommendations, Key or any other Southerner could scarcely attract Hayes's attention in those days of crisis. Nevertheless, the Tennessee senator was a logical choice for those who had followed the decisive December debates. What would be more fitting than to include this representative of the South in the new cabinet, the first who had proclaimed the Southern electorate's demand for peace, in the spirit of the Constitution? But Kellar was indeed proposing a novel plan: to use the appointment of Key to form a coalition in Congress, a coalition that would make Hayes's election possible.

Kellar urged William Henry Smith, leader of the Ohio Gang, to intercede for Key's appointment. If Hayes agreed to appoint Key, then Kellar would "take the aggressive and warmly cooperate with Governor Hayes, & help to lead the conservative national citizens of Tennessee, Arkansas, & Texas." He warned that the decisive moment would soon come, after the Louisiana vote was counted; for then "all the evil influences of Tammany Hall will culminate on Oregon & revolutionary acts will be attempted."[6] Hence, Hayes must act now on Key so that Kellar could effectively pursue his plan.

Once Kellar had set the spark, the news spread rapidly throughout the capital's inner circles. Influential Southerners caucused in Senator Alcorn's Washington home. They commissioned Major Waldron to convey their request to William Henry Smith that Key be given a cabinet post, and they suggested that Key be appointed postmaster general. Thus, they said, Tennessee, Arkansas, and Mississippi willingly would follow Key in support of Hayes. All this Smith quickly passed on to Hayes. The influential publisher of the Chicago *Tribune* also wrote to Hayes and presented the idea of Key's appointment, pointing out that Key had wide support within his state and that Tennessee "is the Key of the Southern situation."[7]

Meanwhile, Congress was a topsy-turvy affair, with the Hayes forces on top one minute and the Tilden forces on top the next. Still, the Southerners held the balance of power, for a protracted filibuster would mean no President at all when Grant's term expired. Then a Pennsylvania Democrat made an effort to repudiate the

Electoral Commission, and Northern and Western Democrats joined him. But the tone Key had set in December had converted some former fire-eaters, and men like Ben Hill of Georgia attacked this move as revolutionary. The former postmaster general of the Confederacy moved that the filibuster be ended and that the count of the electoral vote proceed. Tammany Hall leaders gaped when the Southerners gave this move almost solid support. Kellar's new coalition was working, for he had let it be known that Hayes was about to agree to Key's appointment to his cabinet.

Democrat Congressman Randall called a caucus to lead an attack on erring Southerners. He charged that some Southerners had bargained with Hayes, the very man who would surely rule the South with bayonets; any Southerners who could be party to such bargaining would surely be ruined. While such charges of treachery were permeating the smoky air, Randall suggested that the caucus members initiate a House amendment proposing that the Secretary of State be acting President while another election was held. But the caucus majority voted to postpone action on Randall's resolution until after the Oregon vote was counted.

The crisis was at hand. In the dark hours of February 21, Colonel Kellar, extremely alarmed, made his way to the house of Congressman Foster of Ohio. He pointed out that Hayes's silence on his future Southern policy blocked the defeat of Tammany Hall, that the Tammany men taunted Southerners by saying, "Under Hayes, you have nothing left but unconditional surrender to the Republican Party and its past policy." Kellar insisted that Foster, who was from Hayes's district, speak out publicly and at once on Hayes's Southern policy, before the Northern Democrats began another filibuster.[8]

Foster reluctantly agreed, and while he prepared his speech, the tireless Kellar dashed off another note to William Henry Smith, again urging the appointment of Key to the cabinet as postmaster general, traditionally the controller of patronage. Kellar was sure that "if only the distrust existing between the Southern members and Governor Hayes's friends could be removed, Tammany Hall would shake to its foundaitons."[9]

Foster made his speech. He proclaimed that the "flag shall float over the States, not provinces; over freemen and not subjects." The new administration, he claimed, would "wipe away any and all necessity or excuse for the formation of parties on a sectional basis and all traces of party color lines."[10] The following day, Smith informed Hayes that Kellar's work had been far more effective than anticipated and that Kellar "hopes for the appointment of Senator Key to a cabinet position as being the thing that would at once settle the South."[11]

A definite and specific understanding was reached with Hayes on Key. The appointment would be made. The word could be spread by the lobbyists among those whose votes were needed to tip the balance.

Without further opposition, the decisive Oregon vote was counted; the Electoral Commission accepted the three votes for Hayes, following the same logic Key had used in his speech of December 18. From then on, the Northern Democrats conducted a rear-guard action. Boynton had wired W. H. Smith the details of Key's background so that he could give them to Hayes. Kellar assured Key by letter that he would be offered the cabinet post of postmaster general, that Hayes had read the letter Key had written to Kellar stating his conditions, and that Key should hold himself in readiness to come to Washington.[12]

The bitter fight in Congress was over. The Southerners, all except the die-hard fire-eaters, were satisfied. Key was to be in the cabinet. The remaining votes were counted without serious difficulties. But, like a chicken's body running wild after the head has been chopped off, there were still the flexing of muscles and frenzied movement in various directions. Finally, the last effort for a filibuster ended in a swan-song speech by a fire-eater from Kentucky. He cried out that on this Friday the end had come, that Southern manhood spurned any plea of mercy. On another Friday, he continued, "the Savior of the world suffered crucifixion between two thieves"; and on this Friday, "justice, honesty, fair dealing, manhood, and decency suffered crucifixion amid a number of thieves."[13]

At four o'clock on the morning of March 2, Rutherford B. Hayes was declared the duly elected President. A Georgia newspaper editorialized:

> The South . . . was ready and willing to fight as she was when she sent forth her sons to battle . . . she was ready, at the first tap of the drum, to follow the Democracy [Democratic Party] of the East and West in any sort of movement to defend and preserve them. But the drum-tap was never heard . . . the line was broken, and the men responsible for it have literally "played with the devil."[14]

One of those who had made this possible, one Southerner who had "played with the devil," was at his Chestnut Street house in Chattanooga busily packing for a trip to Washington, while Lizzie and the excited, wide-eyed children helped.

As the newspapers discussed the possibility that Key might be appointed postmaster general, Southern reaction remained mixed but emotional. The *Memphis Appeal* furiously criticized Key's decision to accept the cabinet post.

> A few hungry office-seekers, ready to take service in the party that pays the most, will endorse this treachery of Key, but with the honest masses, the true and reliable Democracy of the South, his course will find no favor. As Postmaster General, the creature of a usurper, sycophants and parasites will swarm and cringe about the seat of ill-gotten power, but Key will live to learn by experience the disgrace he has brought upon a name once honored and respected by his country.[15]

The *Gallatin Examiner* attacked the *Appeal* editorial and praised Key as a citizen, lawyer, soldier, judge, and senator. The *Examiner* cited Chatham, Fox, and John Bright as British examples of statesmen in a government of the opposition. The paper noted that still greater justification for Key's unorthodox appointment lay in the fact that now, for the first time in more than sixteen years, the South would have cabinet representation. Thus, D. M. Key had answered the duty of the hour.[16]

At the same time, many letters and telegrams demonstrated that his course had won over many and had even tamed the hearts of some radicals and fire-eaters. One old Confederate wrote to Key: "It is true that at first I thought it would be wrong in any Democrat to lend countenance to so stupendous a fraud as that which has been perpetrated on our people by the Republican Party, [but when men like you] think differently, then I think differently."[17] In Memphis, the Chamber of Commerce met at the Cotton Exchange and voted overwhelming support for Key's appointment. *The New York Times* said: "Let Mr. Hayes have credit for this rising above his party." And the *Cincinnati Gazette* called the appointment "a tender of a pretty large olive branch" to the South.

In the face of stormy accusations from party regulars that he had embraced an administration that wanted to destroy the Democratic Party in the South, Key minced no words when he told the press that "peace and prosperity are of greater importance than party success" and that he wanted to see "the color line in Southern politics broken."[18]

# 16

## The Postmaster General

Later in March, Lizzie and the children had every room piled with big trunks as they packed amid the music of a serenading brass band and a continuous stream of callers. Some of the ladies who were not among the visitors wagged their tongues about a sellout to the Republicans as they passed the Keys' house on Chestnut Street, but waved and smiled when they caught a glimpse of Lizzie or the girls above the geraniums in the windows.

A few days later, the older Key children arrived at Ebbitt House, much impressed by this stately structure at the corner of Fourteenth and F streets. The Ebbitt was certainly a grand hotel, far more elegant than the Imperial, and filled with distinguished admirals, generals, and celebrities like Mark Twain. The Key girls were fascinated by the hotel's ornate façade, its five floors of windows, and the fancy gilded mansard roof, from which many American flags were flying, as if every day were Independence Day.

Soon the girls explored the hotel—the oblong Crystal Room, which ran the entire length of the hotel's Fourteenth Street front; the grand stairways and new elevator; and the hall leading to the basement room, full of cigar smoke, where the gentlemen drank whiskey. They heard much talk about Washington's prominent figures and its young people, such as the gallant Webb Hayes. Nine-teen-year-old Emma listened with much interest. With her black hair, her sparkling eyes, and lovely personality, she now had grown into a charming young lady.

As D. M. Key watched his daughters invade Washington society, often arm in arm with the beautiful Sherman daughters, he thought how things had improved since the days at Mrs. Shedd's boarding-house and even since his stay at the Imperial. If only his financial situation had improved as well! Lizzie still blamed the war for their lack of money, and much of Key's postwar earnings had gone into the upkeep of their comparatively fine brick house in Chattanooga.

In early March, Key and Lizzie set out to inspect houses for rent in Washington, Lizzie declaring that it had to be a large one to accommodate their big family. The least expensive suitably furnished large house they could find was available for $2,500 a year; it would cost the new postmaster general one-third of his salary. This would hardly leave enough money for Lizzie to keep house in the style of a cabinet member's wife. So they resigned themselves to keeping part of their family in Chattanooga and to staying on at the Ebbitt.[1]

Lizzie Lenoir Key, with her aristocratic background, plunged into Washington's social responsibilities, quite different from the way her homespun husband had reacted upon his arrival in the capital as a senator. She promptly got a brown leather book to record and check off the dozens of names for her regular Tuesday and Thursday calls. For prim Lizzie, it was a welcome relief that the new First Lady, Lucy Hayes, was sweeping the White House clean of the lush trappings of the Grant era. Lizzie was glad to see Mrs. Hayes discourage the famous getup of society queens and disapprove of bustles, long trains, elaborately frizzled hair, and emeralds and diamonds hanging down low-cut dresses. Mrs. Hayes, with her old-fashioned hairdo, her high-necked black silk dresses, was ridiculed by some people, who called her "Lemonade Lucy"; for on her instructions, liquor and wines were barred from the Presidential mansion. Gone was the shoddy magnates' "Vanity Fair," their cham-

pagne and terrapin suppers, not only from the President's house
but from all of official Washington society. Yet, Lucy Hayes
charmed Lizzie and many other visitors with her warm smile and
unaffected Midwestern ways.[2]

However much Lizzie admired "Lemonade Lucy's" abstinence,
Key had not lost his taste for good bourbon and poker. Neither
had the new Secretary of State, who was responsible for the proper
entertainment of the diplomatic corps. Secretary of State Evarts
tried to reason with Lucy, but Lucy was adamant, and the Women's
Christian Temperance Union presented her with an ice-water pitcher
to express their approval. But soon thereafter, unbeknown to Lucy,
someone worked out a splendid compromise. At the "temperance
banquets"—amid the untainted perfume of innocent flowers, on the
table loaded with delicacies—oranges were piled high on large
serving dishes, and there, concealed beneath the healthful fruit, was
potent iced punch, spiked with Santa Croix rum. This strategic
hiding place became to Evarts, Key, and many others the "lifesaving
station."[3]

Not all vestiges of the corrupt and flashy Grant era had vanished
from politics. Clever James G. Blaine tried to stage a new drama
by holding up Key's Senate confirmation as postmaster general.
Blaine rose to the chamber floor and, with a flourish of oratory,
quoted a passage from Key's December speech in which he had
stated that "any attempts to count on Hayes and Wheeler must, if
successful, result in the overthrow of Republican institutions." It
was a deft master stroke. With a censorious air, the inimitable
Blaine took his seat, and indeed Key looked like an inveterate
opportunist.[4]

To obstruct Key's appointment, the radical Republicans arranged
for all names of new-appointment nominees to be sent to committee
for approval. Lamar, Hill, and Gordon, in the best tradition of
Southern chivalry, rushed to the Tennessean's defense; so did much
of the press, even many Republican papers. Blaine, Conkling, and
Cameron gave up their opposition when they realized that their
tactics, though applauded in Congress, were called obstructionist

on the outside. Yet, two fire-eating Democrats refused to the end to vote for the so-called Judas of their party.

No one was more jubilant over Key's success than Colonel Andrew Kellar, who believed that the appointment of Key confirmed that Hayes would now bring about "a general smashup" of the political machine. But this smashup of machine politics, which was tied to the color-line issue, had to be accomplished quickly—before the politicians of the Democratic Party blew the bugle and waved the bloody shirt to close ranks again. The fluid alignment of liberal Republicans and moderate Democrats had to be cemented into a permanent coalition, perhaps even into a permanent third party. But as the early March weeks flew by, Hayes falteringly delayed action on the withdrawal of federal troops from Dixie and the restoration of the South to its full position within the Union—and at the very time when quick action was needed to win over the distrustful Democrats.

March 20, 1877, was to be a day of cabinet meetings, and the new postmaster general gave special attention to his attire. He put on his best frock coat, tie, and overcoat. Yet, despite this elegance, he walked out of Ebbitt House wearing his favorite old beaver hat. Key would not relinquish it for more fashionable headgear, though a reporter had recently described it as the worst-looking dicer ever seen, out of style four years, three sizes too small, and set way back "on the top of his iron gray bristles." Yet, Key was supremely happy wearing this chapeau as he strolled down F Street to the White House, only two blocks away.[5]

As was customary, the cabinet members arrived at the White House carrying portfolios containing reports relevant to the problems to be discussed. At noon, they were all assembled in the upstairs Cabinet Room, which was furnished with an enormous gilded mirror above the fireplace and a piano in one corner. There would be about fifteen minutes for greetings and amenities, and Key soon came to use the time to tell his Tennessee stories and jokes.

The group in the Cabinet Room was varied indeed, and one

embittered radical accorded it the appellation "a bouquet of ugliness." Tall, thin, serious John Sherman was the Secretary of the Treasury. Key and Sherman had developed quite a warm friendship despite their less friendly encounters in former days on the Senate floor. Representing the most liberal Republican wing was the Secretary of the Interior, German-born, red-haired, red-whiskered Carl Schurz, who vied with Key in storytelling. Schurz enjoyed telling stories in every dialect except his native German. Secretary of State William Evarts, who was hated by the radicals and admired by Key, had defended Andrew Johnson during his trial. His homely, unusual face looked as if it were made of brown parchment. It was said that "to see him look sideways out of his carriage is to regret that Hogarth is dead."[6] The Secretary of the Navy was tall, silky-haired Colonel Richard Thompson, who always came to the White House wearing a black silk hat and carrying a cane, both symbolic, perhaps, of his old-guard interests. Well-dressed Attorney General Charles A. Devens was a splendid if overly loquacious speaker and a partner in an eminent law firm. George W. McCrary, the Secretary of War, was sponsored by the lobbyist General Dodge and railroad magnates Tom Scott and Jay Gould.

Whether or not the cabinet was a "bouquet of ugliness," it was indeed a coalition of strange bedfellows, although even Blaine admitted their over-all ability.

The most pressing problem faced by the cabinet at this moment was the crisis in Louisiana caused by its two opposing governments—Packard's and Nicholls'—which both claimed to be legal. Key, along with all other cabinet members except Devens, adamantly stood against using force to uphold the carpetbag Packard government, but proposed sending a six-man investigating commission to Louisiana. Key recommended that John C. Brown, former Tennessee governor, be a member and that Colonel Kellar accompany the commission.[7] The appointment of this commission was a major decision, one that was to affect the future of the Hayes Administration. Yet, as the cabinet members departed from the

White House some time later, they seemed little aware of the significance of their decision.

When the commission arrived in Louisiana, Kellar, the old Memphis Fox, was up to his old tricks. With a handful of money, he bribed enough legislators to desert the carpetbag Packard government and join the Nicholls legislature to help give it a quorum. By April 20, the Nicholls legislature had legal recognition, and four days later the federal troops were ordered back to barracks. The old bells of New Orleans tolled, and torchlight processions continued late into the night.

Thus, a month and a half after Hayes had entered the White House, the occupation of Louisiana and the reign of the carpetbag regime ended at last. To Colonel Kellar, a dream had become reality. As he enjoyed the evening breeze, he watched "the close of the night of the Reconstruction" and "the dawn of the Restoration Era." He wrote to Smith: "Before two years shall have passed, there will be a new earth & a new heaven, and the carpetbagger and old secession leaders will have passed away."[8]

But Kellar's dream was in vain. Hayes's delay and initial procrastination had allowed emotions to boil, and Southern fire-eaters had undermined the confidence of the Southern moderates led by Lamar and Hill. The very idea that the administration had formed a commission to examine and deliberate on the Louisiana controversy rather than simply withdrawing the troops was to Lamar and other Southern moderates "a declaration of doubt" on the President's part. The fact that Key had had Brown added to the commission was not enough to appease them. The delay also antagonized the radical Republicans, who wondered what Hayes was doing. Thus, Hayes was caught in the middle, losing support from both sides.

In the trying days ahead, the postmaster general failed to grasp the problem as clearly as did Lamar. Key too had to walk a tightrope, held at one end by extremist Republicans, at the other by extremist Democrats. And he was without his closest political associate, Andrew J. Kellar, who was in Memphis or New Orleans when Key was most in need of his political acumen. Together they might have worked toward the "new heaven" and the "new earth," but a political combination such as theirs during the election months was not to occur again.

Kellar soon met with acute financial difficulties, which were not accidental but were brought by the concerted efforts of the Bourbon machine to destroy him. The followers of Isham Harris did not forget easily, and they "got" Kellar by ruining him financially. Kellar kept much of his troubles from Key but told him that he was unavailable for any appointment from Hayes, which indeed saddened the postmaster general. Key would have been deeply distressed had he known that Kellar, as reverse followed reverse, would be washed from the center of Key's political life into an endless sea of financial and personal troubles. The Harris machine had wrought its vengeance on Kellar and now would aim it at Key, who was a good target and a bit naive about the methods of cunning men.[9]

Hayes had heard that Southern Republicans were sliding over to the Democrats, and that many Southern Democrats were outraged when he nominated Negro Frederick Douglass for marshal of the District of Columbia. In a mood of frustration, Hayes wrote in his diary: "If a liberal policy toward late rebels is adopted, the ultra Republicans are opposed to it; if the colored people are honored, the extremists of the other wing cry out against it."[10]

Key should have recognized, and maybe he did, that Hayes's political dilemma was similar to Andrew Johnson's. Johnson had tried to create an alliance of moderate Democrats and moderate Republicans, yet Johnson had failed because he was dilatory. Now Hayes was about to fail for the same reason. And what of the attitude of the new postmaster general? What was Key doing while precious political moments were fleeting away?

For one thing, he was unpacking and getting adjusted to his new quarters at the Ebbitt. During those harried early weeks in March, when his appointment was being confirmed by the Senate, he had not been in the best position to bring up the Louisiana question to Hayes, a man he did not yet know. And at first he might have taken it for granted, as had Lamar, that Hayes would immediately withdraw occupation troops from the South. But Hayes did not act. Had Key demanded that Hayes act immediately or risk the Tennesean's resignation, many of the Democrats who had swung toward Hayes because of Key's appointment might have been completely won away from the Southern machine.

Lamar later wrote to Hayes: "Had your order been issued [to withdraw the troops] the day upon which your cabinet was confirmed, not one man in the Republic would have been surprised."[11] Hayes failed partly, as Kellar put it, because he was distracted by the legions of favor-seeking delegations trooping into the White House. But Key too must bear a portion of Hayes's failure to act, although he might have argued that he had hardly met the President and that he was too busy at the time moving into Ebbitt House, replying to piles of letters, and meeting the initial demands of the gigantic Post Office Department. Key had many virtues, but a keen sense of political timing was not always among them. He now was in need of his advisers—Kellar, Brown, and Redfield. But after the triumph of Key's appointment, Key was not adequately in touch with them.

About three o'clock one March afternoon Key left Ebbitt House and walked the few blocks down crowded F Street to the Post Office Building. As he ascended the wide entrance steps, he admired the tall Ionic columns; he preferred the simple, classical lines of the building to the elaborate style of the new edifices springing up around it. Key noticed the restaurant across the street, remembering with pleasure the good oysters served there—one of his favorite dishes.

In the building, he entered a large two-story-high room, where all the clerks from the various Post Office divisions were now assembled. This was indeed a handsome hall, with its tiered, ornamented balconies, columns, black-grilled railings, and rows of impressive desks and swivel chairs. This morning the former postmaster general, James Tyner, gave his farewell address and introduced the new one, David McKendree Key. Now Key too was called upon to address the assembly. As often when speaking informally before a crowd, he felt slightly bashful as he faced his new co-workers.

He confessed that he felt some embarrassment, still being a stranger in the Post Office Department. He told the assembly that any personnel changes—and he intended to make few—would be made only "for good and sufficient cause." He now raised his voice more confidently and announced that the criteria for selecting appointees would be fitness for the job and character and that a postmaster who had satisfactorily served his four-year term would have the opportunity to serve again before another applicant was considered for the job.[12]

The audience, which included several reporters, filed out of the tall doors in a hubbub. Key's words were like dynamite, for this department was known as a vehicle of large-scale patronage. The postmaster general had the power to hire and fire thousands of postmasters, special agents, and mail carriers. He controlled more than 27,000 post offices and the mail-service subsidies for state coaches, railroads, and steamships. Since the days when Andrew Jackson had instituted the spoils system, the postmaster general had been called the "cabinet politician," for he controlled the most gigantic patronage organization in the nation. Grant's first postmaster general, John Angel James Creswell, for example, had promptly fired all postmasters who did not support the radical Republicans. "McCormick's reaper," bitterly commented one newspaper, "which is covered all over with medals and stars, would leave twenty heads standing where Creswell leaves one."[13] In one state, a man became party boss sheerly by using his powers as postmaster in one of the largest cities. Thus, during the Grant Administration, the Post Office Department became an adjunct to the Republican Party's campaign committees.

When liberal Republican reformers like George William Curtis and Carl Schurz made an issue of the need for civil-service reform,

Grant appointed a semireformer, Marshall Jewell, as postmaster general. When Jewell refused to acquiesce to the demands of party politicians, one of them commented, "Why, God damn him! He runs the Post Office as though it was a factory." Eventually, Grant could stand Jewell's "annoyance no longer." He demanded his resignation and ordered James Tyner, the second assistant postmaster general, a seasoned politician, to report to the White House. "I have decided, Mr. Tyner, to ask for your resignation," Grant had quipped while flicking his inevitable cigar, "and to appoint you as postmaster general."[14] One newspaper cracked about this protégé of Senator Morton: "Tyner was appointed, not to see that the mails were carried, but to see that Indiana was carried."[15] Tyner performed just that function; he saw to it that the Indiana delegation supported Hayes in the primary. And during the election, Tyner raised record political contributions from government employees who wanted to keep their jobs. No wonder D. M. Key's new policy pronouncements echoed strangely through the department's high-ceilinged assembly hall.

After this ceremony, ex-Postmaster General Tyner walked with the crowd down the narrow halls and strode out of the south entrance of the building that had so long been his bailiwick. At the bottom of the stairs, Tyner walked toward a fancy carriage in which a heavy-set gentleman was waiting for him—Senator Morton himself. The driver opened the door for Tyner, and the two men sat there and chatted as the shadows lengthened and carriages and streetcars clattered by.[16]

Hayes had not granted Morton's request to retain Tyner as postmaster general, yet Tyner was merely leaving the Post Office Building by one door to go back in by another. He would be appointed first assistant postmaster general. The announcement would be made two days later, and Tyner would insist that Hayes retain in office the second assistant pstmaster general, General Thomas W. Brady, another of Morton's Indiana lieutenants. Brady was as well practiced as Tyner in using his powers to levy campaign contributions. These two politicos would certainly be able to give

Key "advice." After all, Morton and Tyner chuckled, both Hayes and Key had much to learn.

The two men shook hands. Tyner said good night and stepped out of the carriage, which then went clattering down the street.

Democrat Key was in a peculiar position among such Republican colleagues. True, the new postmaster general said that he was glad to have the assistance of Tyner. Key knew that he could not expect to choose all the postmasters in the Republican North and East; the best he could hope for was to temper patronage with an effective merit system. Although Tyner may have originally been appointed to see that Indiana rather than the mail was carried, in his earlier years as a special Post Office agent he had gained detailed knowledge of the department, and as a member of Congress he had served on the Post Office Appropriations Subcommittee. In line with his stated policy, the new postmaster general wanted to make changes only for good and sufficient reasons, and experienced hands were to remain in the department. Thus Key saw the situation; it is doubtful that he could have changed it had he rationalized it differently.

One day, Key heard a growing chatter of Midwestern voices in his outer office. Soon, his secretary ushered in a group of postal clerks who had been discharged by their postmaster and were demanding that he be fired for his lack of party loyalty. The burly Tennesseean fired back that "the post office is not a political institution. . . . If anyone, whether he supports or opposed the administration, neglects his duty by being a busy politician . . . he ought to be removed. But if he attends faithfully to his duties and makes a good and acceptable postmaster he should not be removed, though he sees fit to oppose the administration." The plaintiffs sourly filed out of Key's office, and the new postmaster general's use of the merit system had passed its first test.

Other such cases followed. When a newly appointed special postal agent complained to Key that his widespread postal-inspection duties interfered too much with his party duties, the irate postmaster general issued a stinging reprimand. The agent had not been "appointed to organize and build up an administration party" but "to do the work of the Post Office Department. You serve your party best by doing that work, and I shall take great pleasure in removing an agent and reducing the force when I discover that he has time to attend to party organization and party discipline."[17] The removal of this special agent was to have repercussions.

Many people were jolted by this attitude. The *New York Tribune* commented: "It is no marvel that sensible views like those of Mr. Key shock gentlemen who have been educated to believe that the Post-Office is primarily a party prerequisite and only incidentally a means of distributing mail matter." The *New York Graphic* editorialized that the dream of George William Curtis, Joseph Medill, and Carl Schurz had come true: "Civil Service Reform is really a tangible something at last. Secretary Key has buffeted one of his special agents in a manner that will make the head of every party Ring-master in the country ring with pain."[18]

This was only one set of reactions. A sharp young female writer, Gail Hamilton, charged that Key's daring war whoop of reform, "shouted out in public" to the special agent, was not quite loud enough "to drown the sibilant echoes" of what he had told his brother: that if the Southern Democrats continued to oppose the administration, "the President will be compelled to use his official patronage in such a way as to give him strength in his own party; whereas, should Southern Democrats wisely extend him a support, he will be able to deal his patronage to them liberally."

"Gail Hamilton, acting under the impression that every Key should have a hole . . . is now engaged in filing [Key] down," charged the *Cincinnati Enquirer;* "the most suitable Key hole, in her estimation, . . . would be six feet by three in the Knoxville cemetery." The *Chattanooga Times* vehemently protested that Knoxville was not Key's hometown, adding: "We don't care for Gail. She may buzz like a hornet and sting the Judge if she likes."[19]

Criticism and ridicule of Key rapidly began to mount. The post-master general was plagued by facetious critics even when he quietly traveled down to Pokowamico, a pleasant and secluded spot in Virginia, for a few days of shooting. There, a reporter of the *New York World* bird-dogged Key and produced quite a yarn.

A Negro hackney driver had lost Key's suitcase, which contained his clean shirt, trousers, and treasured demijohn. The postmaster general therefore had been forced to wear the clothes in which he had rooted about in the swamps when some Virginia politicos asked him to an important gathering. Key complained to the reporter (so the reporter said):

> Then I had in the portmanteau a demijohn of Kentucky Bourbon—and such Bourbon! Emancipated spirits in a happier sphere may have had better whiskey, but I doubt it. That's gone too, probably has irrigated the internal improvements of a nigger who can't appreciate the difference between Robertson's county whisky and turpentine with a dash of pain-killer for bitters—which is about the average of Pokowamico liquor. I wrote for another demijohn of it, and I'll be cussed if I can understand why it hasn't come.

Key had also dispatched urgent letters to his wife for new supplies of clothes and underwear, according to the reporter.

Next day, the story continued, Key went to the post office and asked in vain after his parcels. The local postmaster offered his official superior the facilities of his little back office to write more letters to the liquor dealer and to Mrs. Key for clothing. Key had scarcely seated himself at the desk when he "bounded into the air with a spontaneity and exuberance which, as Mr. Murat Halstead would say, were both 'exemplary and memorable.'" Thinking that Key's heavy frame had come down on a bent pin, the postmaster profusely apologized.

But the postmaster general, purple with wrath, had spied his two previous letters, unmailed, on the desk. Key was quoted as saying: "What in the name of Satan do you mean by delaying the mails in this manner? . . . Are you a blind asylum and the whole average

of illiteracy in the Southern States? Isn't the address on this letter
as plain as the nose on Secretary Evarts' face? Answer me, you wall-
eyed swamp angel."

Thereupon the postmaster proceeded to quote Key's own regulations stating that no one but the sender had the power to change
the address on a letter, pointing out that Key's letters had been
addressed to Washington but not to D.C. Therefore, according to a
second set of Key's regulations, they were destined for the dead-
letter office. Then the *World* reporter vividly described how the
postmaster general immediately threatened to take action against
the postmaster, who protested: "Nice sort of civil-service reform
administration, where a postmaster gets bounced for obeying regulations he has been peremptorily ordered to follow!" The *World*
correspondent satirically related other adventures of the postmaster
general, all reflecting his postal reforms.[20]

Key indeed found himself on the horns of the dilemma of reform
versus political patronage when he tried to develop Southern support and to break up color-line politics. These were noble but conflicting goals. Key believed that Hayes had to use patronage powers
to develop Southern support, and perhaps by now he had begun
to realize the great damage done by Hayes's failure to withdraw
the occupation troops from the South immediately after his inauguration. The following fall, Congress would be reorganized as a
result of elections, and this would test whether the liberal Republicans and progressive Southern Democrats could turn their temporary alignment into a permanent alliance and smash a Solid
South based on the race issue.

Key would not pervert the Post Office Department's essential
mission to carry the mail—not even to aid this political maneuver.
Yet he believed, of course, that it was ethical and possible to find
competent Democrats to fill mail carriers' positions and other Post
Office vacancies. Once appointed, however, their job was to deliver
the mail, not votes. Key was aware that such appointments would
win Southern Democratic support for President Hayes in the House.

This was a plausible approach to his dilemma, at least in theory.

As the follow-up to the nation-wide issue that Key had created by firing the special agent, President Hayes sent this order to all department heads: "No officer shall be required to take part in the management of political organizations. . . . No assessments for political purposes on officers or subordinates shall be allowed."[21] Infuriated old-time Republican politicians demanded to know just how the party could function, since so many of its active party members were government employees. Soon Key's desk was stacked high with inquiries about interpretation. The postmaster of Madison, who was the political boss of all Wisconsin, contrived to puzzle and annoy Key by reporting that four of the five members of the Republican State Executive Committee were postmasters. Would the postmaster general explain whether the calling of the convention by the Executive Committee would violate Hayes's executive order? Until he received a cabinet ruling, Key replied, each official should interpret the order for himself; his own interpretation was that merely calling a meeting, as opposed to attempting to control its organization or future action, did not violate the President's order. At the meetings in the Cabinet Room, the postmaster general submitted such cases for rulings, and the cabinet usually agreed with Key's interpretation.[22]

Key, as usual, found himself raked on one flank by the radical Republican bosses and on the other by the Tammany and Southern hotspur Democrats who feared that Hayes-Key political policies might sabotage their machines and crack up the Solid South. The *Montgomery Advertiser,* for example, painted Key as a man ostensibly speaking high-sounding reforms but actually offering "a bribe of 'office' to Southern Democrats in exchange for their support" and threatening them with "a continuation of carpeting misrule if they refused to make the bargain." The *Knoxville Tribune,* which was often sympathetic to Key, now attacked his appointment policy as "Reform without Reformation." When there was a flurry of rumors that Key might be appointed to a Supreme Court vacancy, the *Tribune* applauded this as the heaven-sent solution to Key's increasingly impossible personal position as postmaster general, a job in which "his intentions are liable hourly to misinterpretation. He cannot write a letter of good advice to a complaining or unruly subordinate ... without being charged with 'doing the soft-shoulder work' of the Administration." If he appointed a Democrat, the *Tribune* continued, the Republicans howled; if he appointed a Republican, he was called the tool of Tyner. "He was a clear-headed Chancellor and he would be a just Supreme Judge."[23]

Rumor followed upon rumor. It was said that Tyner, darling of the radicals, would replace Key as soon as the Tennessean was appointed to the Supreme Court. It was said that the radical Republicans had the upper hand over Hayes and would soon demand the resignation of Evarts, Schurz, and Key—that Key would be pushed out and would not be appointed to the Supreme Court. The *New York Herald* asserted that the country would not tolerate the dismissal of these men, that if the Republicans escaped defeat in the autumn elections, it would be because of the presence of men like Evarts, Schurz, and Key in the administration.[24] The *Savannah News* maintained that even if the Northern radicals forced Key's resignation, they could never return to policies destructive to the South; even Blaine, the arch radical, would hardly be willing to defy the clear majority of voters who now objected to such policies.[25]

Key was undismayed, plowing ahead as if he were back on Parson Key's eastern Tennessee farm. Southern patronage was his special province, although he frequently interfered with Tyner's Northern patronage projects when the question of ability or character was involved. Both Southern internal improvements and Southern patronage were necessary if the administration was to control the House and, ultimately, to realign the parties there. Hayes was slow to grasp this and to understand the overriding need to grant Key complete authority in doling out Southern patronage. However, his closest advisers saw it. The ex-leader of the Ohio Gang, William Henry Smith, clearly pointed out this need in his letter to the President of March 22, 1877:

. . . a wide and wise discretion given to Sen. Key now would enable him to so organize things in the South as to give you control of the House anyhow. The same rules of civil service cannot be applied to the South at present as to the North. There must first be an adjustment suited to the new order of things. Wholesale changes are not necessary. But a weeding out of disreputable and objectionable men *at once* seems to be desirable to prepare the way. Key must know how—he certainly can get the men to search out reputable & conservative citizens for the places. Post offices conferred on country merchants, & on county editors would improve the service & put citizens in better humor. Such action would render *nil* the efforts of desperate Democrats North and South who gain only by political turmoil, & who are now preparing to make a desperate attack on you to break you down.[26]

Despite Smith's urging, Hayes persisted in a nation-wide patronage policy giving preference to Republicans in appointing postmasters. Key referred many letters from the South to the President. He showed Hayes, for example, a letter from the chairman of the Virginia Democratic Executive Committee, a newspaper publisher, who had written to the postmaster general in March about the need for a conservative party in the South to replace the radical Republicans. "Mr. Hayes has it in his power now to build up such a party," he wrote, "but my dear Sir *you know* it cannot be done with the *material* of which the *Republican Party* of the *South is composed,* the *native* 'scalawag' is as objectionable as the 'carpetbagger.' "[27] Key also gave Hayes a clipping from the *Lynchburg Virginian* that said that the South had too long been the "football" of the Democratic Party, that Southern conservatives should support Hayes and not let Blaine "bulldoze" the President.[28]

For ten years, Lynchburg had had a "carpetbagger" postmaster who, Key learned, had shown no interest in the community and had "excited the hostility of the colored race against the white." In this case, Hayes finally backed Key in having the carpetbagger replaced by a Democrat. In a similar case in Petersburg, Virginia, another qualified Democrat replaced a carpetbagger. A townsman commented that "the community here rejoiced & hurrah for Key first and Hayes second." In Richmond, an incompetent postmistress —appointed by Grant reportedly because she had been a federal spy during the War—was replaced. In Kentucky, Key had so many Democrats appointed to government positions that Republicans complained to the President. Hayes replied timidly that "an occasional Democrat appointment will not hurt. . . . Possibly a mistake. But good men advised and I suspect it will not hurt."[29] When rumors increased that such Republican criticism was causing Hayes to end Democratic appointments, the President, writing to an old Southern friend, denied it; but, he added, "of course I shall appoint Republicans generally . . . you understand me."[30] Although a clear-cut strategy was needed to win the South, these were days of vacillation.

One newspaper estimated that during Hayes's first five months in office, he bestowed one-third of all Southern appointments upon Democrats.[31] But for fear of antagonizing radical Republicans in the North, Hayes granted several notorious carpetbaggers outstanding appointments, such as that of Consul at Liverpool. For this job, the expense account alone was said to involve a higher sum than the salary of the President. Hayes ruined his chances of gaining support in the South by failing to give Key the authority that William Henry Smith had urged he must have, authority that Kellar had been assured would be given to Key. Whatever power Hayes delegated to Key was the result of Hayes's growing confidence in Key's personal statesmanship rather than the outgrowth of a consistent strategy to win support in the House and realign the parties in the South. Key had indeed protested against Hayes's apathy, but his protest was neither adamant nor decisive enough to matter. Again, Key sorely missed the support of a liaison of men like his old associates Kellar, Smith, Boynton, and Redfield, who might have moved Hayes to action.

# 17

## Erring Brethren

Through his letters, his many meetings with politicians and press, and his addresses from the speaker's rostrum, Key carried on a running dialogue with the South. When it concerned the touchy issue of Southern political traditions, the controversy of this dialogue was accentuated by the curious combination of Key's personal philosophy and the public image he projected. This Southern Democrat, serving in the cabinet of the President he had once accused of lacking the legal right to that office, seemed suspect to many people. He was often represented as a paragon of expediency, a political opportunist—an oafish and garrulous one at that—who nevertheless had managed to be clever politically. Actually, Key was exceedingly modest and too void of personal ambition and diplomatic acumen to achieve real political effectiveness. Despite his unusual insight into the tides of his time, rarely was he politically clever, once separated from Kellar.

But at all times, Key was determined to destroy the power of vindictive politicians who manipulated the South by incitement of racism and sectionalism. Key used every conceivable occasion to fight the self-seeking cliques that plagued the Southern states. Key felt that a moderate middle course had to be found, and if it was not found soon, the strife between extremist segregationists and extremist reformers would make it impossible for men of common sense to congregate on middle ground. He had often spoken out against radical Northern Republicans; but during his first year as postmaster general, he hammered away at the Isham Harrises of the South on many a speaking trip.

Key made the first of these trips in the late spring of 1877. The Southern skies would be bright with sunshine one moment, dark with clouds the next, and sudden showers would chase away expectant crowds at the railroad stations. Key traveled with the Postal Commission to one Southern town after another. The more he investigated the postal system and its relationship to commercial development in the South, the more clearly he understood the situation. He traveled hundreds of miles by train, stopping off at stations and whistle stops to talk to postal agents, businessmen, and politicians. On these trips he confirmed his pet theory that a bit of peace and prosperity interested the masses of Southerners far more than their machine politicians' loquacious, honey-coated slogans and shibboleths about moonlight and roses and the good old days of the antebellum South.[1]

Key's theory was that one of the ways to accelerate the development and prosperity of the South was to speed up the mails. In business transactions, saving time was saving money. And the people who ordered goods from the firms along the postal routes had to be able to depend on quick, efficient deliveries. Key hoped to speed up such postal service and to extend parcel post into the mountain regions of the South. By bringing the mail to these isolated areas, education was advanced too, through the delivery of newspapers, magazines, and books. In these objectives of industrial and educational development and better federal services, Key saw the future of the South—not in the defense of an outmoded agrarian system that had hastened the South's defeat at Vicksburg and elsewhere.

To the machine politicians, Key's pet theory seemed powerful enough to blow asunder their self-serving political system. In many parts of the South, it seemed to the politicians that such developments would threaten the whole Southern way of life—and their own political careers. To stay in office, they had to stoke the fires of Southern discontent, fanning sectionalism, demagoguery, racism, and backwardness. There were, of course, more legitimate problems disturbing Southerners. But Key was convinced that in his home state, for example, Isham Harris and his machine did not voice the problems and aspirations of the farmers, storekeepers, and businessmen who wanted to get ahead economically. They wanted to think of the Civil War now as part of history and to let time work out the race issue. In 1860, Harris already had misrepresented the voice of a small vocal minority as that of the majority of the South. Key well understood that deception. He had helped to perpetuate it in 1860.

In a crowded, hot, spittoon-cluttered courtroom in Knoxville, a town with a real future in manufacturing and commerce, Key hit hard at some of the sacred cows of the South. Perspiring, gesticulating with his big hands, he explained how the Northerners had shrewdly worked to increase the postal routes in the North and East, a salient fact that explained in part the prosperity of these areas in comparison with Southern poverty. Each Northern village, each settlement had a mail route. During the past twenty years, the Northeastern star-route mail services, the horseback and stagecoach routes, had been vastly increased. During the same period in the South, such service had even been cut back, and this had helped to impoverish many a once great Southern town. Key banged the rostrum as he told the crowd how unjust it was that government service had been increased in the North and East and had been curtailed in the South.

The audience cheered: Bully for Key! He had the rebel fire left in him yet! The North and East, as usual, had done them in.

But then the postmaster general fixed the blame, much to everyone's surprise, squarely on the Southern machine politician. His closely cropped hair seemed to bristle as he continued. "We of the South have been fighting on abstractions, while those of the North were working on businesslike principles. Where we have been politicians, they have been statesmen. While we have fought for abstract issues, they have gone on establishing mail routes and improving their facilities for doing business."[2]

Key continued to belabor the Southern machine as he mopped his brow with a handkerchief. Some of the audience now scowled, but others continued to applaud heartily. To the businessmen and storekeepers, Key made sense; but to those who depended on the political machine, Key was just plain dangerous. In Knoxville's *Tribune and Age,* a reporter commented: "The South, if let alone, will demonstrate in the next ten years that she is entirely capable of attending to her own business and that she does not seek or want gratuitous advice . . . if the South is poor today . . . it is because of the supremacy of the carpetbag government."[3]

The *Knoxville Chronicle,* however, retorted that Tennessee was indeed about the poorest of the states but that this could hardly be ascribed to carpetbag government. The state legislature had always consisted predominantly of Southerners, and all the governors had been native Tennesseans. Charging that the legislature had been dealing in "abstractions" for the past seven years, the article urged Tennessee representatives in Congress to combine their energies "to secure appropriations for our rivers. Let us have a Southern Pacific Railroad, improve our Southern harbors, do something to build up Southern commerce." The *Louisville Commercial* asserted: "The Postmaster clearly has the Key of the whole matter. The solid-South school loves to oscillate between abstractions and distractions."[4]

Key boarded the special postal train for Washington and left the Southern press to carry on the argument. In late summer, before the journalists had simmered down, he was preparing to travel northward for another tour. Lizzie again dutifully packed his clothes. She had just sent off Emma and Kate, who did not like to leave the busy social life of Washington, to Mrs. Lefebre's school in Baltimore, and Albert, who looked like a Prussian in his midshipman's uniform, had gone off to the Naval Academy.

The postmaster general had been invited to make this trip with the President, who was also accompanied by Mrs. Hayes, Secretary of War McCrary, loquacious Attorney General Devens, who was by far the best-dressed member of the group, and Secretary of State Evarts, whom the Northern radicals hated as much as they hated Key. Decked in red, white, and blue bunting, the Presidential train was a colorful sight as it steamed toward Rutland and Windsor. The Presidential party traveled through New Hampshire's White Mountains and the Green Mountains of Vermont. They visited the industrial centers of Manchester and Nashua, where great puffs of smoke rose skyward—a taunting symbol of the industrial development that the postmaster general craved for the South.

At every stop, they were greeted by expectant crowds. Trumpets, sounded, swivel guns were fired, and enthusiastic welcomes were shouted, resounding through the countryside. Everywhere, the President's party was feted with receptions, ovations, processions. The postmaster general delivered speeches wherever they went, often in a humorous vein, enjoying his own folksy humor and the bantering back and forth with Hayes in a battle of wits. At one stop, the President, in a very serious vein, introduced Key as the man who "did not fight with us in the war and who voted against me in the last election, but who believes as we do."[5]

In the opera house at Nashua, New Hampshire, and in Concord, the postmaster general spoke at length and before great crowds of people, many of them workers from the mills and printing works. He told the people in Manchester about the economic interdependence of the North and South. It was the same cotton that made the great factories of Manchester hum and Southern farms stay prosperous. To gain broader markets would be to the advantage of both, and the gulf that separated North and South—once based on sectionalism and slavery—would soon be breached forever through common enterprise and cooperation. Of course, both sections had their problems of keeping law and order, as the lawbreaking mobs in the recent railway strikes had demonstrated in the North.

Key's style took. "The presence of Mr. Key in this portion of New England," wrote one Vermont reporter, had "its effect in harmonizing differences and bringing into accord the President's policy

even with many Republicans who stood aloof." The more Key
spoke, the more he was lauded by the Northern press and criticized
in the South. Down in old Cotton Town, the *New Orleans Picayune*
called the trip a case of "The Lecturer and his Illustration," and
said that in New England, "where people were skeptical of the con-
vertibility of a Rebel, Hayes, the exponent of the Southern policy,
was exhibiting Key, the living proof of its efficiency." Then the
*Picayune* attributed these thoughts to Hayes:

> See this man! A few years ago he was clad in gray . . . his ears
> drank the music of the rebel yell. . . . He remained a Democrat after
> the war . . . stood on all the planks of every Democratic platform,
> even that of St. Louis, which charged Seymour, Greeley and Tilden.
> He voted against me. For all that we know he still believes . . . that
> my inauguration was the consummation of the most gigantic fraud
> on record. Yet there he sits, perfectly harmless. . . . He has accepted
> a place in my Cabinet, and meets with me, and Mr. Sherman, and
> Mr. Devens, in consultation with all the composure of Daniel in the
> lion's den.[6]

Another New Orleans paper, the *Daily Democrat,* expressed the
opinion of many of the city's aristocratic families who lived along
lush St. Charles Avenue: "We wish to say as plainly as possible that
Postmaster General Key is misrepresenting the South and Southern
sentiment in the spectacle he is making of himself as the illustration
of the beauties of the Southern policy."

In tobacco country, the *Louisville Courier-Journal* saluted the
political courage of this Democrat in a Republican cabinet. The
paper noted that "the circumstances attending the inauguration of
the President were sufficiently equivocal to make any compromise,
except that of lawful submission to constituted authority, an im-
propriety. For this reason the official tub which Mr. Hayes proposed
to throw to the whale of public opinion went begging until Judge
Key accepted it." Amazingly enough, this was the paper of the same
Marse Watterson who had wanted to lead the South to a second
civil war less than a year earlier. The *Courier-Journal* said that Key

had taken "his political destiny in his hand, put up his political life at a venture," and that his New England speeches were the best anybody had made. "So long as Judge Key does nothing worse than talk peace and good will upon the line of generous concessions on both sides, he will hold his own and can afford the sneers of those who never drew a sword or set a squadron in the field." This could have been a side jab at Isham Harris, who grew more scornful of Key's antics as each day went by.

But it was the radical Republicans who tore hardest at Key during his initial New England speeches. To the papers that adored the influential Oliver Morton and the Adonis-like Roscoe Conkling, the Key-Hayes alliance could not be tolerated. The *Chicago Times* compared it to a temperance revival, with Key the human stave snatched from the rum barrel and on display to give confessions between drinks. "Key has been groveling in the gutter of democracy. He has been a political reprobate of the very worst kind." Asserting that Key had been both a rebel and a Bourbon senator, "the sum of villainies," the *Times* pointed out that he had worked and voted for Tilden. "Among themselves the Hayes people decided that, as they wanted a Terrible Example in the cabinet, they would lift this fallen creature from the political slums in which he had passed his life. . . . They made him Postmaster General."

Such clippings his personal secretary passed on to the impassive Key. After studying them, he puffed out his cheeks and his heavy jowls, grunted a little, and passed them back to the secretary to be firmly pasted into a scrapbook.[7]

While the Presidential train chugged along its way through Vermont, Key had time to think back and recollect. Often he was seated near Evarts, the homely, brilliant lawyer who had defended Andrew Johnson in the famous impeachment proceedings. Key and Evarts often talked of their mutual admiration for Johnson. Now these two had been the subject of personal vilification by radical politicians who had once aimed to discredit the Great Commoner. Evarts and Key recalled how Johnson had been determined to represent the true feelings of the majority of the common people, when the Isham Harrises of the South and the Roscoe Conklings of the North were determined to block such representation. Key knew that Conkling and his allies were determined that Northerners should not know that most Southerners wanted to put the war behind them. To prevent reconciliation, Conkling would never cease to wave the bloody shirt.

Key still wore the same battered beaver hat that had accompanied him into every fight. His wiry hair was gray now, and his face had aged and toughened since he had made the Mississippi elections speech. His experiences had affirmed his old insight that men in Washington had two faces—one that stirred emotions to advance their political careers, another proclaiming quite different private attitudes and opinions.

On this trip, at one stop, the great virtuoso James G. Blaine had rushed with outstretched arms to greet Hayes and all his party. But Key had conditioned himself to be undaunted by friendly hand-shakes that might be followed the next minute by political blasts from both radical Republicans and fire-eating Democrats. He was fed up with the extremists on both sides; they all were a menace, trying to close the vise on the people in the center. He was determined to be above sectionalism, to read the people in the North and in the South alike, and to expose the fact that these politicians were not speaking for the majority, but for ambition's sake were prostituting public office.

Key gazed out of the window of the train at the rolling farm-lands, the steep red roofs and white fences of neat farms, and the prosperous factories near the towns. How different all this was from the gnarled, impoverished Tennessee countryside. Then his gray eyes turned back to the scrap of paper in his hand that he was trying to steady against the jiggling of the train; he was making a note or two for his next speech. The next stop would be Bennington, a landmark in American history, familiar to him from his boyhood history books. There, the Green Mountain Boys, led by General Stark, had defeated General Burgoyne's raiding forces and found immortality. Key was to speak at the anniversary celebration of the battle, before a record crowd of New Englanders. Like Stark, he was trying to win a battle, a battle of ideas instead of muskets. His aim was to disarm his listeners so that they would lay down their prejudices and suspicions and understand that the South did not want another civil war.

But how could he, in one speech, break through hostility and prejudice planted in New Englanders by skilled politicians over a span of years? Key wondered. He, an ex-rebel colonel, would be standing next to the former Union General Hayes. Perhaps he would be able to make light of the prejudices fostered by the Mortons, the Conklings, and the Blaines. After all, the people could see for themselves that ex-rebels were not sinisterly conspiring toward a second civil war but were hoping to make a new life for the South and the whole country. Here was one, they might say, who had spoken against war during the disputed election. Key would beguile them by saying that surely they had "kindly feeling toward the erring brethren of the South." Looking back, he had long felt that the Civil War had been a tragic mistake; now he decided that it was high time for him to admit it publicly. This in itself should help to dispel suspicions toward the South. And what better, what more historic time and place than at the centennial celebration of the Battle of Bennington—a battle fought in a war that had not been a mistake?

This was on Key's mind as the train pulled into the decorated station at Bennington. He had been so occupied with his thoughts that he had not finished the notes for his speech. In the drizzling rain, the crowd stood below a sea of umbrellas. They waved as bangs of dripping cymbals and blares of wet trumpets greeted the Presidential party. The guests were presented with bouquets of flowers. They soon climbed into waiting coaches that would take them to a New England home, where they would spend the night.

The following morning, the rain had stopped. Hayes and his party—seated in luxurious carriages, escorted by columns of police, and followed by a five-mile procession—drove to the battlefield.

Expectations heightened as cheers joined with a sudden brilliant breakthrough of the morning sun.

When Hayes, Key, and Evarts mounted the platform to join the other speakers and guests of honor, they faced a crowd of 40,000 New Englanders. There was the usual flurry of introductions by the local leaders, and then the President spoke.

He was followed by the postmaster general. "A rebel in the late war," people whispered. Reporters never were able to get Key's exact words because of his funny, slurring singsong dialect. His speech was short, but he made the 40,000 listeners laugh and cheer and almost come to tears as his loud hillbilly voice boomed out a few words of humorous ridicule of all their suspicions and preju- dices. Here he was, he cried in his deep baritone, the monstrous ex-rebel colonel whom the man now by his side, Rutherford Hayes, had put into his cabinet. Surely, his generous listeners must have some kindly feelings about their "erring brethren." Who did not now think that the Civil War had been a mistake?

Then he spoke of the Battle of Bennington, of the common heritage of all Americans, of the interdependence of North and South, of their common future. He expressed the true feelings of the majority of Southerners, he told them.

The 40,000 voices swelled in cheers, and hands pounded ap- plause, louder even than that given to President Hayes, and the stocky Tennessean took his seat again on the rostrum.

If Key was right, thought the people, the wavers of the bloody shirt, the Conklings and the Blaines, were wrong. If this man was a typical Southerner, if Southerners were really eager to put the war behind them, how blind Northerners had been.

Waves of the friendly, festive crowds surrounded Hayes and Key and followed them to the ramp of their train. For a farewell, they were showered with confetti, flowers, and cheers. People were still waving and cheering as the engine gained steam and the train puffed out of Bennington. Key stood in the aisle and chatted with Evarts and Devens as the porters prepared the berths. He still felt the tingle of excitement, still heard the cheers of 40,000 New

Englanders as the train rolled through the Green Mountain country, bathed in the evening's last sunlight. Key's thoughts were still with the friendly crowds in Bennington.[8]

That same evening, the telegraphs clicked out reporters' accounts, sending out the news of the day all over the nation, to Maine and to South Carolina alike: Key hald told 40,000 New Englanders that he was one of the "erring brethren," that he had helped lead the South into the unfortunate Civil War, and that now he declared that war to have been a mistake.

Mistake! Erring brethren! From South Carolina, the first state to secede from the Union in 1860, the *Charleston News* indignantly fired back: "Erring be hanged. . . . They did not err. . . . They were right." Key was the Uriah Heep of the South, declared another paper. Key was "eating to much humble pie," snapped the *Baltimore Sun,* and then labeled him "this wretched craven playing the part of a whipped spaniel." The *Galveston Civilian* angrily asked where Key got his authority "to speak for the people of the South during his swing around the circle with the 8 by 7 President? Will Mr. Postmaster Key tell us where and by whom he was empowered to say that the South had made a mistake in attempting to secede from the Union?" The Texas paper characterized him as obsequious, lacking in moral courage and principles, and as a fawning sycophant who had a right to speak for no one but himself. Even the usually loyal *Chattanooga Times* was embarrassed over the hometown senator. In publishing the speech, the paper had deleted the word "erring," making it appear that the postmaster general had said something quite harmless. Later the editor, when taken to task, hastily explained that he assumed the telegraph company surely had made an error in including the controversial word "erring."[9]

But this was not the deepest cut of all. In Cincinnati, a reporter tracked down a tall, well-built visitor from Tennessee—Governor James D. Porter. In manner and appearance, the governor was the prototype of a statesmanlike Southern gentleman. It was he who had sent Key to Washington in the first place. The newsman sat with Porter in the rotunda of his hotel, and, after some talk about other things, the conversation turned to Key. The handsome governor met the questions full face. Yes, D. M. Key had been speaking out of turn, a trifle too much. The South did not need this kind of apology, Porter said, repudiating Key.

Many moderate Southerners agreed with Porter. A place, a time, and a way could be found to accomplish everything; but to many Southerners, Key's place, time, and way were in poor taste, seeming groveling and even disgusting. They had liked and respected him, but they had never expected his sometimes strange but well-meaning conduct to go to such lengths. It appeared that Key had indeed gone too far, that he no longer had the support of the majority of Southerners, not even that of the more moderate Southern politicians.

As criticism grew, embarrassed Key supporters tried to excuse that disputatious word "erring" as a typical display of the postmaster general's well-known humor. Of course, he did not really mean it! The *Bristol News* said that Key, "while being exhibited as a live-caught Southern catamount, falls into the President's happy way of joking over it. . . . Key replies in a jocular vein, and, of course, he humors the joke. The cold print in which his speeches are quoted cannot do justice to the humor of the occasion, and Col. Key has suffered somewhat in the public estimation in consequence."

Similarly, the *Austin Statesman* observed that Key's joke of presenting himself at Bennington as one of the "erring brethren" brought so much laughter that Key delightfully repeated the successful phrase at Lake Winnepesaukee and, "with mock-heroic solemnity," pronounced the lines of the hymn "And while the lamp holds out to burn, the vilest sinner may return." This produced great merriment, maintained the *Statesman,* "and though this fact is stated, so eager are the 'Radical' papers of all sorts to find fault with a Democrat in Hayes's cabinet that they pronounce Key's utterances those of abject cowardice."

Key was deeply disturbed and disappointed as he read these clippings. He was a jokester—at least he tried to be one. In his New

England speeches, he had indeed mixed humor with seriousness, but he would have none of this apology. Despite the attitude of his friend and adviser James Porter, he determined to set the record straight and to continue hammering home the erring-brethren theme in speech after speech throughout the autumn—and, if necessary, without humor. Somehow, his humor had soured.[10]

But there were also newspapers that defended Key. The *Staunton Virginian* asserted that "Key has the courage to say what he believes, and very few dispassionate men will differ from him." The *Virginian* reasoned that those who believed that the South had not erred must maintain that the Union ought to be dissolved and a Southern Confederacy established, with "slavery as its chief cornerstone, to be followed, in the course of time, by a Western and Pacific Confederacy. Is there a sane man in the South now who will not say this would have been an error?" In Alabama, the *Opelika Weekly Times* said that if the postmaster general was guillotined on the next day, he might "place his hand upon his breast, and *consistently and truly* say, I have done well. I have risked obloquy and suspicion. But I have . . . assisted in the freedom of my native South." Halstead's *Cincinnati Commercial* editorialized that perhaps Key had committed

> political hari-kari, but if he has done so he selected a spot on this round globe than which none other could be more appropriate for a patriot. When American citizens of the year 1977 assemble on the battlefield of Bennington to celebrate the heroic virtues of General John Stark and the Green Mountain Boys, they will also remember that it was there that a Postmaster General . . . went so far as to admit that the South erred in its attempt to overthrow the Union of the fathers and found upon its ruins another Republic whose cornerstone was to be human slavery.[11]

When Key returned to Washington, to the Ebbitt House Hotel, and to Lizzie, he gave her the job of putting the proliferating clippings in a scrapbook. This served a double purpose, for as they sat together in their parlor suite, they could analyze again the effects of

Key's speeches, and what real good they were doing. The more they analyzed the more Key became convinced of the good will created in New England by the visit of a one-time Southern rebel. Then it came to him. Why not a former Union general, now President of the United States, visit the South? Hayes must break through the politicians' curtain and directly reach the people in the South. It would take some courage on Key's part after some of the adverse publicity in Dixie, but Key would be his host. Lizzie could not have agreed more. She would entertain the President in the Chestnut Street house in Chattanooga.

Some weeks after the grand Presidential tour was in progress, David Key sat in the elaborate Presidential train car across from Hayes, studying his expression. It seemed one of pleasure, despite the extra jogging of the train as it wound its way through the Tennessee mountains of the Cumberlain plateau, near where Key as a young chancellor had rode horseback. So far this tour had been an unmitigated success. The President's reception in Kentucky and Tennessee was living proof of what Key had been preaching: machine politicians like Harris were obviously not expressing the true feelings of the people of the South.

Key had in hand some clippings to give Lizzie in Chattanooga for the scrapbook. Even the *Knoxville Tribune,* which had been calling Hayes the "pretender" and "His Fraudulency," suddenly gushed praise, which led the rival *Knoxville Chronicle* to comment: "Now, isn't that a remarkable change? . . . We feel like taking our newly-converted 'erring brother' by the hand and bidding him God-speed." A reader of the *Memphis Appeal,* a former Tilden supporter, entreated one of the pro-Harris papers to changes its ways, recommending that every Southerner lay aside his prejudices and meet the administration's overtures "in the honest, manly spirit with which they have been offered." As another newspaper said: "The truth is, that the practical and business interests of the people are coming to the front. Men are getting tired of weary disputes, which only delay prosperity. They want something better; something which will bring bread to the hungry, wages to the workman, life to the mills and mines, and profits to capital."[12]

Key and Hayes mulled over the Louisville visit again. All business had been suspended. A bodyguard of 400 Confederate veterans, led by General Basil Duke, had escorted the President and postmaster general, who were greeted by the governor of South Carolina, General Wade Hampton. In Nashville, they had been greeted with wild cheering and a salute of guns, and soon Hayes and Key, in elegant carriages, were on their way to the capitol. Then came the highlight for Key. Governor James Porter greeted them. The governor's cordial smile and warm handshake alleviated some of the sting of his earlier remarks about Key's speech at the Bennington centennial celebration, as Key recalled with pleasure.

As the Presidential train approached the mountains and ridges of Chattanooga, Key had hoped to explain the relationship of the terrain to the battle once fought there. Small drops of rain started to beat on the window panes. They arrived in Chattanooga in a heavy downpour, and, though it was noon, it was as dark as dusk. The Presidential party kidded Key about the bad weather as the train slowed down and the familiar bell rang out. The rain was pouring down in torrents as the dignitaries entered Union Station. Beneath the black, red, and green umbrellas that lined the ramp, Key found his lifelong friends. Soon Hayes, Key, Evarts, and Hampton were escorted through the station and down Market Street, where the buildings were decorated with drenched bunting.

Since the four speakers were quite accustomed to one another's wit and idiosyncrasies by now, the round of speeches that followed was like an old-fashioned Methodist love feast that Parson Key might have conducted. The audience was an responsive as the Parson's converts had been. Ill feelings his old neighbors might have harbored toward Key were nowhere evident.

Under the frosted chandeliers that evening, 300 guests sat at three long tables at the Stanton, which once had been Crutchfield House. Some of Key's best friends and old neighbors had debated whether to attend that dinner in honor of General Hayes, and some

had come merely out of deference for their old friend Key—not
for the new Key who served under the fraudulent President and
called the honorable Confederate cause an error. But as the applause and the shouting increased for Hayes and Key, even these
old die-hards cheered.

The beaming postmaster general was toasted. "His neighbors,
who know him best," one of the speakers said, "honor and trust him
most." On this night of good feeling, it would have been easy for
"Judge" Key, as his townspeople called him, to speak in a jocular
mood and avoid controversy. But he would not do so; it was a point
of honor. For the Chattanoogans, he had serious words. He felt he
had to render an accounting and talk right to the core of the
prejudice in some of his dear old friends. As the audience hushed
and every head turned toward Key, he stood as straight as a rod,
his big barrel chest out, and in a good-natured but bitterly serious
way explained his position.

At Bennington, he had been cheered even more than the President, he told these Chattanoogans, and he glanced apologetically at
President Hayes, who sat by his side. The New England crowds
had come out to celebrate the centennial of a Revolutionary battle
and to demonstrate their love for those who had bravely fought in
the War of Independence. There had been immense good feeling
toward him—not only toward him personally, but toward Southerners as a whole, Southerners as fellow Americans.

Key paused, and his gray eyes looked searchingly at the attentive
audience. There he saw Governor Porter and many others who had
recently responded to him with embarrassment and disapproval.
He then told the assembly that he knew his remarks at Bennington
had elicited kindly and brotherly feeling toward the "erring brethren" of the South and that this sentiment of brotherhood and
sharing in the traditions of the Republic had motivated the audience to overwhelming applause.

Key then said that he had been surprised to learn that his speech
had not found approval at home, even right there in Chattanooga.
He said he had entered the Civil War as heartily and vigorously as

any man; as he saw it then, it was a right and unavoidable war. But in retrospect, he knew he had made a very serious error. And this he confessed standing almost on the very spot where, nearly seventeen years ago, Bill Crutchfield had passionately pointed out that error in his arguments with Jefferson Davis. Crutchfield, his hair still as red as ever, his eyes shining, his mind full of memories, was there before him now.

"It was an error," Key said, his voice rising with emotion, "an unfortunate error, as the numerous widows and orphans, the 500,000 graves, and the public debt, which we all have to pay, and no result accomplished, could testify." The only good to come out of the war, he concluded, raising his big right hand in the manner of old Parson Key, had been the freeing of the slaves. But for that the South had not fought, Key flatly retorted, as he stuck out his big chin. Then he added some general remarks, a sweet dessert to follow the heavy dish he had just served.

Rounds of applause followed, and President Hayes especially beamed with joy "at the demonstration of approval and esteem for the man whom he called to his Cabinet . . . who has been criticized more than any other member."[13]

The rest of the trip was an anticlimax for David Key—even the mammoth receptions at Atlanta, Knoxville, and Lynchburg—but he was more convinced than ever that rabid newspapers, machine politicians, and gossip cliques who pretended to represent the opinion of the South voiced only the attitudes and desires of a tyrannical and influential minority. Key was now certain that his new insights, the realistic prospect of cooperation and development, could lead the South to a far brighter future. This Presidential tour through the South had been balm to his hope. In this moment of happy triumph, he apparently never considered that the cheering of his fellow townsmen and the warm endorsement by Porter and his old neighbors at the foot of the East Terrace perhaps did *not* fully reflect what many of them really thought either of him or of his ideas.

# 18

---

# The Brink of War Again

So often did he roam through the Washington streets and byways, like a Tennessee mountain cat unaccustomed to his city environment, that the burly postmaster general became known as the "tramp of the cabinet." On a balmy May evening, in 1878, under a starlit sky, Key paced street after street beneath the many bright-colored awnings of the store windows. He inspected the new residences and public buildings that were going up, many in red and multicolored brick, with turrets, ornamented roofs, iron grillwork, and stained-glass windows. They seemed to be clamoring to see which could be the most ostentatious, sporting the greatest confusion of design. Yet Key and the men of his day found these architectural monstrosities fresh and attractive, and the postmaster general thoroughly enjoyed the sight of the new building projects on these nightly walks.

But this evening, he lacked the calm of the stars overhead; echoes of the recklessness of 1860 haunted him at every step. The fire-eaters, taking command of the Democratic Party, had set out on a vendetta to resurrect the election controversy and eject Hayes from office. On May 13, 1878, a Tilden spokesman, Congressman Potter, had introduced a House resolution proposing a reinvestigation of the 1876 elections in Florida and Louisiana. The legitimacy of Hayes's Presidency had been challenged.

Hayes was greatly alarmed. He realized that this was no minor political maneuver, but, as he said, an effort to "lay a foundation for a revolution." If the junta were to gain support in the autumn elections, he feared there would be another rebellion. Preparing for the worst, he declared that any move to put Tilden into the White House at this time would mean one thing: "Mr. Tilden will be arrested and shot. He cannot attempt to take possession of the White House without a fight. That means Civil War, and in that event we shall whip them badly."[1] One senator advised Hayes to organize additional military units to cope with the rebellion.

Key brooded over these calamitous events as he turned down another dark street toward the mall. He shoved his hat back on his gray head and sighed. It seemed incredible that Southern politicians should push again to the brink of war! Letters were pouring into Key's office asking advice as to what course a patriotic Southerner should follow. He had to answer—and quickly. But how? What was he to say?

At Pennsylvania Avenue, he paused, letting a gaily decorated carriage pass before crossing toward the grassy mall. As he paused, he gazed at the Washington Monument and then at the dome of the Capitol, illuminated by a great lantern. That Capitol was a beacon of democracy for all the world; yet once again, constitutional government seemed on the brink of disaster. Once again, there was the possibility that this nation would react like so many Latin American countries and would settle the dispute with a coup or another civil war. This had to be prevented, and Key, a Southern Democrat, had somehow to make his voice heard above the voices of people like Harris and Potter. How could he help to prevent another national catastrophe? Perhaps he should consult with some of his associates before formulating his plan, but it began to take shape as he walked, thought, and meditated among Washington's landmarks representing the march of civilization toward freedom under law.

In newspapers throughout the nation, on May 28, there appeared a "Letter to the South," written by D. M. Key. Pemberton's attack at Gettysburg had been no more ferocious than was Key's attack on the revolutionary wing of the Democratic Party. Key informed the nation that the Potter resolution and the many inflammatory declarations of prominent Democratic politicians and journalists were evidence that Democratic control over both the House and the Senate in the next Congress would result in an attempt to oust Hayes and inaugurate Tilden. No Congress, present or future, wrote Key, had the power to subvert President Hayes's title, once "settled irrevocable by the Forty-fourth Congress in the act creating the electoral commission under which he was legally inaugurated." The postmaster general asserted that "the Forty-sixth Congress will have no more right to ignore him and to recognize the defeated candidate, Mr. Tilden, than Mr. Hayes would have to send a file of soldiers to the House of Representatives" to unseat some congressman that he might think fraudulently elected.

"The leaders in this desperate attempt to Mexicanize our institutions," he said, "rely confidently upon a 'Solid South' to furnish the bulk of the Democratic majority in the next House of Representatives." Key tossed out his favorite barb that the Tammany Democrats had encouraged the South to secede in 1861 and had then deserted her. He asked: "Can the Southern people afford to join this [new] revolutionary movement, with the certainty that when the inevitable hour of peril comes, they will be again left unassisted and alone . . .?" He showered with praise the Southern leaders of 1877 who averted the war danger by compelling the completion of the electoral count under the commission that had been approved by both parties. He expressed surprise that some of these same congressional leaders had "joined in a movement to subvert the results of their former patriotic" deeds and to lead the country to anarchy. The President had restored autonomy to all states and had appointed responsible Southern citizens to Southern offices.

For the Southern people to endorse the revolutionary action of their congressmen was "to admit the truth of the charges that the

people of the South care nothing for the welfare of the Union, desire the downfall of the Republic, and would rejoice to see it again
involved in a civil war." These were stern words. Key then cited the
Potter resolution to prove that members of the Southern Democratic Party could not resist "the mandates of the caucus and the
terrors of the party lash" wielded by Tammany Democrats, men
who were merely seeking political revenge when they called upon
responsible Southerners "to organize and to resolve to support no
person for Congress who has given aid" to the revolutionary schemes
of the mischief-makers. No Southern dreamer "need hope that the
schemes of the men who have engineered the movement to unseat
President Hayes [from his lawful title] can be carried out without
a bloody civil war. To avert this danger, I confidently rely upon the
patriotism and honor of the people of my native section."[2]

This direct, hard-hitting letter infuriated the leaders of the
Southern political machine. Isham Harris crustily remarked that
Key had already "killed himself" politically by accepting the cabinet
position, and now his open letter to the South amounted to a grace-
less attempt to "mutilate his corpse."[3]

From all over the South, the machine politicians heaped insult
upon the man they now called a scalawag. Many Democratic newspapers refused to print the letter in its entirety. One tagged it "the
most consummate piece of impudence" ever perpetrated by a cabinet
officer. The *Nashville American* facetiously termed the letter just
"one of those little mistakes the Postmaster General is fond of
committing." Some papers interpreted the letter to mean that Key
had "at last severed his connection with the Democracy [Democratic
Party]—has, so to speak, burned his ships—and will hereafter be
found in the Republican camp."

But Key had many grass-roots supporters. The *New Orleans
Picayune* granted that few people believed Hayes was elected by the
people, nevertheless, "the Electoral Commission accepted as returns
such as were known to be false and fraudulent. They were counted
and that count was accepted as a finality, in accordance with the law
by which the commission was raised." The article concluded that the

only constitutional process by which Hayes could be removed was impeachment, an alternative "so remote and improbable as to be worth not even a momentary thought." The *Tennessee Republican* editorialized: "Ye who love your homes and your firesides, ponder well what Judge Key so well says." The *Knoxville Chronicle* declared that Key, whose letter had so stirred the ire of desperate Bourbon politicians, had performed a patriotic duty.

The *Valley Virginian* said that Key's letter had created a profound impression on the voters, that Democratic congressmen from Virginia had no sympathy with the Potter movement but had allowed themselves to be driven to its support by the party caucus. The American people had deposed King George, but they had installed "King Caucus."

A letter to the editor of the *Memphis Avalanche* charged that the same newspaper editors who now attacked Key were those who during the war had fought so bravely on paper—well to the rear. They had condemned General Albert Sidney Johnston for retreating too much, they had slandered General Longstreet after the war was over for his failure to support their policies, and now they called Key a craven renegade, although he had shown his devotion to the South "when the danger was somewhat greater than in an editorial chair, or in the Confederate Congress. . . . The War of the Politician is over. The Peace of the Soldier has begun. . . . Keep the soldiers to the front. They felt what war was, and want no more. Let the fire-eating squad go to the rear, where it stood so contentedly four years." Key found this style remarkably like that of his old friend Andrew Kellar.[4]

Key rapidly began to build up support among the more independent Southern Democrats. Texas Democratic Congressman Mills asserted that the postmaster general's letter represented the true sentiment of the South and that the Potter resolution was unwise and unfortunate. This charge came from the former vice-president of the Confederacy, Alexander Stephens.

The activities of Key, Mills, and Stephens crippled the Potter resolution. An attempt by some Tennessee congressmen to counterattack and publish an answer to Key's open letter soon was abandoned as public sentiment continued to grow for the postmaster general.[5] On June 24, the House resolved by an overwhelming vote of 215 to 21 that no subsequent House would have the jurisdiction to revise the decision proclaiming Hayes the duly elected President. The Potter committee, of course, would continue its investigation, but the chances of unseating Hayes were foreclosed. For once, the machine politicians had been delat a devastating blow by Hayes, the man they thought they had discredited to a point where he could never again have a following in the South.

Some time later, Key sat in a big swivel chair, his big fingers thumping rhe leather of its upholstered arms. Overhead the whirling blades of the ceiling fan kept several flies in circulation but could not keep the heavy postmaster general cool. Key was busy signing a stack of postal commissions. Next to the stack of papers, on Key's ornate desk, stood a curious new-fangled and useful contraption, a so-called telephone, which Key's assistant for the railway mail service, Theodore Vail, had rigged up for him. Over this telephone system the postmaster general could talk to his assistants throughout the building.

Key was expecting a caller, and soon his secretary escorted a reporter from the *Philadelphia Times* into the high-ceilinged office. The portly postmaster general swung around in his chair, got up, and greeted his guest with a hearty handshake

Pleased with the Tennessean's good nature and friendliness, the reporter said, "Pretty hot weather, Judge."

"Yes," replied the postmaster general, swabbing his face, "this beats Tennessee."

"By the way, the papers don't seem to be pitching into you much lately."

"No," answered Key, laughing and tossing back his large head. "No, they don't call me an ex-rebel, ex-Confederate, or erring brother quite so often now. Well, I really try to get along easy and not offend any one."

The reporter smiled. "What do you think of the Potter commit-tee?"

Key swung around in his chair to gaze out of his floor-length window at the carriages and streetcars clattering past on F Street below. "Oh, that's a foolish piece of business, and the committee isn't doing anything. They haven't found anything yet; never will find anything. That's my idea. The Democrats made a great mistake. I notice that Alexander Stephens of Georgia, Mills of Texas, and others who voted against the Potter resolution are being received very enthusiastically by their people. The investigation has de-veloped a rascally crowd, and that's about all."[6]

They chatted for some time before the reporter departed. But in the interview, the postmaster general had made some points to ponder, such as the one about Alexander Stephens' warm recep-tion in Georgia after his stand with Key against the Potter resolu-tion. Stephens had ridden around his district in his well-known yellow coach-and-four, which had become a symbol to the Geor-gians. He had been so warmly received that there was talk now about the possibility of an independent party. The press had im-mediately associated this movement with Key, who admitted that he had received a letter from "a prominent Georgian" representing a large group of constituents who wanted to break with the rabid Democratic machine and ally themselves with the administration. There was speculation about starting a new newspaper. Key had told the reporter that this venture would rapidly progress if it received support from the administration and that he planned to discuss the matter with President Hayes. After all, the administra-tion could sponsor enough advertising to ensure the success of a new newspaper.[7]

Key did discuss the Georgia movement with Hayes and pre-sumably expressed his view that support from Hayes would "crys-tallize [it] into a formidable factor in Southern politics."[8] Coming as an aftermath to the postmaster general's victorious open letter, this was the second great opportunity to realign Southern politics and end color-line politics. Hayes was in sympathy with this awak-

ening in the South, but again he displayed his lack of political
acumen and timing, for he failed to take advantage of this opportunity in Georgia and elsewhere.

Seething with factionalism, the Southern Democratic Party was
ready for some kind of renaissance. The question was whether this
renaissance would be one of racism and sectionalism or of enlighten-
ment and a broader national outlook. A dynamic new force in the
nation was the agrarian population—the small farmers, often called
rednecks, who were reared in the Jacksonian tradition and who,
until the 1870's, had supported the Bourbon planter class. The
burden of the small, depressed, backward farm tracts weighed
heavily upon these resentful farmers as they hunched behind their
plows in the scorching sun. For a time, they looked hopefully to the
Hayes Republicans' promises of economic improvement in the
South, but outside of Key's efforts to improve rural mail service,
they found that Hayes's plans were mere piecrust promises.

During the 1873 depression, the small Southern farmers had begun to break with the Southern conservatives and had turned toward
the gospel of easy money for deliverance. They were willing to join
any group favoring inflation—the Silverites, the Greenbackers, and
the anti-railway-monopoly groups of the West. Advocating repudiation of the Southern states' war debt, this resurgent radical agrarian
group gained power as Western and Southern farmers joined hands
with a force that shook the established political organization in
many a state. In the South, this movement was built on a violent
hatred of the Negro, the poor black man who was now coming into
direct competition with the poor redneck on the little farms.

It was this radicalism that Governor James Porter was now trying
to stave off in Tennessee. Porter not only had forgiven Key for his
"erring brethren" role but was now working with him again.
Porter felt strongly on the controversial issue of the debt repudiation. He now convinced the postmaster general, who had become
quite well known through his open letter, to write another such
letter, this time to the citizens of Tennessee, urging them not to
repudiate the debts of their state. This letter triggered talk that

Key would run for governor on a nonpartisan anti-inflation ticket. Apparently he was approached, but we know little about the details of this plan. *The New York Times* reported that the postmaster general opposed the repudiation of the state debt so bitterly that, if necessary, he would personally lead the antirepudiationists of Tennessee. But Key declared elsewhere that he did not aspire to the governorship, and he decided not to run for this office for reasons we do not fully know. He apparently was unwilling to run on a state Democratic platform that was already equivocating on debt repudiation and was opposed to industrialization, railroads, and national banks. The Democrats were also trying to outpromise the Greenbackers, and Key would have no part of that.[9]

In not running for governor, Key made his great mistake. The indications were that the Tennessee Republicans would have given him solid support, Colonel Colyar's industrial Democrats would have backed him, and some agrarians might have followed him because of his association with their hero Andrew Johnson, the Great Commoner. Granted, the Southern Democratic Party was riddled with inconsistencies, and within a few years, Key would not have had a chance politically. But in the year 1878, he had a chance and an opportunity; he could have counted on a large combined Republican and Democratic vote, and he had the prestige gained from his greatest victory—the open letter—after having amazingly recuperated from his earlier political unpopularity.[10]

As it turned out, the election year 1878 saw the inauguration of a Solid South committed to all that Key abhorred. No Republican governors and only three Republican congressmen were elected, and the Republicans lost much support even in the black belts. In Tennessee, for example, of the five counties with a Negro vote of more than 50 per cent, none voted a Republican majority in 1878.[11] Speaking of his Southern policy, Hayes, the man ultimately responsible for this defeat, gloomily remarked: "I am reluctantly forced to admit that the experiment was a failure."[12]

With that year's disappointing election results tormenting his mind, Summerfield Key took up his pen and wrote to his brother, the postmaster general:

> I am hopelessly out of heart with the conduct of the democracy especially. It seems to be without sense, prudence, or patriotism. The blind thirst for office among its leaders has demoralized and degraded the whole mass of the party. For temporary success it is willing to sacrifice its principles, and the good of the country. Everything looks gloomy now. . . . The history of the "solid South" can be written in two words—poverty and disgrace.[13]

# 19

## Star-Route Scandals

For Lizzie Key, social life at Ebbitt House in the late 1870's was a whirling merry-go-round. At forty, she was well-preserved, her hair still lustrous and black, pulled straight back in a knot; she conformed gladly in every way to the severe but gracious ways of the First Lady. As the wife of a cabinet member, she took her social obligations seriously and managed carefully within the family income. She followed her brown leatherette appointment book meticulously and traversed Washington from the houses on Capitol Hill to the buttressed and turreted mansions along Massachusetts Avenue. Lizzie's passion for her husband's political career was deeper than his own, and her sanguine ambition was to see him advance, not to the Governor's Mansion in Nashville, but to the black robes of a Supreme Court justice. President Hayes had offered Key an appointment, she told her children, but "Papa" had declined. He said he could not have retained his large family in Washington on the low salary of a Supreme Court justice.

Men of government service did sometimes increase their income through legitimate means, and it was to this mission that Lizzie addressed herself, in the hope that Key would not have to turn down another such offer. She had more than $1,000 and was looking about for a profitable investment. She was intrigued by the commercial future of the "talking boxes" that Theodore Vail had rigged up in Key's office and all through the Post Office Building. Vail, who had connections with Alexander Graham Bell's new company, invited Lizzie to invest in this young enterprise. But the venture seemed chancy to her, for Bell's company was mired in legal difficulties of patent rights. Lizzie was also considering investing with the enterprising General Brady, the second assistant postmaster general, who had invested with Vail and was also exploiting a supposedly vast gold mine in the West. There was no slippery patent involved in this venture, the General told Lizzie, when he offered her this investment opportunity. At the time, Lizzie was packed to leave for the family's summer stay in Chattanooga; but before her departure for the station, she made a firm decision. She went to the Post Office Department to give Vail her $1,000 to invest in Bell's company, only to find that he had just departed for New York City. Lizzie's train time was approaching as she stood in the narrow hall listening to Brady expound again on the tempting gold mine. She paused, thought, and made her decision. She gave the $1,000 to Brady to buy mining stock. After she had made her investment, she breathlessly rushed out of the building to the waiting carriage and on to the station.

Of course, the gold mine was to fail, and Vail, soon to leave the Post Office to direct the Bell Telephone Company, would win a suit to gain patent rights that would bring the company millions.[1]

Although Hayes had failed to fulfill his promises to the South, Key was determined to carry out his mission to provide the South and West with a mail service second to neither North nor East. While traveling with the Postal Commission, he had investigated the situation in various business communities. In the western part of North Carolina and in the tidewater area of Virginia, despite a web of trade by land and water transport, not one single important mail route had been added since the war. As a Georgia postmaster had said to the commission, "Time is money." Yet the lack of efficient mail service was wasting both time and money. This inspection tour had convinced the commission of the need for the railroads to rearrange their schedules so as to deliver the mails "in New Orleans at half-past seven instead of half-past eleven, and in New York at seven instead of ten, thus saving a business day at either end." The commission, and the postmaster general especially, realized that the South needed more post offices and shorter routes leading to the main lines if the industrial development of the South was ever to approach that of the North.

Especially in need of expedition were the star routes, so called for the asterisk marking them in the U.S. Postal Guide and in maps and for the star adorning newspaper ads seeking contract bidders. Star-route carriers serviced areas not accessible by railroad or waterway, and the routes were leased by contract to private bidders who made deliveries by coach or riders. As star routes carried comparatively few letters and packages over vast isolated areas, they were not self-supporting, but a much needed subsidized government service.

The boom years of 1878 and 1879 saw vast increases in the star routes. Many original contracts had been leased at very low bids in depression years, but they increased in value during this particular phase of Southern and Western economic development, when several major railroads were nearing completion. Once in operation, the railway mail services would replace the temporary star routes, which would greatly reduce the Post Office Department's expenses. Key calculated all this, and he realized that his policy was full of risks. The contracting laws for operating this service, dating back to 1845, were archaic and fraught with opportunity for corruption, and Key "often and emphatically pointed out defects in the contract system and recommended means of correcting them."[2] But Congress, not Key, made the laws.

Consequently, he had to rely heavily upon the honesty and ability of his second assistant postmaster general, Thomas Brady, who was charged by law with the operation of this contract system. Tyner and Brady, both Stalwart Republicans, disagreed on star-route policies, and this disagreement, Key believed, served as a countercheck.

Tyner, as a radical Republican, was opposed to increasing the government's subsidies and services for the West and South, while Brady firmly endorsed Key's policy of expediting these services.

Ever since 1872, the star-route postal service had periodically been accused of corruption by Tammany Democratic and Stalwart Republican newspapers. When these charges were repeated in 1877, Key permitted Talcott Williams, an independent observer, to examine the files in Brady's contract department, and Key asked Williams for a report on his findings. Williams produced no evidence, no basis for the rumors of fraud. Nevertheless, in the summer of 1879, the postmaster general ordered Tyner to make a discreet independent investigation of the entire mail service on the West Coast. After several months of personal inspection, Tyner handed Key a report that seriously questioned Brady's judgment in the expediting of several star routes. Key then asked Tyner point-blank to evaluate Brady's character. Tyner insisted that a more honest man was not to be found. Key then asked Tyner to keep his report confidential, so that Brady would not feel Tyner had invaded his jurisdiction, but said that Tyner should discuss his conclusions informally with Brady.[3]

Next, Key himself, without either Tyner's or Brady's knowledge, examined the files on the star routes in question, and he concluded that "Gen. Brady's action had been based upon strong and convincing documentary testimony, generally endorsed by the members and Delegates of Congress from the States and Territories interested in these routes." Key also found that Brady had sent an experienced special agent to conduct a similar inspection of these routes and that the agent had uncovered no evidence of fraud.[4]

Meanwhile, a mass of requests for new star routes came to the postmaster general's desk, many of them from distinguished men like Lew Wallace, who was governor of the New Mexico Territory, General E. O. Ord of Texas, and General Nelson Miles. Miles argued that increased postal service would attract more settlers to Montana, accelerate its agricultural and mineral development, and serve the more than 1,000 federal troops stationed in the area.

Meanwhile, there was a great clamor in Congress for more star routes, and one Congress alone produced an increase of more than 2,000 new star routes.[5]

If the expenditures of Brady's division continued at that rate, Key concluded, they would exceed appropriations by the time Congress convened in early 1880. Thus, Key decided to force the whole controversial issue into the lap of Congress, which had far greater investigative powers than he. Members of Congress, after all, had demanded the increase of star routes in the first place, and Congress had the power to change appropriations and the faulty contract laws. Key also requested Congress "to limit and restrain the expeditions of the service to cases not exceeding an increase of fifty per cent over the original costs of the route."[6]

Congressional hearings dragged on, amid mounting rumors and publicity about Brady's increased wealth, supposedly acquired through star-route frauds. Key knew of Brady's investment in Vail's telephone company, which now was booming. Angered, the postmaster general paced the floor of his big office, then called in Brady and gave an abrupt order. Until Congress was willing to commit itself on star-route policies, he would suspend extra service. All mail service on the star routes would be reduced to one trip per week, and all routes established since July 1, 1879, were to be discontinued. If the routes were to be restored, Congress would have to do it. Key was sick of congressmen personally endorsing the policies but failing to commit themselves publicly on the issue.[7]

In early April, Congress voted an appropriation of $1.1 million. The President noted that "both branches of the Democratic Congress sustained the inculpated officer, General Brady."[8] Now Key's dilemma was resolved. He felt that Congress had made "an appropriation for the service as Brady had expedited it and as executive officers, we were controlled by its action. It would have been inexcusable in me to have flown in the face of Congress, and to have claimed more wisdom and honesty than that body possessed."[9]

Although Key considered the case closed, a pandora's box had been opened. Politicians of Tammany Hall and of the radical Republican wing were about to ruin both Tyner and Brady in an effort to tear to shreds the last semblance of Hayes's Southern policy. And in that process, they would also get at the maverick politician D. M. Key. The postmaster general had developed the worrisome habit of going directly to the people, North and South, over the heads of their politicians. But could the people possibly trust and defend a man if it could be proved that he had presided over a multimillion-dollar fraud? They would pin this one on Key himself. But this was not yet the moment to do it. They would wait.

# 20

---

# Color-Line Politics

Chattanooga—its green walls of mountains and ridges, its newly paved streets with several new, fancy electric lights, and its elegant new hotel—never looked so homey to D. M. Key as in the late summer of 1880, when the family returned after he had resigned as postmaster general. A crowd was clustered around the railroad station. There were the matronly ladies with their parasols, cigar-smoking and tobacco-chewing businessmen and workers, young mothers and children—they all had come to cheer their hero, who, in the waning days of the Hayes Administration, had accepted an appointment as federal judge for the central and eastern districts of Tennessee. Although without the prestige of a Supreme Court appointment, the new job allowed Judge Key to return to his native town and its fields and mountains, to try cases in the court in Chattanooga and in other courts of the area. Now, above all, he would be able to preach his philosophy of the need for a South reborn in economic progress rather than in the defense of divisive racial issues.

The family spent these last weeks of summer in the cool shade of a mountain on the western rim of Chattanooga Valley, in a new settlement on Walden Ridge called Summertown. The needs of the family, now with nine growing children, had expanded since

Key had departed in 1875. Thus, for $400 he had bought 135 acres of additional land and paid the rustic architect of the mountain, "Uncle Billy" Miles, to build a large two-story log cabin with a shingled roof. By Key's design, the interior of "Topside," as he named his mountain home, was left rough, with beamed ceilings and log walls. Gay and glamorous Emma and her protégé Kate found mountain life stark compared with the goings-on in the capital.

But Judge Key gladly exchanged the tawdry Washington life for the pure, crisp mountain air and the autumn smell of burning hickory logs on the great "Topside" hearth. He happily returned to his old clothes, mountain cap, and soft shoes. He also preferred the mountain-store prices, chickens at fifteen cents apiece, eggs at ten cents a dozen, mutton at seven cents a pound. As he plodded along bridle paths or trundled about the mountain roads in the family carriage, Key now had time once more to look up at the far-stretching arch of the heavens. From the cliffs of Walden Ridge, he could set a "base-line of judgment in regard to man and events of which one in the crowded field of a work-a-day life gets only hasty and confused notions." So wrote one of Key's former Post Office assistants who missed the judgment of the old post-master general in Washington. He reported that things had come to a sorry pass in the department.[1]

Season after season, Judge Key traveled his circuit to hold court in Knoxville, Nashville, and back home in Chattanooga. Opening a letter in his office or reading the papers in a dining car, he often read with alarm about smears of his policies and even of his personal life.

The complicated, sinister plot that was to implicate Key began during the Presidential campaign of 1880. Despite rumors about the dishonesty of Assistant Postmaster General Brady—for Brady was steadily amassing greater wealth—the Republican Presidential candidate, James Garfield, asked both Tyner and Brady to solicit campaign funds from government employees. Senator Dorsey, who was also suspected of alleged deals in connection with the star

routes, was elected secretary of the Republican National Committee. Of course, this alignment of so-called star-route characters in
the election campaign became a fair target for Tammany.[2]

Candidate Garfield not only encouraged assessments of government workers but, to ensure his own election, made lavish patronage
promises and openly agreed to return to the policy of congression-
ally influenced appointments. The merit system had been sup-
planted once more by the spoils system.[3] To the victor belonged
not only the spoils but also the quarrels. Once elected, President
Garfield rudely ignored New York's Republican machine bosses
Platt and Conkling, who were close to Tyner and Brady; he appointed Thomas L. James postmaster general. Soon, the New York
Republicans launched an interparty war, and as Platt and Conkling
attacked James, James counterattacked by resurrecting the star-
route charges and blaming Tyner and Brady. Tammany was delighted to see the Republicans tearing one another apart, and
*The New York Times* added salt to the wounds by demanding a
further investigation of the star-route rumors.

The new administration complied and soon trained its guns on
Brady. The *National Republican* commented: "We have no small
curiosity to see how an administration which is the result of state
buying in October will proceed in May to reform the man who
handled the money."[4] The investigator, P. H. Woodward, who was
supported by Postmaster General James, exposed to the public
the inadequate contract laws, charging Brady with the responsibility for these inept laws, as if he had made them, and accusing
Key of not having tried to change them. One member of the Post
Office Department wrote to Judge Key: "In view of the fact that
you and Brady had often and emphatically pointed out defects in
the contract system and recommended means of correcting them,
one is at a loss to see what special credit remains to the present
administration."[5]

Then Woodward charged that the star-route corruption had been
coordinated into a monstrous conspiracy and that Brady had been
a master coordinator. As the onslaught intensified, the President

removed Brady from office. Judge Key, feeling the investigation was partisan and one-sided, told the press that he did not believe the charges against Brady to be true and that "there is not a word or figure now in these charges that we did not have something of two years ago." *The New York Times* retorted: "[Key] invites condemnation which the public will not be slow to pass upon him."[6]

After being elected President, Garfield was caught in a whirl-wind of pay-offs, and the star-route scandal afforded a tailor-made distraction from the administration's plight. Postmaster General James concentrated his attack on Tyner, issuing a series of scathing statements, until the trembling Tyner realized that if Garfield demanded his resignation, the press would take this as a verdict of guilty. Tyner begged for Garfield's mercy.[7] In July, 1881, President Garfield was shot by a disappointed office seeker. In a sense, the very spoils system that Hayes and Key had striven to abolish had slain Garfield, the man who had reinstituted the system by his campaign promises.

As the President lingered near death, the star-route investigation continued. The James clique burst into headlines with the scandalous news that Tyner had suppressed a report he had prepared for Key on the star routes. Tyner resigned under great pressure shortly after Garfield died, in September. When the press played up the rumor that his resignation had been demanded because he had suppressed the report, Key released the whole story of how he had asked Tyner to make the investigation and hold the report as a confidential paper.[8]

*The New York Times* used the occasion not only to smear Key's policies of accelerated mail services for the South and West, but also to defame the entire Southern policy of the Hayes Administration. The *Times* called Hayes's policy of conciliating the South a dead failure, charging that "the Southern whites thought no more of the President and less, if possible, of Mr. Key, [who was] a respectable elderly political Judge of the South-western type, whose standard of public service and political privilege was better calculated for a Confederate Cross Roads."[9]

The investigation continued amid charges and countercharges of a sellout of the government. In March of 1882, a grand jury indicted both Brady and Dorsey. More than 100 witnesses were paraded before the court. Brady and Dorsey were acquitted; two other defendants were found guilty. There followed charges of a bribed jury, and the verdicts were set aside. Soon, a new trial opened, and more acquittals followed. Key felt that the trial was assuming "quite a scaly appearance on both sides of the case." The partisanship had grown so flagrant that the Tennessean believed that it was no longer within the power of the jurors to determine the guilt or innocence of those concerned.[10]

Ironically, the testimony of railroad executives and military commanders during the trial proved that Postmaster General Key's mail policies had expedited the growth and prosperity of the South and the West. These underdeveloped areas for once had obtained their deserved share of federal aid—aid that their spokesmen had sought since the early days of Calhoun and Clay, but that the North had usually managed to monopolize. Thus, David McKendree Key had fulfilled a historic mission, though he was not to be honored for it.

In Tennessee, Judge Key rode his circuit, a man now more solemn with his contemporaries and sterner with his children, who, he felt, must be prepared to face the acid realities of politics in America.

With the years it became increasingly evident to Key that the high noon of economic opportunity for a new era of Southern politics had been in 1877 and that he had failed to take advantage of it. Now, in the 1880's, storm clouds were about to blot out the light of a Southern renaissance for almost a century. But not all the storms originated in the South. As *Harpers Weekly* noted, the election of 1880 was a contest neither of principle nor of policy; "real party divisions have largely ceased to exist. There are free traders and money men in both parties, and in both men who favor the same general policy for the South and for reform.

But they hold to their own camps from a feeling of mutual distrust."[11] Writing of American politics in the same period, Viscount Bryce observed, in his *American Commonwealth,* that he failed to discover that either party had anything vital to say, any clearly defined program to offer; each seemed to have only the aim of power. For years, Key had prophesied this barrenness and suggested ways of avoiding it, but his proposals had not been heeded. By now, politics had become increasingly depraved, party platforms bereft of meaning.

But the depravity of the 1880's could still worsen, Key realized. On the issue of state fiscal responsibility for debts, he had hoped that the sensible Republicans and the industrial wing of the Democratic Party of his state could unite. The industrial wing of the party, led by Colonel Colyar, was on the threshold of far-reaching financial power, not only in Tennessee but throughout the entire South. Colyar himself was buying a string of Southern newspapers. Key's friend ex-Governor John C. Brown was soon to become head of the Tennessee Coal, Iron, and Railroad Company, and ex-Governor Porter head of the Nashville and Chattanooga Railroad.

This group had the friendly, paternalistic attitude of the old planters toward the Negro, and it subscribed to the dogma that responsible states should honor their debts. These Democrats, as newspaperman Henry Watterson noted, supported "Republican" principles, in the best sense of the word. But except for the 1877 campaign, when they had worked to elect Key to the Senate, they would not join forces with the Republicans because of the stigma that party still carried in the South from the Civil War and the carpetbagger Reconstruction days.[12]

At the same time that this wing of the party dissipated its effectiveness by staying with the solid Democratic South, the other wing —the Bourbon wing—remained entrenched in provincialism, color-line politics, dogmatism, and nostalgia for the ante-bellum South. These old-line Bourbon Democrats remained blind to the need for economic development and willing to play the pawn of Tammany Hall, and they still considered Judge Key and his attitude a threat to their power. That many of them remained Key's personal friends was a tribute to his crusty sense of humor and his formidable personality. Most of them liked the aging judge immensely in the courtrooms and in the family parlors, but behind his back they cursed his politics.

Key found he could live with this generation of reactionaries. But a new group made him fear for the future. The rednecks, the impoverished farmers, and the hillbillies were on the rampage again. Burdened with debt, they blamed the railroad rates on the fat industrialists and railroad moguls whom they saw resplendent with gold watch chains, diamond stickpins, and Cuban cigars. These small farmers sought easy money and state-debt repudiation. They feared the Negroes, feared that they might become more educated and more skilled and so would threaten white farmers' livelihood in competition. They claimed to be the true sons of democracy, walking in the footsteps of Andrew Jackson and Andrew Johnson. But their democracy was a limited white man's democracy of an agrarian proletariat. They were breeding hate, aiming to segregate and degrade the black man.

Key appreciated their hard lot. But he realized also that their resentment of the capitalists and their fear of the Negro were kindling explosive conditions that could shatter the social development of the South. Key, who was sometimes called the successor of the Great Commoner, knew these people well. He sympathized with them in their daily troubles and advised them as he traveled his circuits. He talked to them of corn and hogs and his mountain farm at Summertown. He explained the law to them, and he patiently preached his political and economic philosophy of a new South. He begged them to think beyond the next weekend at the market, beyond the next season, to consider the issues that would affect their children. They applauded Judge Key when he spoke to them, but they did not really hear what he said.

Judge Key kept on preaching, as old Parson Key had done long ago. He sensed that the clock of time ticked dangerously toward a disastrous hour when the poor hillbillies would join with the Bourbons to write racism into the law.

Key never lost sight of this oncoming social disaster. In his humility, he did not see his unfortunate role in the tragedy: he was the one Tennessean who might have led the children of Andrew Johnson away from the Bourbons, who might have united the Democratic industrialists and the Republicans across the state.[13] Key rode his circuit in search of legal justice instead of the campaign trail in search of political office. The power lay not with legal decisions but with politicians.

On a bright and sunny day in the 1880's, the members of the Tennessee Bar Association were smoking their cigars, cracking jokes, and greeting friends as they piled into the courtroom in Nashville for their annual meeting. This day they were to be addressed by the healthy, white-haired judge of the Federal Circuit Court of Middle and East Tennessee, the Honorable D. M. Key. There was lively interest. Judge Key's topic was "The Legal and Political Status of the Negro."

Key had added his finishing touches to the speech on the train from Chattanooga. He still enjoyed the train rides. He traveled first class, in the cars especially furnished for ladies. There he escaped the heavy cigar smoke and spittoons filled with tobacco juice, which frequently slushed onto the floors of the men's cars as the train rattled around the bends of the Tennessee mountains. He realized that few Negroes traveled in the cars and that some railroads excluded them from first-class seats. The Civil Rights Bill of 1875 stated that all persons shall be entitled to "full and equal enjoyment of the accommodations, advantages, facilities, and privileges of inns, public conveyances on land or water, theatres, and other places of amusements." That same year, 1875, the Tennessee State Legislature passed a law that abrogated the bill, but the Circuit Court of the Western Tennessee District ruled this statute unconstitutional.[14] The ruling was often violated, however, and each violation incensed Judge Key. This was one matter he chose to take up with the Bar Association.

Key strongly felt, as he had often instructed his jurors, that throughout all ages, race prejudice had been the source of animosity and war. He had seen roughnecks before his court who had bullied Negroes who entered first-class railroad cars. He had commented in court that "those who are most sensitive as to contact with colored people and whose nerves are the most shocked at their presence have little to be proud of in the way of birth, lineage, or achievements." Judge Key did believe that it was within the rights of railroads to have separate cars for whites and Negroes but that they had the obligation to have alike and equal accommodations. "There is no equality of right when the money of the white man purchases luxurious accommodations amid elegant company and the same amount of money purchases for the black man inferior quarters in a smoking car." Judge Key often told his jurors that the ancients had frequently depicted Justice blindfolded and that the just jury member had to be blind to color.

These opinions Key now explicitly incorporated into his speech. Standing at the bar rail, he studied the members of the Bar Association, recognizing some as Isham Harris Bourbons, others as representatives of the agrarian radicalism, still others as general counsels for the growing industry in Tennessee. He raised his voice and read steadily and firmly from his text. A white and a colored couple pay the same price for their tickets, he said, but "the last two are not allowed upon any grounds to go into the ladies' car—either to smoke or to escape smoke—but the first may go forward into the smoking car at will." The judge indignantly declared that the law would not tolerate such discrimination, that the purchasing power of a dollar in a black man's hand should be as great as that of the same dollar in a white man's hand. He conceded that the railways could establish separate cars for different races but asserted that each should have the same accommodations. Oddly enough, he noted, no one raised any objection to a Negro woman who was a nurse or a servant being seated in the first-class ladies' car.

Over and above legalities, Judge Key then vented his personal feelings:

> For the life of me, I cannot see what injury a neatly dressed, well-behaved colored person does me by riding in the same car. And should he sit in some corner of the same dining room away from my table, I cannot see why my appetite or self-respect suffer by it. . . . I do not insist that it is one's duty to sit next to a colored person on the car or at the table, but I do say I should prefer to sit by a genteel, well-bred Negro than a dirty, filthy, disgusting white man. . . .
>
> I believe as much as anyone in the superiority of the white race. Its natural powers are greater and its capabilities broader. To my mind this furnishes a powerful reason why we should scrupulously extend to the weaker and less capable race every right to which it is entitled.[15]

Judge Key was indeed a man of his time. Despite his deep humanity, he viewed one race as superior in ability to another. But to him, unlike most of his fellow Southerners, this was all the more reason to guard zealously the moral and legal equality of the two races.

Key maintained that one of the rights to which each citizen was entitled was jury duty. The Federal Civil Rights Act of 1875 had made discrimination in jury service illegal, and this portion of the act had been held constitutional by the Supreme Court in 1883. Hence, Key declared, to deny the place of a Negro on a jury was to deny him a right. He added that he had never found a so-called professional juror of the black race, that the Negro jurors in his experience had discharged their duties faithfully.

Judge Key finished and sat down heavily. He got the usual round of applause, the cheers, the warm handshakes. Ever since the Mississippi election speech, more than a decade earlier, he had become skeptical of this warm afterglow, the jolly-good fellow routine. But he stood up again, smiling, leaning his bulky body against the mahogany rail, under the big glass globes lighting the high-ceilinged, smoky chamber. He shook hands with one colleague after another, but he would not deceive himself. Ten years ago, these same Southerners were closer to moderation than they were now.

Reactionary winds were blowing with hurricane strength. Tom-toms of hate were sounding. Bloody shirts were waving. Class conflict was on the march. Once Key had told a reporter that the prime exploiter of class conflict, Communism, would one day be the greatest peril to America. After the European revolutions of 1848, European immigrants had brought Marx's ideas to the United States. In 1869, the first American section of the First International was established. The growth of Communism pointed to the dangers of societies that built caste systems and permitted no fluidity among social groups, no chance for a man of ability to climb beyond the confines of his own group, no release for pent-up emotions except to attack the so-called exploiters.[16]

The whole South could have learned from Chattanooga in more ways than one, Key believed. Whereas in the national and state elections political lines were closely drawn, in the Chattanooga elections no party had a guarantee of office; if either political party presented a bad man, party lines were crossed. What is more, of the voting population, 44 per cent were colored. Chattanooga had had a Negro on the city council, and it had worked well indeed.[17]

In some respects, this valley town had accepted the ideas Key had preached, and one of the best vehicles for the communication of these ideas was the *Chattanooga Times,* the thriving newspaper of Key's friend Adolph S. Ochs, a son of a Bavarian Jew. One of its reporters wrote of the town: "We think those who fought the battles of the war were brave and noble. We think those who fight them over in these times . . . are fools. The scars of the minie ball, of grape, canister, cannon ball and shell may be seen in the trees [of this town]. . . . The man from Massachusetts and the man from South Carolina stand upon an equal plane in Chattanooga."[18]

This was true, for even those who lived on the terraces no longer felt quite so divided from the Confederates at the foot of the hill, many of whom were becoming increasingly prosperous. Minority groups mixed well. Adolph Ochs was making the *Times* into such a success that it had become unpopular to attack him or any other man for his Jewish background.

But even in Chattanooga, suspicions were growing. Some of the townspeople complained that Chattanooga Negroes were becoming increasingly fond of display and parades. They remarked that, even on minor occasions, some Negroes would appear in the gaudiest colors, wearing ribbons and frills, sashes and great badges. Chattanooga Negroes had their societies, and each society seemed to have a noisy band, with such names as the Glorious Promise and Circles of Great Expectations, Sons and Daughters of the Gilded Dawn, and Knights and Ladies of the New Dispensation. As their grand marshals, chief knights, and lord high moguls paraded up Market Street and down Broad Street, on the Fourth of July or Emancipation Proclamation Day, some Chattanoogans took their toggery and mysterious rites as a portent of a black attempt to take over the whites.

About this, one of Key's associates of the bar commented in a way that reflected Key's own thought: "Nothing the colored folk did, said, were, or thought was more grotesque than this thought. It was baseless if not base fear, and the whites who feared were as fit subjects for contempt as were the blacks who paraded for amused pity . . . . The only grounds for fear were . . . the white people who encouraged every ambition and foible of the black man, in order to utilize his vote."[19]

Through the 1880's, Judge Key observed all this with increasing alarm and frustration.

# 21

## Epilogue

Shortly after the turn of the century, on a cold February day in Chattanooga, a seventy-six-year-old man, heavy-set, with a large crop of snowy white hair, was surrounded by an adoring group of red-necked mountaineers and hillbillies. They were all clustered on the wide stone steps of the Federal Court Building, a bleak, gray structure marked by twin four-storied towers with the cupolas so typical of that day. At a glance, it appeared that the old gentleman's health was not the best, that he should be indoors on such a day. But he was not given to bowing before the weather or the scoldings of wife, daughters, and doctor. This man loved to tramp through the streets and was proud that once, in Washington, he had been called the "tramp of the cabinet." Besides, he had just walked out of the very courtroom where he had retired as federal judge scarcely six years before. Everyone there, from the spittoon cleaner to the court clerk, overflowed with affection for him, which was an elixir far better than any the doctor could order.

On the steps of the courthouse, Judge Key chatted vigorously with an array of Tennessee moonshiners, discussing bourbon, mountain dew, and farming. They and their lawyers had concluded that the "free coinage" of liquor was not in that class of criminal law *malum in se,* or things wrong in themselves, and had no business being in *malum prohibitum,* or things prohibited by law.

The lanky men surrounding Key had come into town from small farms and from far up on the ridge near Summertown. They were a colorful lot. One was thin, a bit stooped from plowing, and long-haired, with a sandy beard; he had one suspender doing the work of two. A buddy wore a piece of rope for a belt. Another, a youngster, had pink cheeks, bewitching blue eyes—the type a jury would exonerate despite absolute proof of guilt. Their knives generally were used for whittling, their long rifles for shooting squirrels, turkeys, and quail; but they would also shoot to defend their still. Sometimes, gun battles would go on in the hills and hollows, but there were fewer liars and perjurers among the moonshiners than among the well-dressed people who tried to manipulate the votes in this fine city of Chattanooga.[1]

Judge Key, a few years back, had consternated many an upright citizen by letting some moonshiners out of jail for the harvest when they promised that they would return after it was over. When Key was about to request retirement, among the petitions begging him to stay on the bench—many from eminent judges like William Howard Taft—was a lengthy petition from the moonshiners of his circuit. They had Key's sympathy because they were poor, for their small farms up in the hills were not productive enough; but he often deplored their radical politics—especially their hatred of the Negro. He would try to reason with them, for he saw with sorrow what was happening across the South.[2]

After a few moments of free counsel, Judge Key waved farewell, crossed the busy throughfare, and walked toward Market Street, where, thirty-nine years before, he had driven with Lizzie one evening to meet Jeff Davis. Crossing at the corner, he admired the gold-domed structure that Ochs had recently built for the *Chattanooga Times.* The judge smiled to himself as he crossed the paved street and thought how Ochs had gone on to even greater things—he was now running *The New York Times.* Ochs had opposed color-line politics as much as Key had. And, like the judge, he had represented a South interested in industry and economic development—not in refighting the war or pitting one social group against another. At the corner of Market Street, Key watched some gay bicyclers, then crossed to the site of Crutchfield House, where now stood a new hotel.

The judge tipped his hat to some passers-by, cocked it back on his gray head, and turned down Market Street. It was now lined with rows of high telephone poles, some with five or six cross boards supporting a vast web of black wires. Key remembered how Vail had made his millions with Bell. He was glad Lizzie had not invested in their company. Such wealth would have been associated with star-route frauds and would have brought the Keys dishonor and misery. That smear was forgotten around Chattanooga now, and he was glad.

The winter sun was setting, a ball of glory over the canyon to the west. A few electric lights were flashing on. Soon the hush of night would lie over the sprawling town. The last rays cast long shadows on the cliffs near Walden Ridge, at Summertown, where the judge had spent his last summer. It had been a dry winter, and the stream that would soon rush by Mabbitt Spring was quiet as a tomb now amid the dead leaves.

As the sun sank behind the mountains, Key paused to look back, ignoring the pain in his side. The South as a whole was not like Chattanooga Valley; the South was his sorrow. The bright hopes of 1877 had vanished into a bleak prospect of social disaster and economic stagnation, as he had foreseen. The small farmers and rednecks had organized into powerful Grange associations, had even for a time dominated the Democratic Party in the state. In a play for votes, the Bourbon Democrats had moved to repudiate the state debts and, Key sadly reflected, had chased away outside capital and slowed down Southern economic development and prosperity. The radical agrarian politicians, wearing their wool hats, shouted for segregation of the Negro and for his elimination at the polls. And so Jim Crowism had come to one state after another in the 1890's.

True Southern conservatives, who had overthrown the carpet-baggers and assumed power in the South in 1877, had passed no segregation laws for the following twenty years. Conservatives like Key, Lamar, and Hampton had restrained the passions of extremists. They believed that there were different types of men among both white and black and that intelligent, creative Negroes like Booker T. Washington ought to be supported. They understood that the Negro should be encouraged to reach a higher economic and educational level. As one Southern governor had said of the Negroes: "If we do not lift them up, they will drag us down."[3]

Segregation did drag the South down. Negroes migrated from the country into the slums of the cities and became more and more isolated from the white man's economy and culture. Now, slowly but surely, Negroes were being forced out of the small businesses that they had successfully operated. The radical Southern whites were driving the Negroes to a new radicalism of their own. Booker T. Washington, with faith that the reforms in the South would come from within, had encouraged young Negroes to work for their own education and emancipation. Now he was branded by radical Negroes—as Key had been branded by radical whites—as unmanly, lacking in courage, and a maverick.

In 1892, the Populists, led by Tom Watson of Georgia, threw a bombshell into Southern politics in a bid for Negro votes when they sounded the trumpet call for Negroes to demand equal rights. Panic-stricken by the support the Negroes gave the Populists, many Southern Democrats joined the forces of reaction to promote Jim Crowism and racial isolationism. Tom Watson, however, eventually left the Populists, became one of the most extreme racists, and ran for the Senate on the Democratic ticket. This was but one of many signs.

As the judge walked down Market Street for the last time, he knew that the witches' brew was complete, that the nightmare he had feared for decades was upon the land. The wounds of war were open and bleeding again, and the spokesmen for this "new" South were not men like Colonel Key. They were not men who had matured on the battlefields of the Civil War; they were the Watsons and the "Pitchfork" Ben Tillmans, urging the land of secession to crush the "nigger." These men spelled disaster for the South.

It was dark when Judge Key turned into the tree-shrouded walk to his Chestnut Street house. The rows of violets that once his gay little redheaded daughter Sarah had tended were long since gone. The chill from the river deepened the pain in his side. On the porch steps, he glanced back a second time. Maybe his dreams did not have to end this way—not if the South elected statesmen instead of time-serving politicians. But perhaps Judge Key's real pain was that he knew that had his personal force matched his personal vision, he might have prevented this tragedy at the high noon of now lost opportunities. There was no longer any middle ground for men of good will.

He turned the knob, stepped heavily inside, and faltered, his left hand closing the door on the valley of hope. He pulled off his beaver hat and slipped his right arm around Lizzie, his beloved wife. She had been waiting for him at the door and now held him up lovingly. He had to admit that he was ill.

On February 5, 1900, Judge David McKendree Key was laid to rest on a tree-covered knoll at the foot of Lookout Mountain, a mountain that rises up broadly, leveling off abruptly, like Key's hopes and aspirations, which came to an end in Chattanooga Valley.

# Notes

## CHAPTER I

1. *The Daily Critic* (Washington, D.C.), March 6, 1877.
2. Descriptions of the inauguration week in Washington are found in *The Capital*, *The Washington Critic*, the *Washington Sentinel*, *The Sunday Herald*, the *National Republican*, and the *Memphis Avalanche*.
3. *The Capital* (Washington, D.C.), February 18, 1877.
4. The best accounts of the disputed election are contained in C. Vann Woodward, *Reunion and Reaction: The Compromise of 1877 and the End of Reconstruction* (Boston: Little, Brown & Co., 1951); Paul L. Haworth, *The Hayes-Tilden Disputed Presidential Election of 1876* (Indianapolis: Bobbs-Merrill Co., 1906); John Begelow, *The Life of Samuel J. Tilden* (New York: Harper & Bros., 1895). It is interesting to note that accounts before that of Professor Woodward were not based upon documentation revealing Key's role in this election, that even Woodward's book did not use the Key Papers. Many of Key's attitudes toward the dangers arising during the disputed election are in his speech in the *Congressional Record*, 44th Cong., 2d Sess., December 18, 1876, V, 262–64.
5. Description from clippings in the Key Scrapbook, especially *Cincinnati Commercial*, August 23, 1875; *Chattanooga Times*, August 18, 1875; the Donelson Memoirs.
6. Description from *National Republican* (Washington, D.C.), March 7, 1877.
7. For these and other comments about Key, see *Brownsville Democrat*, March 15, 1877, and *Raleigh Observer*, March 15, 1877, in the Key Scrapbook.
8. For Key's attitudes, see letter from Key to Andrew J. Kellar, *New York Tribune*, March 8, 1877; letter to the editor, *Memphis Avalanche*, March 8, 1877; interview with D. M. Key, *Chattanooga News*, undated (probably 1895), in the Key Scrapbook. For background on the Southern race problem, see C. Vann Woodward, *The Strange Career of Jim Crow* (New York: Oxford University Press, 1955).
9. Comments on Key's nervous habit of fumbling his hat and the origin of the hat are in clippings in the Key Scrapbook, one from the *Hartford Times*.
10. *The Daily Critic* (Washington, D.C.), March 6, 1877. The reconstruction of the White House, as well as Washington, D.C., in general, is derived from photographs and sketches in the Library of Congress and in the National

Archives; De Benneville Randolph Keim, *Washington: Its Public and Private Edifices, Interiors, Monuments, and Works of Art* (Washington, D.C.: B. R. Keim, 1881); *New Washington: or, The Renovated Capital City* (Washington, D.C.: Chronicle Publishing Co., 1874); Mary Clemmer Ames, *Ten Years in Washington* (Hartford, Conn.: A. D. Worthington, 1873), pp. 168–70.

11. *Memphis Avalanche,* March 7, 1877; letter from D. M. Key to Andrew Kellar, undated, in the Key-Patten Papers.

CHAPTER II

1. Description in this chapter from Kate Cummings, *Gleanings from the Southland* (Birmingham, Ala.: Roberts & Sons, 1895), pp. 89–90; William Cullen Bryant (ed.), *Picturesque America* (New York: D. Appleton & Co., 1872), I, 53; Gilbert E. Govan and James W. Livingood, *The Chattanooga Country, 1540–1951: From Tomahawks to TVA* (New York: E. P. Dutton & Co., 1952); *Gazette* (Chattanooga) and *Advertiser* (Chattanooga), 1861 editions; and photographs in the Chattanooga Public Library. *Chattanooga News,* undated article (probably 1910) by Nell Cooke Patty, on file in the Chattanooga Public Library, describes many antebellum and postbellum Chattanooga homes, including Key's. See also *Chattanooga Times,* April 2, 1933, quoting Campbell's Business Directory of Nashville, 1857. Jefferson Davis' railroad journey can be traced in *Appleton's Railway and Steam Navigation Guide* (New York: D. Appleton & Co., 1861), pp. 247–48.

2. Lewis Shepherd, *Personal Memoirs* (Chattanooga, Tenn.: privately printed, 1915), pp. xi–xiii, 104; *Chattanooga Times,* clipping titled "Two Judges in Contrast," undated, in Key-Patten Papers; *Courier-Journal* (Louisville), August 21, 1875; letter from D. M. Key to John S. Mathes, June, 1899, reprinted in *Chattanooga Times,* February 18, 1900, p. 1.

3. *Gazette* (Chattanooga), January 22, 1861.

4. Henry M. Wiltse, "History of Chattanooga," unpublished ms., Chattanooga Public Library. This voluminous manuscript contains a wealth of description of events, noted characters, and racial attitudes in nineteenth-century Chattanooga.

5. See Varina Davis, *Jefferson Davis: A Memoir* (New York: Belford Co., 1890), II, 2–7.

6. Oliver P. Temple, *Notable Men of Tennessee from 1833 to 1875: Their Times and Their Contemporaries,* comp. by Mary B. Temple (New York: The Cosmopolitan Press, 1912), pp. 109–10.

7. Davis, *op. cit.,* II, 6–7.

8. *Ibid.*

9. Temple, *Notable Men of Tennessee . . . ,* p. 110. Even in retrospect, Key called Davis' speech "very moderate in character"; "nothing in it personal or offensive in expression or manner."

10. *Ibid.*; Zella Armstrong, *The History of Hamilton County and Chattanooga Tennessee* (Chattanooga, Tenn.: Lookout Publishing Co., 1951), I, 125.

11. Temple, *Notable Men of Tennessee . . . ,* p. 111; Armstrong, *op. cit.*

12. Key's subsequent relationship with Davis evidently was not satisfactory. See Chapter III on Key's attempt to gain Davis' ear.

16. *Cincinnati Commercial*, January 20, 1877.
17. Quoted in the *Memphis Avalanche*, January
18. Letter from T. C. Lowe to Key, February

### CHAPTER XIV

1. Woodward, *Reunion and Reaction*, pp. 110–1
2. Letter from John Sherman to Hayes, January
Williams, *The Life of Rutherford Birchard Hayes*
Co., 1914), I, 521; letter from W. H. Smith to
in the Hayes Papers.
3. Woodward, *Reunion and Reaction*, pp. 114,
4. D. M. Key, "Open Letter to the South," *Th*
1878, p. 5.
5. *Congressional Record*, 44th Cong., 2d Sess., J
913; Haworth, *op. cit.*, p. 221.
6. Allan Nevins (ed.), *Selected Writings of A*
Columbia University Press, 1937), pp. 172–73; F
7. Letter from Andrew Kellar to W. H. Smi
W. H. Smith Papers; see also Kellar's letters to 3
8. It is impossible to tell exactly when Kella
understanding, and this scene is a reconstruction
from Andrew Kellar to D. M. Key, February 1
letter from Joseph Medill to Richard Smith, Feb
Papers; letters from Andrew Kellar to W. H. Smi
in the W. H. Smith Papers.
9. Edward Mayes, *Lucius Q. C. Lamar* (Nashv
of the Methodist Episcopal Church, South, 1896)
10. Letter from Andrew Kellar to D. M. Ke
Key Papers.

### CHAPTER XV

1. Conversations with Mrs. Sarah Key Patter
*Times*, October 20, 1935.
2. Letter from Andrew Kellar to Key, February
3. Key was undoubtedly aware of the ext
Lamar. Furious attacks against "traitors" to Dix
uary, when a Democratic newspaper, the *Washin*
gomery Blair, charged that L. Q. C. Lamar had
the Presidency to Governor Hayes in exchange
Actually, Lamar had even refused to talk with (
1876, as Murat Halstead and Andrew Kellar k
was so infuriated over the accusations that he
challenging Blair to a duel. See Mayes, *op. cit.*, p
4. Letter from Key to Kellar, February 16, 18
*Avalanche*, March 8, 1877. See the handwritte
Key to Kellar in the Key Papers.

*Chronicle* and other newspapers. The *Mem*
is dated August 20, 1875.
4. *Nashville American*, November 2, 187
ilton, the bank issue had always been spicy k
Bank of the United States had passed from
Andrew Jackson's colorful fight with the
For years afterward, the federal governme
banking; but in 1863, a federal banking
this step was taken not so much to contro
provide a sound and adequate currency an
Underwood Faulkner, *Economic History of*
Macmillan Co., 1928), p. 239. For the
Alexander, *op. cit.*, p. 168; Emory Q. Ha
(New York: The Macmillan Co., 1928), F
*American State Debts* (Durham, N.C.: Du
and William A. Scott, *The Repudiation o*
Y. Crowell Co., 1893), pp. 138–41. On t
Hesseltine, *A History of the South 1607–1*
1936), p. 678. This was the first major iss
with the Bourbons, and it illustrates the
on his political and racial attitudes.
5. The controversy reached such a peak
resign. Letter from James Porter, Novembe
are found in letter from a friend in Winch
in the Key Papers.
6. Letters from Key to his wife, Decer
quent background information also from
ary, February, 1876, in the Key Papers.
7. *Congressional Record*, 44th Cong., 1
8. Letter from Key to his wife, Februar
9. Letter from Key to his wife, March
10. *Ibid.*; *Congressional Record*, 44th C
Matthew Josephson, *The Politicos, 1865–*.
Co., 1938), pp. 204–7; Gail Hamilton
*James G. Blaine* (Norwich, Conn.: Henr
11. William D. Foulke, *Life of Oliv*
Merrill Co., 1899), II, 365–73.
12. Letter from Key to his wife, Marc
no thanks to Gordon, Morton's tactics wer
voted against him [Pinchback]," wrote k
vote of thirty-two against twenty-nine. . .
apprehensions of the lady members of se
that Mrs. Pinchback, though colored, is
to demand her social rights."

### CHAPTE

*General Note:* Key's letters were of
Washington life, and much of this mat
Washington without footnoting. Additio

4. Key's attitudes are best reflected in h
and 30, 1863, in the Key Papers.
5. *Battles and Leaders* . . . , pp. 485–86
6. Letter from Summerfield A. Key to Mr
Key to his wife, April 25, 1863, in the Key
7. *The War of Rebellion*, XXIV, Part I,
of this and subsequent events are found in
(1955), 354–55.
8. *Tennessee Historical Quarterly, ibid.*,
berton, *Pemberton: Defender of Vicksburg*
North Carolina Press, 1942), pp. 150–313.
9. Pemberton, *ibid.*, p. 152; *Battles and*
10. *Battles and Leaders* . . . , *ibid.*; Port
11. *The War of Rebellion*, XXIV, Part
12. *Ibid.*, Part III, p. 987; *Tennessee His*
13. *The War of Rebellion*, XXIV, Part
14. Porter, *op. cit.*, p. 85.
15. Alexander S. Abrams, *A Full and De*
*burg* (Atlanta, Ga.: Intelligencer Steam Po
16. *The War of Rebellion*, XXIV, Part
17. Porter, *op. cit.*, p. 85.
18. *Ibid.*; *Chattanooga Times*, February

### CHAPTER

1. Conversations with the late Mrs. Sara
2. *Ibid.*; "A Half Hour with Elizabeth I
M. Key," *The Lookout*, January, 1924.
3. Crutchfield served as an adviser on g
cluding General Grant. See Temple, *Notabl*
4. "A Half Hour . . . ," *loc. cit.*
5. Conversations with the late Mrs. Sara
are also found in letter from S. A. Key to I
Key Papers.
6. The Lenoir mansion is well described
ing J. A. Gertel, *Hand in Hand Through*
St. John's Hospital Church Charity Founda
7. Conversations with the late Mrs. Sara
*loc. cit.* This was a period during which
there were rumors of his death. See S. A.
in the Key Papers.
8. S. A. Key to D. M. Key, January 15
9. Such conditions are described in let
Johnson, September 1, 1865, in the Joh
Washington, D.C.
10. *Cincinnati Commercial*, August 23,
Key's attitudes on Johnson during this peri
44th Cong., 1st Sess., January 11, 1876.
11. The pardon, dated June 15, 1865, b

### CHAPTER III

1. On February 9, 1861, Tennesseans at the polls rejected a proposal to call a secessionist convention. Hamilton County, which included Chattanooga, voted 1,445 to 445 against the convention. See Charles W. Lusk, "Some Phases of Chattanooga History During the Civil War" (unpublished ms., 1933, Chattanooga Public Library), p. 8.
2. The majority of Tennesseans still hoped for compromise. See James W. Fertig, *The Secession and Reconstruction of Tennessee* (Chicago: University of Chicago Press, 1898), pp. 25ff.
3. Armstrong, *op. cit.*, I, 125; Shepherd, *op. cit.*, pp. 98–99.
4. John B. Lindsley, *The Military Annals of Tennessee, Confederate* (Nashville, Tenn.: J. M. Lindsley & Co., 1886), p. 60.
5. Tennessee State Legislature, extra session, April, 1861, Public Act 1, Tennessee State Archives; Fertig, *op. cit.*, pp. 26–27; Wiltse, *op. cit.*, pp. 251–52; *The War of the Rebellion: A Compilation of the Official Records of the Union and Confederate Armies* (Washington, D.C.: Government Printing Office, 1882), Series I, IV, 240–45.
6. Wiltse, *op. cit.*, pp. 251–52.
7. Merton Coulter, *William G. Brownlow: Fighting Parson of the Southern Highlands* (Chapel Hill, N.C.: University of North Carolina Press, 1937), p. 141; Oliver P. Temple, *East Tennessee and the Civil War* (Cincinnati: Robert Clarke Co., 1899), pp. 180–81.
8. Letter from Henry Lenoir to Mrs. D. M. Key, May 6, 1861, in the Key Papers.
9. *Union and American* (Nashville), August 24, 1875, quoting a *Cincinnati Commercial* article signed "L.R.," in the Key Scrapbook.
10. Temple, *East Tennessee* . . . , pp. 341–43.
11. Letter from Key to his wife, May 19, 1861, in the Key Papers; Temple, *East Tennessee* . . . , p. 187.
12. Letters from Key to his wife, June 10, July 30, 1861, in the Key Papers. In Hamilton County, 1,260 opposed and 854 favored secession, although Chattanooga proper voted four to one for secession. See Temple, *East Tennessee* . . . , p. 199; Philip M. Hamer, *Tennessee: A History 1673–1932* (New York: American Historical Society, Inc., 1933), II, 551.
13. See W. J. Worsham, *The Old Nineteenth Tennessee Regiment, CSA* (Knoxville, Tenn.: Paragon Printing Co., 1902), pp. 8–13; Bell Irvin Wiley, *They Who Fought Here* (New York: The Macmillan Co., 1959), pp. 22–38; letters from Key to his wife, June 10, July 30, December 14, 1861, in the Key Papers.
14. Lindsley, *op. cit.*, pp. 372–73, 521; letters from Key to his wife, July 30, September 27, 1861, and February 14, 1862, in the Key Papers; see also Jonathon D. Hale, *Champ Ferguson: A Sketch of the War in East Tennessee* (Cincinnati: privately printed, 1862).
15. Letter from Key to his wife, July 30, 1861, in the Key Papers; Worsham, *op. cit.*, pp. 9–11.
16. U.S. Congress, House Committee on Invalid Pensions, HR 3634, *Pensions to Certain East Tennesseans*, 51st Cong., 2d Sess., 1891, p. 1. See

also Temple, *East Tennessee . . .*
*Mountaineers of Tennessee* (Kn[...]
Hamer, *op. cit.*, II, 564–65; The
17. Humes, *op. cit.*, p. 133; W[...]
*Sherman* (New York: Charles W[...]
*sions . . .* , p. 2.
18. *The War of the Rebellion,*
G. Brownlow, *Sketches of the Ri[...]
*Narrative of Personal Adventure[...]*
Childs, 1862); Temple, *East Tenn[...]*
19. The entire account of this
February 14, 1862. It reflects the
not mention Key's specific activiti[...]
death. See also Key's letters to his [...]
December 14, 1862, in the Key P[...]
*in Bradley County, East Tennes[...]*
pp. 113–14; Temple, *East Tennes[...]*

1. See Kate Cummings, *A Jour[...]*
*of Tennessee* (Louisville, Ky.: Jo[...]
*Tennessee: Historical and Biograp[...]*
1893), p. 177; letter from Key to [...]
2. Key later noted this in his sp[...]
3. Attitudes reflected in Key's l[...]
4. Letter from Key to his wife, [...]
*of Rebellion*, X, 628–29.
5. Letters from Key to his wife[...]
the Key Papers; *The War of Reb[...]*
6. Armstrong, *op. cit.*, II, 294; [...]
(Atlanta, Ga.: Confederate Publis[...]
7. Background on these events i[...]
1145; Lindsley, *op. cit.*, pp. 522–[...]
(eds.), *Battles and Leaders of th[...]*
*Leaders . . .*) (New York: Centur[...]

1. Information on the Lenoir p[...]
principally from pictures, mement[...]
Patten.
2. See *The War of Rebellion*, X[...]
II, Part II, 462–70; Sherman, *op.* [...]
3. For these and other events o[...]
*Mississippi* (New York: The Blue[...]
"The Defense of Vicksburg," in B[...]
William C. Everhart, *Vicksburg:* [...]
National Park Service, 1954), His[...]

---

when Key took the oath prescrib[...]
29, 1865. It is possible that Key's [...]
that moved Johnson toward amne[...]
to S. A. Key, July 28, 1865, in th[...]

C[...]

1. Much of the background mat[...]
see also J. T. Trowbridge, *The S[...]*
*Cities* (Hartford, Conn.: L. Stebbi[...]
*History of Chattanooga* (Knoxvill[...]
2. Letter from Key to his wife, [...]
3. Letter from Key to his wife, [...]
4. *Chattanooga Republican*, De[...]
5. Wiltse, *op. cit.*; for the Loya[...]
Munson Coan (eds.), *Personal R[...]*
York: The Commandery, 1891).
6. Wiltse, *op. cit.*
7. *Ibid.*
8. Letter from Key to M. H. C[...]
1872, in the Key Papers. For Ke[...]
25, 1909, article by Judge Lewis [...]
Crossville, Tennessee, March 18, [...]
Sarah Key Patten. For backgrou[...]
Alexander, *Political Reconstructi[...]*
bilt University Press, 1950), an[...]
*stitutional History of Tennessee* ([...]
9. Speech of May 29, 1870, qu[...]
21, 1875.
10. For the visit to Washingt[...]
(Nashville), August 24, 1875, q[...]
by "L.R.," in the Key Scrapbook; [...]
by John S. Mathes; conversations [...]
11. For Key's attitudes on Jo[...]
*Record*, 44th Cong., 1st Sess., Jan[...]
12. Quoted in Howard K. B[...]
*Johnson and Reconstruction* (Ne[...]
13. *Congressional Record, loc.* [...]

1. *Chattanooga Times*, June 2[...]
went with Key to Johnson's fune[...]
article by H. V. Redfield; *Congr[...]*
11, 1876, p. 342; *Diary of Henr[...]*
printed, 1875).
2. *Chattanooga Times*, Februa[...]
3. *Union and American* (Nas[...]

---

2. *Congressional Record*, 44th Cong., [...]
257–62.
3. *Ibid.*, pp. 262–64. Key's relationshi[...]
in his letters.
4. *Ibid.*
5. Letters from Kellar to W. H. Smith, [...]
Smith Papers; Garfield Diary, December [...]
Papers.
6. Quoted in the *National Republican* [...]
1876. For the Mosby reference, see the *N[...]*
7. *National Republican*, December 20, [...]
ber 21, 1876.
8. *Congressional Record*, 44th Cong., 1[...]
9. *Senate Executive Documents*, 43d Co[...]
The story of the railroads and the subsid[...]
*Reunion and Reaction.*
10. Letter from Boynton to W. H. Smit[...]
Papers.
11. Letter from Hayes to W. H. Smith, J[...]
A similar letter was written on December [...]

### CHAPTER [...]

1. *Cincinnati Commercial*, January 15, [...]
well as that of most other Tennesseans in [...]
Austin P. Foster, *Tennessee: The Voluntee[...]*
Publishing Co., 1923).
2. Will T. Hale and Dixon L. Merritt, [...]
Lewis Publishing Co., 1913), II, 401.
3. *Battles and Leaders . . .* , I, Part II, [...]
*of Tennessee* (Indianapolis: Bobbs-Merrill [...]
Foster, *op. cit.*; undated clippings in the K[...]
4. *Memphis Avalanche*, January 3, 187[...]
5. *Ibid.*, January 8, 1877.
6. Joshua W. Caldwell, *Sketches of the* [...]
ville, Tenn.: Ogden Bros. & Co., 1898), p[...]
ary 22, 1877.
7. *Cincinnati Commercial*, January 15, [...]
8. *Nashville American*, January 13, 187[...]
9. *Memphis Avalanche*, January 19, 18[...]
10. *Cincinnati Gazette*, January 17, 187[...]
ary 13, 1877, in the Key Papers.
11. *Nashville American*, January 19, 18[...]
12. *Memphis Avalanche*, January 20; N[...]
13. *Nashville American*, January 18, 18[...]
14. *Memphis Avalanche*, January 20, 18[...]
22, 1877.
15. *Memphis Avalanche*, January 21, 18[...]

---

26. Letter from W. H. Smith to Hayes, March 22, 1877, in the Hayes
Papers.
27. Letter from N. B. Meade to D. M. Key, March 10, 1877, in the Hayes
Papers.
28. *Lynchburg Virginian* clipping sent by L. S. Marye to D. M. Key, April
17, 1877, in the Key Papers.
29. Williams (ed.), *Diary and Letters . . .* , III, 436.
30. Letter from Hayes to Guy Bryan, June 13, 1877, in the Hayes Papers.
31. *Louisville Commercial*, August 21, 1877.

### CHAPTER XVII

1. Numerous clippings in the Key Scrapbook.
2. *Knoxville Chronicle*, June 1, 1877, in the Key Papers.
3. Clipping dated June 3, 1877, in the Key Scrapbook.
4. Clippings in the Key Scrapbook.
5. *New York Herald* clipping, dated August 23, 1877, in the Key Scrapbook,
and various unidentified clippings.
6. *New Orleans Picayune*, undated clipping in the Key Scrapbook.
7. Clippings in the Key Scrapbook, August, 1877.
8. Descriptions and account are principally from clippings in the Key Scrapbook.
9. Clippings in the Key Scrapbook, many undated, but approximate dates are
August 28–30, 1877.
10. Key repeated his "erring brethren" remarks on September 8, 1877, at
the National Reunion of Army Veterans in Marietta, Ohio. The controversy
blazed again in the press, and attacks upon the postmaster general reached such
proportions that it was rumored he would resign and devote himself to private
business. In Key's defense, the *St. Louis Republican* said that only one factor
could force Key's retirement: Southern intolerance.
11. Clippings in the Key Scrapbook.
12. *New York Tribune*, quoted in the *Memphis Appeal*, undated clipping in
the Key Scrapbook.
13. *New York Tribune*, undated clipping in the Key Scrapbook.

### CHAPTER XVIII

1. Williams (ed.), *Diary and Letters . . .* , III, 482–84. Senator Hoar advised Hayes to organize military units. See also Theodore C. Smith, *Life and
Letters of James Abram Garfield* (New Haven, Conn.: Yale University Press,
1925), II, 666.
2. *The New York Times*, May 29, 1878.
3. *Memphis Avalanche*, undated clipping in the Key Scrapbook. The *Avalanche* charged that Harris believed "first in his party, next in himself and his
political friends, and lastly in his country." Naturally, said the *Avalanche*, he
conceived of Key's patriotic act as political suicide; yet even Harris had admitted that "not more than one man out of ten in Congress" really wanted to

reopen the Presidential question. Hence, Harris merely believed in obeying the party caucus; "this is what the *Avalanche* calls machine politics."

4. Quotes from clippings in the Key Scrapbook, June, 1878, and undated.

5. *Knoxville Chronicle,* June 8, 1878.

6. *Philadelphia Times,* clipping, dated July 8, 1878, in the Key Scrapbook.

7. *Philadelphia Times,* undated clipping; *Atlanta Constitution,* July 23, 1878; *New York Tribune,* undated clipping quoting the *Atlanta Constitution,* in the Key Scrapbook.

8. *Ibid.*

9. *The New York Times,* January 13, 1878.

10. See letter from Joseph H. Thompson, April 7, 1877, and from B. P. Anderson, January 22, 1878, in the Key Papers. Thompson wrote: "In the future the democratic liberals will naturally follow you and Hayes and if by some bold stroke the President could snatch from the *Bourbon Coils* a few of the old line whigs now acting with that party the Hayes party will have been formed on an irresistible basis." Not only would the Tennessee industrial wing led by Colonel Colyar follow, but the "Andy Johnson element (to which I belong) will stand by *you* come what will."

11. Vincent Paul De Santis, "Republican Efforts to Break up the Democratic South, 1877–1892," unpublished Ph.D. dissertation, Johns Hopkins University, 1952, pp. 93–99.

12. *National Republican,* November 23, 1878.

13. Letter from S. A. Key to D. M. Key, November 22, 1878, in the Key Papers.

CHAPTER XIX

1. Letter from Mrs. Sarah Key Patten to the author, January 30, 1957; clippings and mementos in the Key-Patten collection.

2. Letter from George M. Drake, Post Office Department, to D. M. Key, May 31, 1881, in the Key Papers. On the initial contract, the Post Office by law had to accept the lowest bid, on the increase or expediting service, however, there was no competition. See J. Martin Klotsche, "The Star Route Cases," *The Mississippi Valley Historical Review,* XXII, No. 3 (December, 1935), 408. See also Eugene C. Savidge, *Life of Benjamin Harris Brewster* (Philadelphia: J. B. Lippincott Co., 1891), pp. 121–27.

3. *The New York Times,* October 31, 1881; *Nashville American,* October 24, 1881, article entitled "Star Route Frauds," sent by Key to Hayes, in the Hayes Papers.

4. Letter from Key to Hayes, November 2, 1881, in the Hayes Papers.

5. *U.S. Congress, House,* Misc. Doc. No. 31, *Testimony Before the Committee on Appropriations in Relation to the Postal Star Service,* 46th Cong., 2d Sess., 1880, pp. lv, lxxxi, 31, 67.

6. *Nashville American,* October 24, 1881.

7. Even *The New York Times* (February 21, 1880) praised Key's courage: "[Key] is forced to this measure by his determination to obey the law, and keep his expenditures within the appropriation—a view of official duty which Gen. Brady . . . has completely ignored."

8. Williams (ed.), *Diary and Letters . . . ,* IV, 10.

9. *Nashville American,* October 24, 1881.

CHAPTER XX

1. Letter from George M. Drake to Key, June 27, 1881, in the Key Papers; Elizabeth B. Patten, "A History of Summertown," unpublished paper, August 30, 1953; letter from Key to Hayes, July 30, 1881, in the Hayes Papers.

2. *New York Herald,* May 5, 1881.

3. Robert G. Caldwell, *James A. Garfield* (New York: Dodd, Mead & Co., 1931), p. 338.

4. *National Republican,* May 2, 1881.

5. Letter from George M. Drake to Key, May 13, 1881, in the Key Papers.

6. *The New York Times,* May 6, 1881.

7. Letter from James Tyner to Garfield, June 23, 1881, in the Garfield Papers.

8. *Nashville American,* October 24, 1881.

9. *The New York Times,* October 31, 1881.

10. Letter from Key to Hayes, March 3, 1883, in the Hayes Papers. Historians Ellis Oberholtzer, Leonard White, Harry Barnard, Martin Klotsche, and George F. Howe condemn the star-route policies as an example of mass corruption. Brady himself said: "I am responsible for all that was done while I was at the head of the contract bureau, and am proud of the fact that I was in a position to respond to the wants of the country in its recent and still continuing wonderful era of prosperity. No man who comes after me, whatever his pretensions may be, dares set his face against the liberal policy inaugurated by Judge Key."—*The New York Times,* October 31, 1881. It has been impossible for the author to determine how much of Brady's wealth possibly came from corruption; much of it did come from his telephone investment. Key's liberal policies were highly beneficial, as the testimony clarified. In such an expansionist situation, with faulty laws, corruption undoubtedly existed. The definitive study of the star-route case is yet to be written, however.

11. *Harpers Weekly,* XXIII, No. 1151 (January 18, 1879), 42.

12. Daniel M. Robinson, *Bob Taylor and the Agrarian Revolt in Tennessee* (Chapel Hill, N.C.: University of North Carolina Press, 1935), pp. 19–20.

13. Letters in the Key and Key-Patten Papers; see especially the letter from Joseph H. Thompson to Key, April 7, 1877, in the Key Papers.

14. See Robert Destry (ed.), *Federal Reporter* (St. Paul, Minn.: West Publishing Co., 1881), V, 499–502. In 1881, when the Republicans were in control of the governorship and of one house, the Tennessee State Legislature passed a statute requiring railroad companies to furnish separate cars or to partition cars so that Negro passengers who paid first-class rates would have first-class accommodations. This statute has sometimes been called the first "Jim Crow" law in the South, but it should not be classified with the stricter segregation laws of the 1890's. See Stanley J. Folmsbee, "The Origin of the First 'Jim Crow' Law," *The Journal of Southern History,* XV, No. 2 (May, 1949), 235–37.

15. D. M. Key, "The Legal and Political Status of the Negro," speech before the Tennessee Bar Association, undated, in the Key-Patten Papers.

16. *Philadelphia Times,* interview with Key, July 8, 1878, in the Key Scrapbook.

17. Key, *op. cit.*

18. Henry M. Wiltse, "Chattanooga: Past, Present, and Future," *Times Printing Co.*, 1885.

19. Wiltse. "History of Chattanooga."

CHAPTER XXI

*General Note:* Description from the *Chattanooga Times* editions of the period and other Chattanooga sources previously cited.

1. Wiltse, "History of Chattanooga."

2. Letters in the Key and Key-Patten Papers; letter from William Howard Taft to Key, January 8, 1894, in the Key Papers.

3. See Woodward, *The Strange Career of Jim Crow,* pp. 16–30.

# A Note on Sources

Principal sources are the Key Papers, in the Chattanooga Public Library, and what the author has termed the Key-Patten Papers and the Key Scrapbook, on loan to him by Mrs. Sarah Key Patten at the time of her death, in 1958. It is assumed that this second valuable collection will reside in the Chattanooga Public Library for consolidation with the first collection. This same library is the depository for many other important sources, especially the Wiltse manuscript, and early Chattanooga newspapers.

The Hayes Memorial Library at Fremont, Ohio, has the Hayes Papers, as well as copies of the "Memoirs of Thomas C. Donaldson" and of the William Henry Smith Papers. The Library of Congress contains the Garfield Papers and an invaluable collection of pictures and newspapers, including the *Memphis Avalanche,* the *Louisville Courier-Journal, The New York Times,* the *New York Tribune,* and the Washington *National Republican.*

The author is indebted far beyond what the footnotes would indicate to two pioneer publications. The first is *The Chattanooga Country,* by Gilbert E. Govan and James W. Livingood; the second is *Reunion and Reaction,* by Professor C. Van Woodward. The latter book first set the disputed election in perspective and downgraded the Wormley Conference as a decisive event in the bargain. Interestingly enough, interviews with Key, reflected in the Key Scrapbook, indicate his skeptical view of the importance of that conference. Professor C. Van Woodward did not have access to the Key or the Key-Patten Papers; therefore, his history does not reflect Key's full role in the disputed election.

# Index

245